HIGH SCHOOL
of YOUR DREAMS

Nancy Nicholson

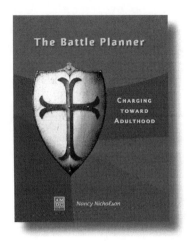

A companion lesson planner is also available:

The Battle Planner

Charging toward Adulthood: Training for Battle

by Nancy Nicholson

ISBN: 978-0-9858343-3-3

Cover and interior art: Michael D. O'Brien, http://studiobrien.com

For Little Folks
P.O. Box 571
Dresden, OH 43821
www.forlittlefolks.com

Distributed by
Catholic Heritage Curricula
P.O. Box 579090, Modesto, CA 95357
1-800-490-7713 *www.chcweb.com*

For more titles by Nancy Nicholson, visit www.chcweb.com!

Dedicated with thanksgiving
to the radiant example
of one
for whom Faith and life
were synonymous:

Pope John Paul II

CONTENTS

INTRODUCTION

What This Program Isn't— and What It Is

This program is *not* a 'pre-packaged' entity in which each text, course, assignment, and daily schedule is already cast in stone. The courses are *not* laid out as inflexible lessons nor day by day, precisely to allow teacher and student the freedom to select courses tailored to the student's interest, choose books and assignments that fit the student's learning style, and allow flexible time frames for completion. Rather than fostering a sense of panic by forcing a student to fit into a nightmarishly rigid course of study, this program is the *High School of Your Dreams.*

The *High School of Your Dreams* was conceived as Catholic homeschoolers expressed to Catholic Heritage Curricula an urgent desire for a high school program that allows:

- wider course selection

- broader choice of texts and materials reflecting the abilities and 'educational track' of the student

- coursework that can be modified for students who struggle with academics but shine in practical skills

- flexibility in presentation, including the option of an experiential, rather than textbook, approach

- means of demonstrating mastery of a course of study that may or may not necessitate a diploma

Survey responses indicate that Catholic homeschoolers want a high school program that can be made to fit the student, not one in which the student is made to fit the program. One would not order from a stranger a box of generic clothing and have any hopes that the garments would fit the recipient, or be appropriate for the local climate. Similarly, a course of study designed to 'fit all' often fits none. One can expect a happier educational outcome with the *High School of Your Dreams,* since those selecting courses, materials, and approaches enjoy a close familiarity with the student!

High School: It's a Fit!

The passing years continue to prove that homeschooled students are acquiring a quality education outside the commonly-recognized school setting. One of the better-known examples of educational achievement outside the traditional school structure, and minus a 'pre-packaged' program, is related in *Homeschooling for Excellence*. This chronicle of the Colfax family's homeschooling experience culminated with their sons' acceptance into and subsequent graduation from Harvard, *all without a traditional education or diploma*. The Colfax family demonstrated that homeschooled students, implementing a variety of individualized approaches to learning, can gain an education rivaling that of a quality private school.

Further, the secular society in which we live not infrequently fails to recognize that each person is made in the image and likeness of God and is therefore of infinite value, independent of his or her physical magnetism, lightning-fast pitch, or towering intellect. An elitist mentality hints that those who graduate medical school are more worthy of honor than those who follow non-collegiate career paths. Nothing could be further from God's Truth. Each individual is a precious and unrepeatable miracle, not because of what he does, but because of who he is: a child of God. Those who use their God-given gifts to the best of their ability, in whatever capacity, give glory to God not according to man's measure, but according to God's. Thus, the most acclaimed physicist and an unsung auto mechanic are on equal footing. Indeed, if the alternator on the physicist's vehicle gives up the ghost, he may hold the auto mechanic in higher esteem than himself.

Recognizing that Our Lord has created each student to be an unique individual, and in response to requests from Catholic homeschoolers, Catholic Heritage Curricula has developed an approach to high school that can be tailored to fit virtually any learning style and goal. This approach 'works' not only for those whose career track demands a college degree, but also for those whose ambitions necessitate a training program not offered in college. Regardless of their ambitions, students in the *High School of Your Dreams* have the freedom to select materials most appropriate to their educational 'track,' interests, and abilities.

Before Reading Any Further...

DON'T skip paragraphs, pages, or sections of this manual.

DO read this manual from cover to cover. Sections that, at first glance, seem not to apply to your student may nevertheless contain useful ideas and information that will ignite your son or daughter's enthusiasm throughout high school.

Required Subjects for High School Graduation for All Students

Courses listed are standard for most states, but there can be minor variations from region to region. Please do check regulations and requirements within your own state and for Canada, as some states/provinces have slightly different requirements for graduation.

- American Government: 1/2 year, or 1/2 credit
- English: 4 years, 4 credits
- Geography: 1/2 year, 1/2 credit
- U.S. History: 1 year, 1 credit
- Mathematics: 2 years, 2 credits
- Physical Education: 1 1/2 years, 1 1/2 credits
- Science: 3 years, 3 credits
- Social Studies: 1 year, 1 credit
- Speech: 1/2 year, 1/2 credit
- Electives: 8 [total of 8 credit hours]

Total credit hours for graduation: 22

Please note that students are welcome to earn more than the minimum 22 credits required for graduation!

Suggested Subjects for High School Graduation for the College Bound

Those who plan to pursue a rigorous college program might wish to base their high school program on the following course of study, suggested by most top colleges and universities.

- American Government: 1/2 credit
- English: 4 credits
  including Grammar, Literature, and Composition
- Foreign Language: 3 or 4 credits
  with a strong focus on at least one language
- Geography: 1/2 credit
- U.S. History: 1 credit
- World History and/or Social Studies: 1 credit
- Mathematics: 3-4 credits
  including Algebra, Geometry, and Trigonometry and intro to Calculus for those seeking a degree that necessitates strong math skills
- Physical Education: 1 1/2 credits
- Science: 4 credits
  including Biology, Chemistry, and Physics; lab time preferred in at least one science
- Speech: 1/2 credit
- Electives: remainder

Total credit hours for graduation: 22

Remember that students may earn more than the minimum 22 credits required for graduation; scholars with their eyes on an Ivy League school should sign on for the maximum number of credits in Foreign Language, Math, and Science.

High School of Your Dreams: What Would YOU Like to Study?

'Is there some way we can study auto mechanics/apologetics/family management/Russian?'

Yes! What would *you* like to study? Certainly, the student will want to fulfill basic requirements for graduation, but there is a good deal of freedom in how those requirements are met. For instance, math credits may be earned by taking Consumer Math, Practical Math, or Algebra, Geometry, Trigonometry, and Calculus.

While Biology is recommended, those on an apprenticeship track may substitute science courses such as Agricultural Science and Midwifery, while the college-bound who plan to specialize may add courses like Astronomy and Fetology. Perhaps one aspires to the priesthood or religious life, or simply desires to delve deeper into the treasures of our Holy Faith; Latin, Theology, and a Vocations unit are options.

Further, those who are interested in a particular field [e.g., meteorology or aeronautics], have the freedom to research possible topics necessary for certification or a degree in that field; those topics, rarely offered in most schools, can then be included in their high school course of study.

Which Book—or Perhaps Video Series—Would You Like to Use?

In public and private schools alike, texts are pre-selected. In some instances, the texts are beneath the ability of the student and fail to challenge or provide the level of mastery that the student seeks. Frequently, while the subject itself is not beyond the grasp of the student, the pre-selected text is too 'dry,' or perhaps technical beyond the ability of the pupil.

High School of Your Dreams allows an unlimited choice of texts and materials that better suits the abilities and 'life track' of the student. Perhaps some are mechanically gifted and plan a career in Auto Mechanics; a college prep Biology text is not necessary for this career path. Pupils planning non-degreed careers who still desire Biology credit might choose to learn the subject with videos or less rigorous texts, while the student aspiring to a doctorate in medicine has the liberty of selecting both the most rigorous Biology text and as many supplemental or enrichment materials as desired.

In the same way, scholars might not wish to limit their study of English Literature to commonly prescribed studies of Shakespeare and Beowulf, but would be pleased to include or even substitute readings from Chesterton, Newman, and Faber. Texts and supplemental materials used in the *High School of Your Dreams* are not limited to those listed under course titles; the user has complete freedom to select materials.

Flexibility in Presentation: Select a Track/Approach That Fits the Student's Learning Style

The standard classroom approach to teaching most core subjects revolves around the study of a textbook coupled with teacher-led discussions and/or lectures. This volume offers greater flexibility in presentation, not excluding the aforementioned textbook approach, but also including a wide variety of research-based studies and hands-on experiential learning not frequently found in the standard classroom.

Other programs apart from the standard classroom may offer an exemplary classical education, which nevertheless fails to adequately prepare the student for the less-than-classical occupation that he desires to pursue. Furthermore, science, history, English, and other classes frequently set instructional levels to prepare participants for college, although not all students share this goal. Some students may lack the ability to pursue college studies; far more are perfectly capable of college-level work, but have true gifts and career goals in non-academic fields such as welding, clothing design and construction, and landscaping. In this volume, methods of study are tailored to the 'track' that best fits the student's goals, whether 'College Track,' 'Community College/Vocational School Track,' or 'Apprenticeship/School-to-Work Track.'

How Are Credits Granted?

Public and private schools commonly assign credit based on a 36-week school year, totaling 5 classroom hours per week per subject, or 180 hours per year. [One might briefly note that most schools grant an hour's credit for classes that end after only fifty minutes, and still give credit for a full 180 hours even when a student has missed a number of classes.] *High School of Your Dreams* follows the same system for awarding credit, primarily because it is the system with which institutions are most familiar.

To earn credit for any given subject, the student will record the time spent studying that topic, including seatwork, fieldwork, and homework, on the *Monthly Hours' Chart*, included in this volume. [See Table of Contents.] For every 180 hours recorded study in a particular subject, 1 credit is awarded for the class.

For example, the 'College Track' pupil might log forty-five minutes reading and taking notes on amphibians from his Biology text on Monday; on Tuesday note thirty minutes of researching the life cycle and anatomy of frogs on the internet; pass two muddy hours at a nearby pond observing amphibian habitat and catching specimens on Wednesday; an hour dissecting a frog, illustrating, and labeling the results on Thursday and forty-five minutes studying for a Biology test later that evening; and finally log fifteen minutes taking a test on Friday. Total Biology hours charted for the week: five hours and fifteen minutes. [One might note that this system of gaining credit is also recognized by Clonlara School; those who wish may use *High School of Your Dreams* for all their course work, but by submitting their coursework to one of these institutions, earn their diploma through Clonlara, or North Atlantic Regional High School, which utilize a similar system.]

For those who intend to apply to an Ivy League college, it is recommended that the student not only complete the textbook study, but select supplemental materials and experiences from *High School of Your Dreams* to ensure the greatest exposure to the subject matter. This enriched exposure is particularly beneficial in one's chosen field of study, and may exceed the total hours required for a given class. That is, one aspiring to a degree in Entomology might not only complete a biology text, but insect-related books, videos, and field hour projects as well.

Pupils who exceed 180 hours may assign the hours to another course. For instance, 'Stephanie Student' is enrolled in both Journalism and English Composition. Using an experiential approach to Journalism, Stephanie has for three years written, edited, and published a magazine for Catholic youngsters. Stephanie spends about 30 hours per month on the magazine, or 360 credit hours per year. Recognizing that her experiential learning contains elements of Journalism and English Composition, Stephanie has divided this time investment between the two classes. Thus, she has earned her three full years' credit for both Journalism and English Composition. Should Stephanie desire, she might further divide the time spent on the magazine among Journalism, English, and Career Development, or Business Cluster [typing, computer applications, bookkeeping and subscriber accounts, customer service, and banking].

Additionally, using this system of credits, the student is free to accelerate and complete a class in less than a year, or take more than one year to finish if necessary or desired. The fabled Stephanie might also have utilized the hours of writing and editing of her magazine primarily for English credit, thus completing her high school English requirements in two years rather than the traditional four. Or, she might have found that the computer applica-

tions, bookkeeping and subscriber accounts, customer service, and banking also necessary to the production of the magazine, totaled only 140 hours in one year—not sufficient for a full credit. Nevertheless, if Stephanie 'banked' those 140 hours and added them to hours earned the following year, she might, over a two year period or less, have realized 180 hours and gained full credit for Business Cluster. [Note that the *same* hours can't be used twice, for two different courses. Rather, 'banked' hours are hours in excess of the 180 gained in one class and assigned to another.]

Perhaps this system seems too generous, too 'easy' to be labeled a legitimate educational system. One should bear in mind that, in a typical public school classroom, Stephanie Student might be earning Journalism credit for occupying a seat while chatting with friends, coloring her nails, downloading music from the internet and, perhaps, working on a Journalism assignment. Indeed, in a public school setting, Stephanie will even earn credit for the days on which she is absent. The Catholic homeschooled student who offers his schoolwork to the glory of God and responsibly exerts a full hour of effort for each hour of credit, has legitimate right to credits earned.

Let us examine another example of the freedom to tailor the course to fit the student and his unique learning style. 'Art Aficionado' plans to follow the 'Community College/ Vocational School Track,' with the goal of becoming a commercial artist. He may decide to earn English credit by reading of Chanticleer and Partlet from Chaucer's *Nun's Priest's Tale*, or perhaps absorbing himself in G.K. Chesterton's *Father Brown* mysteries. In place of a written report, Art decides to sketch Chanticleer and Partlet, or illustrate a scene from *Father Brown*. Although a portion of Art's English project includes sketching, his sketches nevertheless engage him in, and earn credit for, the study of literature. Credit is assigned for all time spent on the subject, whether reading, composing, or sketching.

Composition doesn't rank high on Art Aficionado's list of favorite subjects. But an afternoon passed viewing a traveling exhibit of Van Gogh's work at a local art museum inspires Art to research and compose a short paper about the artist's life as reflected in his work. Art finds English Composition less burdensome, and is far more motivated, when he is free to write about topics that engage his interest.

A final example illustrates how the *High School of Your Dreams* meets the educational and occupational goals of 'Joe Carpenter.' Joe has for the past two summers assisted in the home construction business owned by Vincent Ferrer, a parishioner in Joe's church. Joe exhibits natural skill in carpentry and has his heart set on a career in construction, beginning via an apprenticeship with Mr. Ferrer. Joe's high school studies are based on an 'Apprenticeship/School-to-Work Track.' His English credits derive variously from reading Louis de Wohl's classics, carpentry texts, and attending seasonal Shakespearean theatre productions in his community. Joe's composition practice centers primarily on a daily journal recording construction experiences and outcomes including erecting walls and roof, wiring, pouring foundations, and a detailed account of concrete repair after a neighbor's dog raced through wet cement. Finally, Joe has twice volunteered with a team of Catholic youth, repairing and refurbishing homes of limited-income elderly residents in run-down city neighborhoods. Time amassed in all these activities counts toward Joe's credits for graduation.

Stephanie, Art, and Joe all daily record their hours for each subject on a monthly chart. Stephanie has chosen to use credit and transcript forms from *High School of Your Dreams* to document her high school years; she will submit these records, along with SAT scores and a portfolio of her magazines and other high school projects to Franciscan University of Steubenville for admission to that university.

Art and Joe, too, chart their hours. Art, however, will enroll in sculpture and art history classes at his local community college during his senior year of high school. By doing so, and submitting his *High School of Your Dreams* transcripts and portfolio of high school work to community college admissions, Art opens the door to continuing his education at a vocational school, community, or state college. His community college credits are then accepted by other institutions in place of a high school diploma. Joe will transition directly into an apprenticeship in Mr. Ferrer's construction business, but will also add to his *High School of Your Dreams* credits and transcripts by signing up for a community college course in electrical wiring.

Recording Credit Hours and Using Transcripts

Credit hours, as previously mentioned, are earned by keeping careful track of time expended on every part of every subject. Students should fill in *Monthly Hours' Chart* as they complete coursework each day. [Fill these in pencil, so that times may be adjusted if students add time later in the evening.] When 180 hours are earned, the student has earned one credit for that class.

Remember that the majority of classes will have 'overlapping' credit possibilities. For example, researching and writing a report on earthquakes for Earth Science might include three hours of reading the text and supplementary materials, two hours of internet research, two hours creating a computer-generated PowerPoint presentation of earthquake data, and two hours of writing, for a total of nine hours. All nine hours may be used for Earth Science credit. However, note that hours are expended on computer use and composition. Those hours, if desired, could be subtracted from Earth Science credit and used instead for Computer Science or English Composition. Of course, you may need to use all the hours for Earth Science! [Note that the *same* hours can't be used twice, for two different courses. Rather, 'banked' hours are hours in excess of the 180 gained in one class and assigned to another.]

Be certain to note on the *Monthly Hours' Chart how* student time was spent in each class, so that hours might be 'banked' later, if desired!

Transcripts are simply a listing of credit hours and grades awarded as each 180 hours of class time is completed.

Please see Forms and Charts for reproducible credit hour recording charts and transcripts contained in this volume.

Documenting Achievement: Diploma, GED, or Portfolio?

Catholic homeschoolers for years have been accepted without accredited diplomas, not only at noted institutions like Franciscan University of Steubenville and Thomas Aquinas College, but in secular colleges across the United States and Canada. In place of a diploma, institutions measure ability by PSAT, SAT, and ACT scores, and gather information on student coursework, transcripts, accomplishment, and community volunteer activity documented in portfolios provided by the family. While admission requirements differ among colleges, both Canadian and U.S. homeschooled students are routinely accepted into college based on these test scores and family-provided proof of education.

U.S. and Canadian universities also accept students who, instead of presenting a high school diploma, demonstrate their ability to compete at college level by successfully completing a few classes at a local community college before transitioning to university. Further, by enrolling in a class or two, the student may ask his/her teacher to write letters of recommendation to colleges on the student's behalf.

Essentially, most universities ask simply that students keep and provide a detailed description of their high school curriculum, but neither require that students *'follow a prescribed or approved homeschooling program'* nor provide 'formal transcripts.'

Rather than formal transcripts and diplomas, most colleges and universities look instead at a prospective student's SAT and ACT scores, and for a 'clear sense of intellectual growth and a quest for knowledge.' Many colleges and universities go so far as to state that homeschooled students sometimes have a potential *advantage* over non-homeschooled students, as they have enjoyed the freedom to pursue their own, independent course of study.

In addition, not all students are college-bound; some are gifted in carpentry or construction, and would thrive in an apprenticeship that transitions to a desired profession. According to survey results, Catholic homeschoolers are transitioning into the workforce through both formal and informal apprenticeships. Thus, a student who demonstrates interest and skill in auto mechanics might apprentice himself, gain credit hours toward graduation with hands-on training, and finish high school with a trade.

Pupils from every 'track' are encouraged to create portfolios of significant high school course work, activities, and accomplishments. An 'activity and project' portfolio is an effective means of documenting accomplishment not only to a potential employer, but also for high school graduation and community college admissions, coupled with SAT/ACT scores. [Colleges often view an impressive history of volunteer service in the community and other significant experiential education, coupled with average SAT/ACT scores, as favorably as high SAT/ACT scores coupled with little or no community service or activity.]

A portfolio might include:

• before and after photographs of vehicles undergoing repair and restoration

• photographs of garments sewn

• photos of the garment in use [e.g., layette at a Crisis Pregnancy Center]

• photos of construction projects in which student participated

• student's artwork

• student-composed musical scores

• reference letters from contractors for whom the student worked

• reference letters from managers of volunteer programs in which student participated

• photos of community volunteer activity in progress

• a brief composition, accompanying and describing the purpose/goal/outcome of any of the above projects

Do save a wider sampling of papers and projects than one might think necessary. When it is time to compile a physical record of the high school years, discarding excess materials is far easier than scrambling to fill a skimpy portfolio.

Another alternative for transitioning from high school, used by Catholic homeschoolers responding to the survey, is the GED. Graduates have used the GED, in conjunction with SAT/ACT scores and without, as a springboard into the armed forces, vocational schools, community colleges, and university. Information on GED preparation is included in the *Career Development and College Prep* section of this manual.

Students who prefer to do so may earn an accredited diploma, using *High School of Your Dreams,* under the 'umbrella' of Clonlara School, or North Atlantic Regional High School. This program's *Required Subjects for High School Graduation for All Students* match Clonlara requirements. North Atlantic Regional High School's course requirements differ slightly but, since they require significantly fewer hours and credits, utilizing *High School of Your Dreams'* program to earn NARHS's diploma is equally simple. Both Clonlara and North Atlantic Regional High School are completely compatible with the format, freedoms, and flexibility afforded by *High School of Your Dreams*, but with diploma added.

For students who wish to earn a diploma from Clonlara or NARHS, these organizations do charge an annual fee, and have a few additional requirements including portfolios and documentation of hours earned through *High School of Your Dreams*. More information can be obtained by contacting Clonlara School at www.clonlara.org, 734-769-4511, or North Atlantic Regional High School at www.narhs.org, 800-882-2828.

Thus, Catholic homeschooling students have numerous, routinely used options for demonstrating completion of high school requirements and readiness for college or career, including the earning of an accredited diploma, but also through testing [SAT, ACT, GED], community college classwork, and apprenticeships. Remember that an accredited diploma alone is no guarantee that a student will be accepted by a college; conversely, the student with solid SAT scores and a portfolio brimming with evidence of a motivated young adult will likely be welcomed at university, diploma or not.

Please also see the *Career Development and College Prep* section of this manual, which is not only an elective class for credit, but also a source of college prep information.

Admission to Military or Military Academies

Increasing numbers of homeschool graduates are being accepted into the military, and at military academies. In general, military academies put more emphasis on SAT, ACT, and transcripts than on diplomas. However, requirements for homeschool enlistees are currently in a state of flux; for up-to-date information on admission requirements to the U.S. Naval Academy or the U.S. Navy, for example, see http://www.academyadmissions.com/admissions/advice-to-applicants/home-schoolers/ and www.usna.edu/Admissions/steps.htm, or contact a local recruiter. For information about military careers in general, see www.khake.com/page33.html.

Courses are not laid out as inflexible lessons nor day by day, precisely to allow teacher and student to select courses tailored to the student's interest, choose books and assignments that fit the student's learning style, and allow flexible time frames for completion.

Resources for Courses Offered in This Manual

High School of Your Dreams presents educational approaches and resources for all classes necessary to meet high school graduation and college admission requirements. Used book outlets, nationally recognized Catholic and secular publishers, public libraries, websites and more are sources for widely used texts and supplemental materials including videos, CD's, and links to even more websites for further topical research.

In addition, each subject in *High School of Your Dreams* is keyed both to Church teaching on the topic, and opportunities for hands-on, experiential learning and volunteer experiences. A broad range of resources is provided that the student might have the widest possible flexibility in presentation/ learning style/track for a course that fits the unique interests, individual learning style, and needs of each student.

Core Classes and Electives: Tailoring Your 'Wish List' to Fit Your Desired Course of Study

Core classes are, quite simply, those that are required for graduation. Electives are all other classes chosen by the student, according to his interests, abilities, and life goals.

While core classes are those required for graduation, there is nevertheless considerable choice involved in selecting core classes. Four years of science might be comprised, for the medical-school bound, of Biology, Chemistry, Physics, and Anatomy. The student with a keen interest in landscaping might select his three 'core' years of science from hands-on, experiential classes in Botany or Plant Science, Earth Science, Biology, Environmental Science, or Geology.

It is recommended that students investigate professional fields that interest them to determine what course of study will best prepare them for their career choice. This search can be made online, in college catalogs, or the public library. For example, one who wishes to follow a career in nursing will face enormous struggles in college if he/she has not completed, at minimum, high school Biology. It is extraordinarily difficult to tackle college-level Chemistry, Anatomy, Health, and Biology courses required for a nursing track without previous introductory exposure to at least some of these subjects. Investigating college requirements for one's chosen field, and including some or all of those classes as core subjects at the high school level, considerably boosts performance in college-level courses.

Electives are not necessarily less challenging than core classes, but can play a significant role in career preparation because of the valuable exposure they may give to a chosen field, beyond the core subjects. For example, the student who senses that Our Lord is calling him or her to religious life might, in addition to World History, add elective study of Latin, Medieval/Church History, Theology, and/or Apologetics. One whose interests lean toward a career in Catholic media might add as electives photography, journalism, and communications, as well as apologetics and theology.

Some ideas for elective classes beyond those listed in this course: agribusiness, cinematography, dentistry, economics, herpetology, landscape architecture, photography, and surveying. If you are interested in exploring these topics, it is not difficult to use the format for electives included in this volume as a springboard for your own, home-tailored elective. Those looking for course outlines may find all these subjects and more, with activities and projects already keyed to the topic, in *Pilgrims of the Holy Family* [available through CHC], *Boy Scout Requirements* [available from new and used book dealers] and in the Boy Scout Merit Badge Handbooks [available through an internet search by title and Merit Badge Series, e.g., *Veterinary Medicine: Merit Badge Series*].

Electives grant the freedom to pursue your interests. The student captivated by photography, for example, might begin laying out his course by visiting stores that sell photographic equipment, bookstores, library, and the internet to gather sources of information about photography. Next, he might select those that most capture his attention, or which appear to be the most 'user friendly' as base texts or materials. What equipment is needed? What would the student like to accomplish? Does he know someone whose hobby is photography? Arrange a meeting during which the student can share his interest with the hobbyist. Read, research, and brainstorm projects to meet goals. Take notes, then list areas of interest and possible projects. From the list, select three projects. [Perhaps the student would like to serve the Body of Christ by creating an attractive album of life-changing success stories for a Crisis Pregnancy Center waiting room!] Beginning with the easiest and shortest of the three proposed projects, make an outline of steps that will be followed to finish the project. Set time goals for the project; make a timetable chart and stick to it. Keep a log recording daily activities and time expended for credit hours on the *Monthly Hours' Chart* in the back of this volume. Record what worked and what didn't and how problems were solved. How were goals accomplished?

Core classes are somewhat limited to a general field of study [e.g., three years of science], but often still allow freedom of topic choice within the field [e.g., Botany, Health, Meteorology]. Elective choices are limited only by one's imagination.

Gathering Materials to Teach Your Very Own Electives

If your student is interested in a subject not mentioned in *Boy Scout Requirements* or *Pilgrims of the Holy Family*, a trip to the library or bookstore to browse the shelves by topic will provide titles well in excess of need. But remember that your course needn't be based entirely on texts!

Turning first to books: it would not be physically possible to carry from the store all available titles in the 'Automotive Repair' or 'Computers' sections. By thumbing through the pages, the student may narrow his area of interest, and then obtain the winning books via inter-library loan, or purchase new or used at local book dealers or online.

Browsing book selections in the library [or borrowed through inter-library loan] or bookstore before purchase also increases the likelihood that the student will find a book that most closely matches his interests and learning style. [See Table of Contents for *Resources for Widely Used Books*.] Many used book websites, e.g., www.amazon.com, display book icons along with selected titles. A click of the mouse 'opens' to the book's Table of Contents or sample page. Do search both by title and author.

Additionally, specialty magazines for topics from auto mechanics to science, [e.g., *Popular Mechanics, Scientific American*], historical novels and biographies, videos, and interactive CDs are all legitimate means of learning. The same young person who slumps into his chair at the appearance of a history text may race to the mailbox for the latest issue of *American History* magazine. 'Education' does not have to look like a textbook.

Does your student aspire to be a taxidermist, cake decorator, or arborist? County extension classes and personal contact with those who practice these and other professions may present training or apprenticeship positions. Again, 'education' is not limited to textbooks.

Finally, the internet offers an unending variety of interactive sites, websites with up-to-date research articles, and even materials specifically designed for educational purposes, free for downloading.

Any or all of these resources can form the basis for elective courses and add depth and 'spice' to seemingly dry core subjects. As you read through the core subjects and electives offered in *High School of Your Dreams*, you may decide to follow the formats suggested, but substitute other topics and materials, creating a course uniquely your own.

> *DO read this manual from cover to cover. Sections that, at first glance, seem not to apply to your student may nevertheless contain useful ideas and information that will ignite your son or daughter's enthusiasm throughout high school.*

Volunteer Hours

Students are encouraged to engage in volunteer work within their communities. Perhaps the best reason for volunteering is that it provides the opportunity for charitable outreach to the needy Body of Christ, including but not limited to projects providing home repair or construction for the destitute, working at crisis pregnancy centers, or as hospital aides, serving in soup kitchens, and as assistants in parochial and public school classrooms. However, colleges often look for community involvement in student portfolios, and volunteer exposure that relates to a career path not only allows the student experience in his field of interest, but can be a valuable addition to an employment resume.

Volunteer hours are easily amassed at 2 hours per week per year, or 75 hours per summer, or even as some have done in one summer by serving a 2-week mission with a religious order in the inner city. Those seeking volunteer positions will find numerous possibilities listed under individual course titles in this volume. Please also see the Table of Contents for a complete listing.

Providing Those 'I have no confidence that I can teach this' Courses: Calculus, Chemistry, and Others

Do you begin to tremble at the specter of teaching Chemistry or Biology, particularly to the college-bound student? There are options! Some may choose to enroll in online science or writing classes, at a community college, or perhaps seek out a retired teacher as a private tutor. In many states, homeschool students are allowed to enroll in a local high school or parochial school for one or two classes only. Alternatives do exist for parents who are committed to schooling at home, but who would welcome a little external help with an occasional class or two.

With the advent of virtual Biology Lab and synchronous history and calculus classes, it is no surprise that homeschool students are turning to online enrollment for those college-prep classes that may challenge the parent as well as the student. Online schools are growing at such a pace that a comprehensive listing here would soon be outdated. However, one can sample online offerings by checking out www.compuhigh.com [affiliated with Clonlara School], which offers Biology, Chemistry, Math, Writing, and other courses. [Typing 'online high school' or 'virtual high school' in your internet search engine will reveal a wealth of possibilities.]

Some math and chemistry curricula providers such as Saxon and The Great Courses market instructional DVDs and videos for home instruction. Students who wish to seek instruction outside the home may enroll in one or two community college classes, thus providing both instruction and a diploma-less transition from high school to college. Enrollment can also earn both high school and college credit in classes such as Chemistry, easing the burden for those homeschooling parents who lack either the desire or funds to transform the kitchen into a fully-equipped chemistry lab.

Finally, by calling local high schools or through personal contact, it can be surprisingly easy to locate retired teachers who are willing to teach or tutor an individual or small group of students. [Remember that the ranks of 'retired' teachers include mothers who taught 'publicly' for a time, and then returned home to teach their own children.]

Touring a Course: 'Track' by 'Track'

First, if you haven't already, please read from the preceding pages *Core Classes and Electives: Tailoring Your 'Wish List' to Fit Your Desired Course of Study*. Next, turn to **Biology** in this volume.

Under the heading, **Biology,** is a listing of widely used texts. As noted in the *Key to Abbreviations*, abbreviations identify whether a text is secular [S], has a Catholic [C] or non-Catholic Christian [NCC] author or viewpoint. [CP], or 'college prep,' indicates that the text is either more rigorous or one that is commonly assigned to college-bound students. [T/AK] signifies text with answer key, and so forth. Note that some courses are available with a video or CD presentation. Please see *Key to Abbreviations* in the Table of Contents for a complete listing of abbreviations.

Rather than being limited to one text, the student/teacher may choose from this list that text which most closely suits the student's interests, abilities, and goals. Books may be purchased new from publisher or book dealers, or bought quite reasonably priced from used book dealers. Auditory learners may also select audio books. [A sampling of publishers and new, used, and audio book dealers is contained in this volume.]

Supplemental Reading offers an opportunity to delve more deeply into the subject, particularly in specialty areas. For example, a student who is taking Biology with an eye on medical school and following the *College-Track: Flexible Textbook Approach* might wish to include supplemental materials that teach anatomy and Catholic bioethics. Those using the *Community College/Vocational School: Independent Study Approach* and the *Apprenticeship/School-to-Work Track: Experiential Approach* might select less rigorous texts and supplemental reading, or perhaps choose a video series coupled with independent investigation of *Research* or *Possible Essay Topics.*

Links provide invaluable access to current events and up-to-date research materials related to the topic. These links frequently reflect Catholic teaching and, for those who want to focus their study on one particular aspect of the course [such as Fetology within the study of Biology], can be used to gather information for *Research* or *Possible Essay Topics.*

Church Teaching offers documents that add spiritual depth to the subject. As with *Links,* students from all three 'Tracks' will find *Church Teaching* to be a significant resource for writing papers, reports, and supplemental reading. More importantly, young adults drawing on *Church Teaching* to enrich their view of the course will begin to comprehend that our Holy Faith should and does permeate every aspect of our lives.

Possible Essay Topics are provided that the student might demonstrate a grasp of the subject he has researched, and an opportunity to practice composition skills that are necessary for all courses at the college level, and certainly useful for those on other vocational tracks. In addition, these essay topics should spur thought and discussion by which pupils may examine the subject from a 'Catholic worldview.' Surely, part of the motivation for Catholic homeschooling is to expose the student to the profound wisdom and moral clarity of our Holy Faith, that he will see the world through the eyes of Jesus and His Church. What might be Our Lord's 'worldview' of euthanasia? Of abortion? Of legislation that flies in the face of holy wisdom? Certainly, Biology, Government, and Social Problems can and must be examined with vision magnified by Faith. Indeed, *Ad norman decreti,* from the *Documents of Vatican II,* declares that those who teach cannot claim to be educators 'if there is no trace of their Catholic identity in their teaching.'

For students who find texts to be restrictive, *Research* topics are presented for in-depth studies of several facets of the subject. Those who plan a career that requires the greatest depth of understanding might center their study around a rigorous text, but use *Research* to explore specific aspects of their chosen field or career applications of the course.

By delving into biographies or works by notables listed in *Famous Names,* individuals might explore their contributions to, or experiences in, a given field. This exposure may further ignite interest in supplemental reading and reports, allowing pupils to gather knowledge of a subject in a more flexible manner than a text might afford.

Finally, while *Experiential Learning/Career and Vocational Bridge* is certainly accessible by all 'tracks,' this category will surely appeal most of all to the hands-on learning style of students pursuing the *Apprenticeship Track/ School-to-Work: Experiential Approach. Experiential Projects,* particularly in core subjects, are varied to include topics appealing to all 'tracks.' [For more hands-on learning and apprenticeship ideas located within the United States and Canada, please see the Table of Contents for *Volunteer/Paid/Career Bridge Positions*; *Hands-on the Arts: Museums and Theaters*; *Hands-on History Sites*; and *Hands-on Science Sites.*]

Texts; Supplemental Reading; Links; Research; Church Teaching; Possible Essay Topics; Famous Names; and *Experiential Learning,* offer engaging, diverse, yet connected 'avenues' for learning, including a Catholic viewpoint in nearly every course. Students are not necessarily assigned coursework from each and every one of these suggested approaches to learning. Rather, they may select assignments from as many or as few of these 'avenues' as fit their abilities, engage their interest, and lead to the attainment of their goals; students receive credit for all hours and effort expended, no matter which avenue is chosen. This variety of educational approaches makes welcome *every* student in the *High School of Your Dreams.*

The secular society in which we live not infrequently fails to recognize that each person is made in the image and likeness of God and is therefore of infinite value, independent of his or her physical magnetism, lightning-fast pitch, or towering intellect.

Experiential Learning/Career and Vocational Bridge

'Process Project' and 'Following in Their Footsteps, Finding Your Own Path' Hands-On Projects

Students who thrive with hands-on may wish to approach and gain credit for subjects through the *Experiential Learning* avenues of *Process Projects* and *Following in Their Footsteps, Finding Your Own Path.*

Process Projects are loosely comprised of four parts—1. Exposure to subject and collection of information 2. Goal-setting 3. Process 4. Demonstration of learning. While the sample provided below is for a quilting project, pupils can easily substitute projects of their own choosing to fit virtually any course, following the same four-part outline.

Process Projects Sample Outline

1. Exposure to subject and collection of information [see **Links, Suggested Reading,** etc. for resources]
   a. Select and gather books, videos, resources [quilt books; quilt class at sewing shop]
   b. Locate mentor [neighbor who quilts] or select hands-on experience [Ladies Circle Quilting Club]

2. Set goal [sewing baby quilts for Crisis Pregnancy Center]

3. Process: brainstorm, plan, record steps to reach goal:
   a. Contact mentor and attend Quilting Club meetings
   b. Select and purchase fabric and pattern
   c. Cutting and piecing
   d. Assembling top
   e. Assembling layers
   f. Quilting process
   g. Presentation of quilt to CPC staff or moms

4. Demonstration of Learning: written and/or pictorial record of quilt project

    a. Write at least one paragraph [or include one photograph] of each of the steps above

    b. Link each of the above paragraphs into a written narrative or report of the project; if using photos, create an album just for this project, with samples of fabric and perhaps comments from CPC or moms who received quilts

Following in Their Footsteps, Finding Your Path is an approach particularly well-suited to study those fields which might require tools or skills beyond the immediate reach of the student, e.g., veterinary medicine, helicopter mechanic, attorney. Your own parish is an excellent place to make these professional contacts.

Whether using the format of *Process Projects* or *Following in Their Footsteps, Finding Your Path* the internet provides a wealth of contacts that add a Catholic perspective. In addition to utilizing the **Links** provided with each course, one may gather information by using search engines. For example, a student creating a *Process Project* relating to quilting might search on a topic as obscure as the *Catholic Contribution to Quilting*. For example, typing [catholic+quilts] in the 'search' box provides links that include information about quilted vestments sewn for 'underground' priests during the Elizabethan persecution of Catholics.

Remember, whether using a standard textbook approach, *Process Projects,* or *Following in Their Footsteps*, bear in mind that hours and proof of work equal course credit.

Following in Their Footsteps, Finding Your Path

1. Research the history of subject/skill/trade.

    a. What is the history of _____?

    b. In what ways was this skill useful?

    c. How is this skill used today?

    d. Name some people who are prominent in this field today; what is their contribution to the field?

2. Select and interview someone who currently practices this skill/trade. [With permission, photographs of the professional and his work may be added to this paper.]

    a. How and when did they first become interested in this skill?

    b. Do they follow this trade as a hobby, or as a means of support?

    c. In what ways has this field/skill changed since the person first began his/her involvement?

    d. In what ways do they use this skill to help others?

    e. Do they belong to a group or association of _____?

    f. What steps or course of action would they recommend to someone who wished to pursue this skill/trade?

    g. Do some activities in this trade require more educational preparation or other training than the student expected? If so, describe.

    h. In what ways is the practice of this skill different from what the student anticipated?

    i. If you, the student, were active in this field, what contributions might you like to add, and to what purpose?

    j. How might your Catholic Faith and desire to utilize your talents for the glory of God influence your work in this field?

3. Report on your findings.

For those who may have the opportunity to observe or assist the professional at work: Depending on the nature of the skill/trade, student may seek permission to observe or 'shadow' the professional as he practices his trade for a period of time. If the student is able to observe, he may also ask permission to photograph the professional at work.

> *Texts and supplemental materials used in the High School of Your Dreams are not limited to those listed under course titles; the user has complete freedom to select materials.*

Selecting from Listed Materials

Books, videos, websites, and other materials listed as resources under each course heading represent viewpoints ranging from Catholic to secular. The wide variety of resource options allows the user to select materials appropriate to the pupil's educational goals and mental and spiritual readiness; remember that you are preparing your student to step into a secular world!

Some beliefs embraced by our secular society are clearly immoral, while others might simply be imprudent or inappropriate to present depending on the age and maturity level of the individual. Teaching a child of six to drive an automobile would be inappropriate; it would be equally inappropriate *not* to provide instruction in safe driving skills to a young adult. In a similar fashion, good parenting and teaching include first guiding the student, and then releasing him, wisely prepared and armed with the armor of God, into a secular world.

Please note that Catholic texts and materials are listed where available, but students on a college track should be aware that college courses invariably present a secular view. For example, the student will be exposed to evolutionary theory in university-level science courses. Even orthodox Catholic colleges will discuss the evolutionary viewpoint, yet at the same time present Church teaching on the subject. At both high school and college level, students routinely scrutinize selections from classics like *Oedipus Rex*, Chaucer's *Canterbury Tales* and Shakespearean dramas that portray or make reference to violent and immoral activity. Therefore, during the high school years when parents are available for guidance, and for the student to be fully prepared for college courses, it is not necessarily imprudent to study secular materials alongside those that present Catholic teaching. [Users of this program will also note that references to Church teaching documents are included for nearly every subject.]

Thus, books, videos, and websites listed as references for the courses in this volume are not 'recommended' or 'preferred,' but rather widely used options from which to choose, depending on the intended field of study, educational goals, and the mental and spiritual maturity of the student. As noted in the *Key to Abbreviations*, authors and viewpoints may be secular, non-Catholic Christian, or Catholic. In order to customize the education of each student to match his or her interests, abilities, and goals, the selection of materials is left entirely to the discretion of those who use this program. Descriptions of most books' contents can be found by doing a book search, by title, from new/used book dealers such as www.alibris.com or on www.amazon.com; click on 'Books.' [Enter a book title, and a 'thumbnail' of the book cover will appear. Clicking on the thumbnail will allow a scan of the book's table of contents and more.] Further, customer reviews generally accompany most books offered on www.amazon.com.

Again, please check used book websites and dealers, by book title and by author, before purchasing new. *Numerous* titles are available used for $3-$9, as compared to $20-$40 new.

Resources for Widely Used Books, Video/CD, Audio, Church-related Documents

Listed texts, books for supplemental reading, videos, and websites are drawn from *widely used* resources—not necessarily *recommended* resources! However, all are identified as Catholic, non-Catholic Christian, or secular. Please check the *Key to Abbreviations*.

Alibris—www.alibris.com—excellent source of low-priced new and used books, in and out of print, & audiobooks

American Textbook Committee—1-510-557-5300, americantextbookcommittee.org—U.S. History

www.audiobooksonline.com—for the auditory learner; discount prices

Audio-Forum—www.audioforum.com [catalog with 285 courses in 103 languages]

Barron's Educational Series—1-800-645-3476; www.barronseduc.com

Key to Abbreviations Preceding Book Titles or Church Documents

AK=answer key included

AKA=answer key available separately

C=Catholic author or viewpoint

NCC=non-Catholic Christian

OI=online instruction, classes

CP=for college prep or most rigorous track

B=basic instructional level, lower level reading

S=secular

T/AK= tests and answer key included in text

TM=teacher's manual

V/DVD=video, DVD

CCC=Catechism of the Catholic Church

www.bookfinder.com—excellent source of low-priced new and used books, in and out of print

www.booksontape.com—for the auditory learner

Catholic Heritage Curricula [CHC]— 1-800-490-7713; www.chcweb.com

Cliff's—www.cliffsnotes.com—not only abbreviated versions of numerous classics, but also 300-400 page texts [biology, chemistry, physics, French, Spanish and more], with answer keys and tests

www.coloringconcepts.com— 1-707-226-6207—science coloring books with text

www.conceptualphysics.com

Follet Education Services— www.fes.follett.com—used texts from numerous secular companies

Globe Fearon—1-800-321-3106; www.pearsonschool.com—variety of texts with answer keys, teacher's manuals, and interactive lab CD's. Call for catalog.

Heritage Resources—1-204-745-3094; www.heritageresources.ca—Canadian; non-Catholic Christian homeschool catalog

Homeschool Science Presss— www.homeschoolsciencepress.com— science lab manuals for homeschool

Ignatius Press—1-800-651-1531; www.ignatius.com—Catholic books

Kaplan—www.kaplan.com— information on testing, test prep books, PSAT, SAT

www.mathusee.com—math courses

Merit Badge Books— meritbadge.org/wiki/index.php/Boy_Scout_Portal— complete listing of all Boy Scout Merit Badge courses and requirements

National Catholic Bioethics Center— 1-215-877-2660, www.ncbcenter.org—publications and links dealing with life issues

Pauline Books and Media— 1-314-965-3512; www.pauline.org— Church documents, publications

Pearson Prentice Hall— 1-800-848-9500; www.phschool.com—variety of texts with answer keys, teacher's manuals, and interactive lab CD's.

Rosetta Stone—1-800-767-3882; www.rosettastone.com—foreign language programs

Saxon Publishers—1-800-225-5425; http://saxonhomeschool.hmco.com— math texts

Sophia Institute Press— 1-800-888-9344; www.sophiainstitute.com— Catholic books

Standard Deviants—1-866-386-0253; www.sdteach.com—courses on DVD

Stella Maris Books—1-817-924-7221; www.stellamarisbooks.com—Catholic books

TAN—1-800-437-5876; www.tanbooks.com—Catholic books

Texas A & M, Instructional Materials Service—979-845-6601; www.myimsservices.com or https://store.im.tamu.edu—Ag, vocational texts

The Great Courses—1-800-832-2412; www.thegreatcourses.com—video/DVD courses and audio books. Many video/DVD/audio courses have accompanying texts available.

Thomson-Nelson—1-800-268-2222; www.nelson.com—Canadian texts

Thomson-Peterson— www.petersons.com—PSAT, SAT, ACT, GED prep,

www.zenit.org/en—International, orthodox Catholic news organization; Church-related documents and news

Essential for All Levels:

Internet access—virtually every field now requires computer skills, internet

Catechism of the Catholic Church [CCC]

dictionary

Vatican II: Documents of Vatican II, Vol. I & II, Austin Flannery, O.P.

thesaurus

Recommended for college-bound:

Book of Catholic Quotations, John Chapin—excellent quotes around which to build essays, or to use in essays

FAQs

Q: *How much will it cost to educate my children using this method?*
A: The cost is determined by the curricula and source of materials. Purchasing used texts [see Table of Contents for book dealers] and borrowing from libraries can result in a low-cost, high quality, high school education. In addition, *Links* spotlights websites that offer volumes of relevant articles by acclaimed experts in their fields, free for downloading. Finally, since books purchased are yours, when courses are completed books may be used for subsequent children or re-sold to book dealers.

Q: *I'd like to find out a bit more about the contents of listed texts before purchasing. Where can I find reviews?*
A: Check the Table Of Contents for *Resources for Widely Used Books*. Most texts listed in this manual can be reviewed online at web addresses as noted, or by doing a web search by book title, particularly at sites offering used books for sale, e.g., www.alibris.com.

Q: *We'd like to continue with a 'classical education' approach, but are beginning to wonder whether our children are going to be adequately prepared for either college or a career. Do you have any suggestions?*
A: *High School of Your Dreams* allows the family to incorporate college prep, career preparation, and a study of the classics into one program. One is free to select that course of study which best suits the individual student.

Q: *Frankly, I am worried about transcripts and diplomas for college acceptance. Don't I need to be enrolled with a school that will furnish these?*

A: In a word: no.

Essentially, most universities ask simply that students keep and provide a detailed description of their high school curriculum, but neither require that students *'follow a prescribed or approved home-schooling program'* nor provide 'formal transcripts.'

Rather than formal transcripts and diplomas, most colleges and universities look instead at a prospective student's SAT and ACT scores, and for a 'clear sense of intellectual growth and a quest for knowledge.' Many colleges and universities go so far as to state that homeschooled students sometimes have a potential *advantage* over non-homeschooled students, as they have enjoyed the freedom to pursue their own, independent course of study.

Q: *Why does* High School of Your Dreams *include text books that contain some 'politically correct' teaching?*

A: First, no up-to-date Catholic biology or environmental science texts exist at this time; if any such texts existed, this program would place them at the top of the list. Nevertheless, students [particularly the college bound], will be exposed to current social philosophy 'in the world.' *High School of Your Dreams* seeks to prepare students to face challenges to their Faith and beliefs by listing resources that both present, and effectively counter, politically correct materials. Catholic authors or viewpoint are easily identified by looking for the C= notation by titles, and a quick examination of *Supplemental Reading* titles and *Links.*

Q: *Our son wants nothing more than to work with his hands, and hopes to apprentice with a local contractor part-time during high school. He also hates writing. Can he do this and still meet requirements for high school graduation?*

A: Yes. Please read through *High School of Your Dreams* for the full picture; your son may even discover in this volume an acceptable alternative to what he may see as 'dry English Composition.'

Q: *Do I have to do assignments from each category: Possible Essay Topics; Research; Famous Names; and Experiential Projects?*

A: No. For any of the courses, the student might elect to follow a textbook approach alone, selecting and following a text and taking tests to demonstrate mastery. Another student may approach the course by watching videos, reading biographies suggested by Famous Names, and writing reports on those who pioneered or were instrumental in the field. Still others may wish to follow the Experiential Learning track. Ultimately, assignments and approach for each course are determined by ability, interest, and goals of the student.

Q: *I notice that, in many of the courses,* High School of Your Dreams *doesn't recommend one particular text. Why is that?*

A: Several texts, books, and approaches are listed, because *High School of Your Dreams* recognizes that no single text 'fits' all students' learning styles and goals.

Q: *Why do some of the courses have more websites than texts?*

A: Listed links connect the student to course materials, topical exposure, and professional contacts. Broad exposure to a student's field of study opens previously unknown vistas which in turn can aid in the selection of appropriate texts and materials. For example, browsing links in the field of Criminal Justice reveals more than 100 eye-catching Criminal Justice-related careers from forensics chemist to CIA operative. Links provide motivating information on the course of study necessary to reach those career goals, and connections to materials that appeal to the student.

Q: *Do students have to look up all those Church documents?*
A. No. However, Church documents illuminate the subject with the Light of Christ. They are therefore a valuable resource, not only for essays and other reports, but to lay a Catholic foundation and vision for what might become the student's life work. Which of us, given the choice, would not choose a skilled auto mechanic or physician whose practice is also anchored in the depths of God's love?

Q: *My daughter has a midwifery text recommended by our midwife. Does she have to use the text suggested for the course?*
A: No. Listed materials aren't *recommended,* but rather those *commonly used* for the subject. Whether texts, websites, or suggestions for essays, projects and reports, the choices are yours. *High School of Your Dreams* provides the possibilities; you decide which combinations will work best for your student to achieve his educational and vocational goals.

Q: *What is accreditation?*
A: Accreditation is a voluntary process, done by various private organizations. Most people are unaware that there is neither a single, "official" authority, nor a single, agreed-upon standard that determines whether or not a school is granted accreditation! Neither is there a legal standard that designates one accrediting agency as superior to another, nor agreement amongst accrediting agencies as to what standards a school must meet to be granted accreditation.

Failing inner-city schools are accredited, but the majority of their students fail to meet standards for college admission. In contrast, non-accredited homeschool students have a high rate of college admission, often on scholarship, for colleges look far less at accreditation than they do at SAT and ACT scores and prior evidence of student performance. (Accreditation of *colleges* is another subject entirely; colleges set standards as to which courses they will accept for credit from another *college*.)

Thus, "accreditation" of a K-12 program reveals little about the school/provider, either to a prospective student or to a prospective college; it is essentially meaningless as a measurement of academic excellence.

Q: *Are homeschoolers accepted to college without an accredited diploma?*
A: Catholic homeschoolers for years have been accepted without accredited diplomas, not only at noted institutions like Franciscan University of Steubenville, the University of Dallas, and Thomas Aquinas College, but in secular colleges across the United States and Canada. In place of a diploma, institutions measure ability by PSAT, SAT, and ACT scores, and gather information on student coursework, transcripts, accomplishment, and community volunteer activity documented in portfolios provided by the family. While admission requirements differ among colleges, both Canadian and U.S. homeschooled students are routinely accepted into college based on these test scores and family-provided proof of education.

U.S. and Canadian universities also accept students who, instead of presenting a high school diploma, demonstrate their ability to compete at college level by successfully completing a few classes at a local community college before transitioning to university.

In addition, not all students are college-bound; some are gifted in carpentry or construction, and would thrive in an apprenticeship that transitions to a desired profession. Catholic homeschoolers are transitioning into the workforce through both formal and informal apprenticeships. Thus, a student who demonstrates interest and skill in auto mechanics might apprentice himself, gain credit hours toward graduation with hands-on training, and finish high school with a trade.

An 'activity and project' portfolio is an effective means of documenting accomplishment not only to a potential employer, but also for high school graduation and community college admissions, coupled with SAT/ACT scores. [Colleges often view an impressive history of volunteer service in the community and other significant experiential education, coupled with average SAT/ACT scores, as favorably as high SAT/ACT scores coupled with little or no community service or activity.]

Another alternative for transitioning from high school used by Catholic homeschoolers, is the GED. Graduates have used the GED, in conjunction with SAT/ACT scores and without, as a springboard into the armed forces, vocational schools, community colleges, and university.

Thus, Catholic homeschooling students have numerous, routinely used options for demonstrating completion of high school requirements and readiness for college or career, including testing [SAT, ACT, GED], community college classwork, and apprenticeships. Remember that an accredited diploma alone is no guarantee that a student will be accepted by a college; conversely, the student with solid SAT scores and a portfolio brimming with evidence of a motivated young adult will likely be welcomed at university, diploma or not.

Some responses from our recent homeschooling high school survey:

—Of those with students who had graduated homeschool, 73% chose not to use a program with 'accredited' diploma, yet these students had no difficulty gaining admission to college. That is, these 'non-diploma' students were accepted at essentially the same rate at the 27% minority who had graduated with a diploma.

These figures reflect that fact that 'non-accredited' students are routinely accepted by colleges, who pay far more attention to prior student performance and SAT and ACT scores than they do to diplomas.

—80% of these graduates received scholarships

—nearly half of the graduates received grants

—16% graduated college with honors (a far greater rate than public schooled students!)

Q: We have been using another program for high school for the past two years, but would like to switch to High School of Your Dreams, *as it seems a better fit for us. Can we do this without losing credit or having to start all over again?*

A: Absolutely. Any credits earned thus far may be applied to *High School of Your Dreams* for complete credit. It's as simple as including all previously-earned credits in your student's high school transcripts when he begins *High School of Your Dreams*.

EXAMINING THE THREE 'TRACKS':
Which Leads to Your Student's Goal?

College Track: Flexible Textbook Approach

The *High School of Your Dreams* provides the college-bound student a challenging course of study, but at the same time offers a choice of texts, supplemental materials, means of creating coursework that fits the student's interest, and hands-on enrichment. Utilizing a textbook as the sole source of information about a subject often guarantees a painfully dry learning experience; including supplemental readings and experiential activities in the course expands and enlivens the learning experience.

Moreover, the freedom to select core subjects, electives, materials, and method of study affords a serious student the opportunity to better prepare for upper-level instruction in his chosen field than might be possible in a public school. One who aspires to the practice of veterinary medicine may find in a public school that science classes relevant to his chosen field are limited to Biology and Chemistry. The *High School of Your Dreams* allows the student to expand his studies to include Anatomy, Animal Husbandry, or any other elective related to veterinary medicine that might capture his attention. As have other respondents to Catholic Heritage Curricula's High School survey, the student may also volunteer as an aide in a veterinary practice. But let us begin at the beginning.

Required Subjects for Admission to College

First, read over the *Required Subjects for High School Graduation for All Students*. For those with sights set on an Ivy League college, select the maximum number of years for sciences, math, English, and languages; state colleges are generally less demanding depending on the student's major. Scholar- ships are more readily available to those who have followed the most rigorous course of study; the student who is most serious about college success will set for himself the most serious course of study.

Texts marked 'CP' [college prep] are suggested for the college bound; inclusion of supplemental/enrichment materials is also recommended for the broadest exposure possible.

To the Student: What Will I Study in College?

Ask the Holy Spirit for vocational guidance! As you near the end of your eighth grade year, you might wish to set aside St. Joseph's Day [March 19th] for young men, and the Feast of the Annunciation [March 25th, when Our Lady learned of her vocation] for young women, to make a Holy Hour before the Blessed Sacrament, asking for guidance and direction as you prepare for your high school years.

If you are unsure of your vocational goals, you may wish to read through *LifeWork: Finding Your Purpose in Life* or other materials mentioned in this program under *Career Development*. Obtain catalogs by writing to colleges or universities, or find college websites online. Browse fields of study which interest you, taking particular notice of subjects mandatory for the degree program. You might be surprised to learn, for example, that completion of college-level Zoology, Biology, Algebra, Chemistry, and Technical Drafting may be necessary for a degree in Environmental Sciences, or that Psychology and Biology are required subjects for those pursuing a degree in Criminal Justice. Knowing something of college class requirements in your chosen field will help to guide your selection of high school subjects. And keep track of the hours spent in researching your vocational plan; these research hours are part of your education, too.

To the Teacher: Guided Class Planning and Scheduling

The well-prepared college freshman will have satisfied requirements not only for high school graduation, but will also have mastered courses required for college admission and, just as importantly, learned to plan his time well. It is recommended that this planning, which will include selection and purchase of texts and materials, begin several months before the freshman year of high school commences.

Look over classes required for graduation and those suggested for college admission. Using *Suggested Subjects for High School Graduation for the College Bound* as a guide, fill out the *High School: From Freshman to Graduate* form. [See *Forms and Charts* in Table of Contents]. Guide your student in selecting those classes that will best prepare him for the college major he plans to pursue. If he is undecided about a major, selecting electives that reflect his various interests may gradually reveal a field of study.

Note that the four-year plan is not set in stone; courses can be reassessed annually and modified as needs and interests change. It is, nevertheless, recommended that the freshman year commence with a completed *High School: From Freshman to Graduate* form.

Once the four years' course of study has been determined, instruct your student to read the following selections from this volume: 'How are Credits Granted?,' 'Core Classes and Electives: Tailoring Your Wish List to Fit Your Desired Course of Study,' 'Gathering Materials to Teach Your Very Own Electives,' [see Table of Contents] and 'To the College-Bound Student' [below]. Together, brainstorm approaches and potential assignments that might both appeal to the student and achieve his educational goals.

Next, help your student to select appropriate texts, videos, and other materials for his freshman year. Texts and materials may be picked from the list provided with each course, or from titles, not on the list, with which the teacher is already familiar. [If desired, further information about listed titles can be found by typing the title into an internet search.] Whatever his chosen field, the student will want to select the most challenging course of study in both core and elective courses relating to that field. Doing so will lay a solid foundation for post-high school study.

When texts and materials have been purchased, assign the student the task of scheduling required reading and assignments, using the *Class Lesson Plan Form*. [Instruct the student to record hours invested in course development; these hours, logged under the title of 'Career Development and College Prep,' will be the first earned toward graduation.] Upon completion of the *Class Lesson Plan Form*, the student will submit the schedule to his teacher for consultation, possible modification, and approval.

Finally, just before school starts, students may transfer their first assignments from the *Class Lesson Plan Form* into the daily *Battle Planner*; let the school year begin!

To the College-Bound Student: Planning Your Class Schedule

One characteristic of the successful college student is that he has learned to plan his time well. Part of that planning consists in knowing to look over a course syllabus at the beginning of the semester and develop a schedule to allot the time necessary for completion of required reading and assignments. Your first assignment from the *High School of Your Dreams* is to develop a preliminary schedule of your coursework for the year, class by class, and then submit the schedule to your teacher for consultation and approval.

Stepping Up to the Plan

1. Make two copies of the *Class Lesson Plan Form* [see Table of Contents for *Forms and Charts*] for each course that you are taking this year.

2. Turn to the page on which the first course you have chosen is listed in this volume.

3. Using the sample page of the *College Track: Class Lesson Plan Form* as a model, list chosen text and material titles on the form.

4. Count the total number of pages in the text that you plan to use.

5. Divide the total number of pages by the 36 weeks of a standard school year.

6. The resulting number of pages represents the *approximate* number of pages to be read from the text in a week's time. Enter that number on the *Class Lesson Plan Form*. [The 36 weeks is not a mandatory figure, but is simply a standard number of weeks around which to begin scheduling. The highly motivated student may complete the course in less than 36 weeks, or perhaps follow a family schooling schedule outside the given number of weeks. Another option is to note the number of chapters in a text and equitably distribute them over the weeks of the school year.]

7. Now look over your supplemental materials, including videos and books. Is there a particular chapter in the primary text that focuses on the same material? It is best to schedule supplemental materials with text chapters that address similar topics.

8. Add supplemental materials to the schedule.

9. The number and length of essays/research papers that college students are expected to write will vary from course to course. Students using this high school program are offered a variety of suggested topics for research papers and essays, but may certainly substitute their own topics.

Drawing either from suggested topics or ideas of your own, add to your year's schedule, at minimum, two short essays [2-3 pages] each for English Composition, science, and history courses. On the lines provided under 'Supplemental Materials and Essay Topics,' enter the tentative topics on which you will write. Schedule one longer essay [5-10 pages] for at least one of those courses.

In time, you may find that one particular aspect of the subject catches your interest, and you'd like to learn more about that topic. If so, you may certainly substitute a topic of your choice, replacing a previously scheduled topic for the papers, but must still submit a total of at least two papers by the end of each course.

For English Composition, students should follow a writing schedule as suggested by the English Composition program they are using. If the student is utilizing a program with no suggested schedule, the pupil should plan to compose, at minimum, one short essay every three weeks.

10. Hands-on projects or tests may be substituted for one of the three papers, at the discretion of the teacher.

11. Is this course essential to your college major? Would you like hands-on experience in this field? If so, which

of the *Experiential Learning/Career and Vocational Bridge* activities catch your eye? List them, and any others that might come to mind, on your form. Make note to locate and contact professionals in this field. You may use hours amassed as volunteer hours, or as additional credit hours for the course.

12. When you have completed filling out this form, attach it to the second blank copy. Fill out the blank copy week by week throughout the year, making changes in assignments where appropriate.

13. In the same way, fill out forms for the rest of your courses.

As you progress through the year and are exposed to the riches of new discovery, you will likely wish to modify topics, readings, and other portions of your schedule. You are welcome to make modifications, tailoring the class to fit your interests and educational goals; this is the *High School of Your Dreams.* Beginning the year with a *Class Lesson Plan Form* for each course, however, gives you a framework on which to build.

Finally, keep in mind that your ability to grasp similar subjects at the college level is directly proportional to the degree to which you challenged yourself to gain knowledge of the subject in high school. After thoughtful and prayerful consideration, submit a completed *Class Lesson Plan Form* for each course to your teacher for consultation and approval.

A Word About Writing and Test-Taking Skills

Unlike the one-on-one familiarity fostered between student and teacher in the homeschool setting, a classroom teacher in the public school has little opportunity to interact with students on an individual basis and therefore, without testing, may be unaware of deficits in the student's knowledge. Thus, public schools employ frequent testing to measure student mastery. By contrast, it is rare that the homeschool student's level of mastery is not obvious to both student and teacher, even without the benefit of testing.

Still, the high school student will find that occasional test-taking is a necessary part of career preparation, whether the career track includes vocational training or college. By being subjected to occasional timed tests, pupils hone study skills and gain valuable practice for competency tests, mid-terms, or finals that he will face in apprenticeships, vocational classes, or college.

Similarly, the scholar who is comfortable with expository writing will find himself far better prepared for college than the student whose writing experience has been largely limited to creative writing. Expository writing is used to inform the reader; it is the form of writing used for essays, essay questions on tests, and research papers. Students who are practiced in this type of writing will be less intimidated by the inevitable papers that he will be asked to compose, not just in college 'comp' classes, but in virtually every college course.

From chemistry students to welding students, all will face testing at some point and will ultimately be glad to have test-taking skills. Likewise, basic format writing can be useful, not only to the college student, but also to a mechanic explaining to a skeptical customer why a truck needed the questioned repairs. Hence, while the *High School of Your Dreams* grants the student freedom to approach every course in the way that best fits his learning style, students at every level, whether 'College Track,' 'Community College/ Vocational School Track,' or 'Apprenticeship Track,' should challenge themselves to the best of their ability. That challenge should include acquiring writing and test-taking skills.

Because interests, learning styles, and levels of maturity are unique to each student, this volume avoids recommendation of texts or materials, but rather lists a variety of materials commonly used and approved by others. It is up to the parent and student together to decide which materials will provide the best 'fit.'

However, this volume makes one exception to the rule; there is one text that is recommended to students in *High School of Your Dreams*. It is titled *Jensen's Format Writing*, by Frode Jensen, and specifically guides the student, step by step, through expository writing. Students on the 'College Track' would do well to complete the book; those on a less rigorous track will benefit from exposure to the basic writing methods with which *Jensen's Format Writing* begins.

Selecting a College: Catholic Colleges that Love Homeschoolers

College-bound students should seriously, prayerfully consider enrolling in an orthodox Catholic institution. For the most part, the staff and academic support and spiritual and social environment are incomparably superior to what the student might find at a secular institution.

Ave Maria University—www.avemaria.edu, 1-239-280-2500

Belmont Abbey College—www.belmontabbeycollege.edu, 1-888-222-0110

Catholic Distance University—www.cdu.edu, 1-888-254-4CDU

Christendom—www.christendom.edu, 1-800-877-5456

College of St. Mary Magdalen—www.magdalen.edu, 1-877-498-1723

Franciscan University of Steubenville—www.franciscan.edu, 1-740-283-3771

John Paul the Great Catholic University—www.jpcatholic.com, 1-858-653-6740

Our Lady Seat of Wisdom Academy—http://seatofwisdom.org, 1-877-369-6520 [Canada]

Our Lady of Corpus Christi—http://ourladyofcc.org, 1-361-289-9095

St. Thomas More College—www.thomasmorecollege.edu, 1-800-880-8308

Thomas Aquinas College—www.thomasaquinas.edu, 1-805-525-4417

University of Dallas—www.udallas.edu, 1-972-721-5000

University of St. Thomas—www.stthom.edu, 1-713-522-7911

Wyoming Catholic College—www.wyomingcatholiccollege.com, 1-877-322-2930

Visit www.cardinalnewmansociety.org/ TheNewmanGuide.aspx for current info on faithful Catholic colleges.

Applications, Financial Aid, Testing

Sophomores should plan to take the PSAT for practice, then repeat the test in their Junior year. [National Merit Scholarships are based on PSATs.]

In the Senior year, students should plan to take ACTs and SAT in late winter. [Those applying for Ivy League schools should take the SATs in the Fall. September of the Senior year is not too soon to apply to Ivy League schools. Students taking the SATs and ACTs in the Fall so that scores might be available for early admission may also wish to re-take the SAT in late winter.]

Also see *Career Development and College Prep* course in this volume.

Community College/ Vocational School Track: Independent Study Approach

Planning Your Course of Study

What are your vocational goals? If you are unsure, ask the Holy Spirit for vocational guidance! As you near the end of your eighth grade year, you might wish to set aside St. Joseph's Day [March 19th] for young men, and the Feast of the Annunciation [March 25th, when Our Lady learned of her vocation] for young women, to make a Holy Hour before the Blessed Sacrament, asking for guidance and direction as you prepare for your high school years.

After Holy Hour, you may also wish to read through *LifeWork: Finding Your Purpose in Life* or other materials mentioned in this program under *Career Development*. Find community college and vocational school websites, or acquire copies of their catalogs, then browse fields of study which interest you, taking particular notice of subjects mandatory for the degree program. You might be surprised to learn, for example, that a degree in Environmental Sciences requires completion of college-level Zoology, Biology, Algebra, Chemistry, and Technical Drafting, or that Psychology and Biology are required subjects for those pursuing a degree in Criminal Justice. Knowing something of community college/ vocational school requirements in your chosen field will help to guide your selection of high school subjects. And keep track of the hours spent in researching your vocational plan; these research hours are part of your education, too.

Keep in mind that scholarships are more readily available to those who have followed the most rigorous course of study; the student who is most serious about community college/ vocational school success will set for himself the most challenging course of study in his chosen field, both in core and elective courses relating to that field.

Methods of Gaining Credit: Community College/ Vocational School Track

The *High School of Your Dreams* provides the student a challenging course of study, but at the same time offers a choice of texts, supplemental materials, means of creating coursework that fits the student's interest, and hands-on enrichment. Utilizing a textbook as the sole source of information about a subject often guarantees a painfully dry learning experience; including supplemental readings and experiential activities in the course expands and enlivens the learning experience.

Moreover, the freedom to select core subjects, electives, materials, and method of study affords the focused student the opportunity to better prepare for post-high school instruction in his chosen field than might be possible in a public school. One who aspires to a nursing career may find in a public school that science classes relevant to his chosen field are limited to Biology and Chemistry. The *High School of Your Dreams* allows the student to expand his studies to include Anatomy, Fetology, Midwifery, or any other elective related to nursing that might capture his attention. As have other respondents to Catholic Heritage Curricula's High School survey, the student may access volunteer experiences to gain hands-on knowledge of his chosen field.

But let us begin at the beginning. The student may wish to use texts marked 'CP' [college prep] in his chosen field of study, but has the freedom to select means of acquiring knowledge beyond texts, including *Research* selections [in this volume], supplemental readings, audio books, videos, and experiential activities. 'Field hours' from experiential activities outside the classroom, including job sites, apprenticeship, and volunteer hours, are valid means of gaining course credit.

To the Teacher: Guided Class Planning and Scheduling

A student preparing to enter community college or vocational training will have satisfied requirements not only for high school graduation, but will also have a good grasp, at an introductory level, of courses that he will encounter in his chosen field of study. Just as importantly, he will have learned to plan his time well. It is recommended that this planning, which will include selection and purchase of texts and materials, begin several months before the freshman year of high school commences.

Look over classes required for high school graduation and those that will likely be encountered, post-high school, in the student's chosen field of study. With these courses in mind, fill out the *High School: From Freshman to Graduate* form. [See *Forms and Charts* in Table of Contents]. Guide your student in selecting those classes that will best prepare him for the field of study that he plans to pursue. If he is undecided, selecting electives that reflect his various interests may gradually reveal a vocational bent.

Note that the four year plan is not set in stone; courses can be reassessed annually and modified as needs and interests change. It is, nevertheless, recommended that the freshman year commence with a completed *High School: From Freshman to Graduate* form.

Once the four years' course of study has been determined, instruct your student to read the following selections from this volume: 'How are Credits Granted?,' 'Core Classes and Electives: Tailoring Your Wish List to Fit Your Desired Course of Study,' 'Gathering Materials to Teach Your Very Own Electives,' and 'To the Student,' below. Brainstorm together approaches and potential assignments that might both appeal to the student and achieve his educational goals.

Next, help your student to select appropriate texts, videos, and other materials for his freshman year. Texts and materials may be picked from the list provided with each course, or from titles, not on the list, with which the teacher is already familiar. [If desired, further information about listed titles can be found by typing the title into an internet search.]

When texts and materials have been purchased, assign the student the task of scheduling required reading and assignments, using the *Class Lesson Plan Form*. [Instruct the student to record hours invested in course development; these hours, logged under the title of 'Career Development and College Prep,' will be the first earned toward graduation.] Upon completion of the *Class Lesson Plan Form*, the student will submit the schedule to his teacher for consultation, possible modification, and approval.

To the Community College/ Vocational School-Bound Student: Planning Your Class Schedule

One characteristic of the successful student is that he has learned to plan his time well. Part of that planning consists in knowing to look over a course syllabus at the beginning of the semester and develop a schedule to allot the time necessary for completion of required reading and assignments. Your first assignment from the *High School of Your Dreams*, is to develop a preliminary schedule of your coursework for the year, class by class, and then submit the schedule to your teacher for consultation and approval.

Stepping Up to the Plan

1. Make two copies of the *Class Lesson Plan Form* [see Table of Contents for *Forms and Charts*] for each course that you are taking this year.

2. Turn to the page on which the first course you have chosen is listed in this volume.

3. Using the sample page of the *Community College/Vocational Track: Class Lesson Plan Form* as a model, list chosen text and material titles on the form.

4. Count the total number of pages in the text that you will use.

5. Divide the total number of pages by the 36 weeks of a standard school year.

6. The resulting number of pages represents the *approximate* number of pages to be read from the text in a week's time. Enter that number on the *Class Lesson Plan Form*. [The 36 weeks is not a mandatory figure, but is simply a standard number of weeks around which to begin scheduling. The highly motivated student may complete the course in less than 36 weeks, or perhaps follow a family schooling schedule outside the given number of weeks. Another option is to note the number of chapters in a text and equitably distribute them over the weeks of the school year.]

If you are using a video series in place of a text, similarly divide the number of lessons or units for distribution throughout the school year.

7. Now look over your remaining supplemental materials. Find like topics that focus on the same material covered in chapter or lesson headings, above. It is best to schedule supplemental materials with 'core' text or video chapters that address similar topics.

8. Add these supplemental materials to the schedule.

9. The number and length of essays/ research papers that community college/ vocational students are expected to write will vary from course to course. Students using this high school program are offered a variety of suggested topics for research papers and essays, but may certainly substitute their own topics.

Drawing either from suggested topics or ideas of your own, add to your year's schedule, at minimum, one short essay [1-2 pages] for each elective course. Plan one longer [3-4 pages] essay or research paper for your favorite class.

On the lines provided under 'Supplemental Materials and Essay Topics,' enter the tentative topics on which you will write.

In time, you may find that one particular aspect of the subject catches your interest, and you'd like to learn more about that topic. If so, you may certainly substitute a topic of your choice, replacing a previously scheduled topic for the papers.

[For English Composition, students should follow a writing schedule as suggested by the English Composition program they are using.]

10. Hands-on projects or tests may be substituted for some essays, at the discretion of the teacher.

11. Is this course essential to your chosen field of study? Would you like hands-on experience in this field? If so,

which of the *Experiential Learning/ Career and Vocational Bridge* activities catch your eye? List them, and any others that might come to mind, on your form. Make note to locate and contact professionals in this field. You may use hours amassed as volunteer hours, or as additional credit hours for the course.

12. When you have completed filling out this form, attach it to the second blank copy. Fill out the blank copy week by week throughout the year, making changes in assignments where appropriate.

13. In the same way, fill out forms for the rest of your courses.

As you progress through the year and are exposed to the riches of new discovery, you will likely wish to modify topics, readings, and other portions of your schedule. You are welcome to make modifications, tailoring the class to fit your interests and educational goals; this is the *High School of Your Dreams*. Beginning the year with a *Class Lesson Plan Form* for each course, however, gives you a framework on which to build.

Finally, keep in mind that your ability to grasp similar subjects at a post-high school level is directly proportional to the degree to which you challenged yourself to gain knowledge of the subject in high school. After thoughtful and prayerful consideration, submit a completed *Class Lesson Plan Form* for each course to your teacher for consultation and approval.

A Word About Writing and Test-Taking Skills

Unlike the one-on-one familiarity fostered between student and teacher in the homeschool setting, a classroom teacher in the public school has little opportunity to interact with students on an individual basis and therefore may not be aware of deficits in the student's knowledge without testing. Thus, public schools employ frequent testing to measure student mastery. By contrast, it is rare that the homeschool student's level of mastery is not obvious to both student and teacher, even without the benefit of testing.

Still, the high school student will find that occasional test-taking is a necessary part of career preparation, whether the career track includes vocational training or college. By being subjected to occasional timed tests, pupils hone study skills and gain valuable practice for competency tests, mid-terms, or finals that he will face in apprenticeships, vocational classes, or college.

Similarly, the scholar who is comfortable with expository writing will find himself far better prepared for post high school studies than the student whose writing experience has been largely limited to creative writing. Expository writing is used to inform the reader; it is the form of writing used for essays, essay questions on tests, and research papers. Students who are practiced in this type of writing will be less intimidated by the inevitable papers that they will be asked to compose, not just in college 'comp' classes, but in virtually every college course.

From chemistry students to welding students, all will face testing at some point and will ultimately be glad to have test-taking skills. Likewise, basic format writing can be useful, not only to the college student, but also to a mechanic explaining to a skeptical customer why a truck needed the questioned repairs. Hence, while the *High School of Your Dreams* grants the student freedom to approach every course in the way that best fits his learning style, students at every level, whether 'College Track,' 'Community College/ Vocational School Track,' or 'Apprenticeship Track,' should challenge themselves to the best of their ability. That challenge should include acquiring writing and test-taking skills.

Because interests, learning styles, and levels of maturity are unique to each student, this volume avoids recommendation of texts or materials, but rather lists a variety of materials commonly used and approved by others. It is up to the parent and student together to decide which materials will provide the best 'fit.'

However, this volume makes one exception to the rule; there is one text that is recommended to students in *High School of Your Dreams*. It is titled *Jensen's Format Writing*, by Frode Jensen, and specifically guides the student, step by step, through expository writing. Students on the 'College Track' would do well to complete the book; those on a less rigorous track will benefit from exposure to the basic writing methods with which *Jensen's Format Writing* begins.

> *A course of study designed to 'fit all' often fits none.*

Apprenticeship/School-to-Work Track: Experiential Approach

Planning Your Course of Study

What are your vocational goals? If you are unsure, ask the Holy Spirit for vocational guidance! You may also wish to read through *LifeWork: Finding Your Purpose in Life* or other materials mentioned in this program under *Career Development*. As you near the end of your eighth grade year, you might set aside St. Joseph's Day [March 19th] for young men, and the Feast of the Annunciation [March 25th, when Our Lady learned of her vocation] for young women, to make a Holy Hour before the Blessed Sacrament, asking for guidance and direction as you prepare for your high school years.

If you are already considering an apprenticeship in a particular profession, locate and contact someone practicing that profession. Arrange for a personal or telephone interview to learn what educational requirements are necessary to the profession; the information may also be obtained through an internet search.

One might note, for example, that carpenters and electricians need math and science skills. Becoming familiar with the educational requirements of your chosen field will help to guide your selection of high school subjects. The diligent student who is most serious about settling into a successful apprenticeship will set for himself the most serious course of study, both in core and elective courses relating to that field. And keep track of the hours spent in researching your vocational plan; these research hours are part of your education, too.

Methods of Gaining Credit: Apprenticeship

The *High School of Your Dreams* offers the student a challenging course of study, but at the same time includes a choice of texts, supplemental materials, hands-on experience, and means of creating coursework that fits the student's interests.

Moreover, freedom to select core subjects, electives, materials, and method of study affords the focused student the opportunity to better prepare for post-high school instruction in his chosen field than might be possible in a public school. One who aspires to a career in landscaping may find in a public school few or no classes relevant to his chosen field. The *High School of Your Dreams* allows the student to expand his studies to include Botany, Environmental Sciences, or any other elective related to landscaping that might capture his attention. More significantly, as have other respondents to Catholic Heritage Curricula's High School survey, the student may access volunteer or apprenticeship experiences to gain hands-on training in his chosen field.

But let us begin at the beginning. The student may wish to use texts marked 'CP' [college prep] in his chosen field of study, or 'B' texts [basic instructional level], but has the freedom to select means of acquiring knowledge beyond texts, including *Research* selections [in this volume], supplemental readings, audio books for the auditory learner, videos and, most of all, experiential activities. Experiential, hands-on activities outside the classroom, including job sites, apprenticeship, and volunteer hours, are valid means of gaining course credit.

A Word About Writing and Test-Taking Skills

Unlike the one-on-one familiarity fostered between student and teacher in the homeschool setting, a classroom teacher in the public school has little opportunity to interact with students on an individual basis and therefore may not be aware of deficits in the student's understanding without testing. Thus, public schools employ frequent testing to measure student mastery. By contrast, it is rare that the homeschool student's level of mastery is not obvious to both student and teacher, even without the benefit of testing.

From chemistry students to welding students, all will face testing at some point and will ultimately be glad to have test-taking skills. Likewise, basic format writing can be useful, not only to the college student, but also to a mechanic explaining to a skeptical customer why a truck needed the questioned repairs. Hence, while the *High School of Your Dreams* grants the student freedom to approach every course in the way that best fits his learning style, students at every level should challenge themselves to the best of their ability. That challenge should include acquiring writing and test-taking skills.

Because interests, learning styles, and levels of maturity are unique to each student, this volume avoids recommendation of texts or materials, but rather lists a variety of materials commonly used and approved by others. It is up to the parent and student together to decide which materials will provide the best 'fit.'

However, this volume makes one exception to the rule; there is one text that is recommended to students in *High School of Your Dream*s. It is titled *Jensen's Format Writing*, by Frode Jensen, and specifically guides the student, step by step, through expository writing. All students can benefit from exposure to the basic writing methods with which *Jensen's Format Writing* begins.

To the Teacher: Guided Class Planning and Scheduling

A student preparing to enter an apprenticeship will have satisfied requirements not only for high school graduation, but will also have a good grasp, at an introductory level, of skills that he will encounter in his chosen field of study. Just as importantly, he will have learned to plan his time well. It is recommended that this planning, which will include selection and purchase of texts and materials, begin several months before the freshman year of high school commences.

Look over classes required for high school graduation and those that will likely be encountered, post-high school, in the student's chosen field. With these courses in mind, fill out the *High School from Freshman to Graduate* form. [See *Forms and Charts* in Table of Contents]. Guide your student in selecting those classes that will best prepare him for the vocation that he plans to pursue. If he is undecided, selecting electives that reflect his various interests may gradually reveal a vocational bent.

Note that the four year plan is not set in stone; courses can be reassessed annually and modified as needs and interests change. It is, nevertheless, recommended that the freshman year commence with a completed *High School: From Freshman to Graduate* form.

Once the four years' course of study has been determined, instruct your student to read the following selections from this volume: 'How are Credits Granted?,' 'Core Classes and Electives: Tailoring Your Wish List to Fit Your Desired Course of Study,' 'Gathering Materials to Teach Your Very Own Electives,' and 'To the Student,' below. Brainstorm together approaches and potential assignments that might both appeal to the student and achieve his educational goals.

Next, help your student to select appropriate texts, videos, and other materials for his freshman year. Texts and materials may be picked from the list provided with each course, or from titles, not on the list, with which the teacher is already familiar. [If desired, further information about listed titles can be found by typing the title into an internet search.]

When texts and materials have been purchased, assign the student the task of scheduling required reading and assignments, using the *Class Lesson Plan Form*. [Instruct the student to record hours invested in course development; these hours, logged under the title of 'Career Development and College Prep,' will be the first earned toward graduation.] Upon completion of the *Class Lesson Plan Form*, the student will submit the schedule to his teacher for consultation, possible modification, and approval.

To the Student on an Apprenticeship Track: Planning Your Class Schedule

One characteristic of a successful building contractor is that he knows how first to assess what is required to complete a job, then logically plan, step by step, a schedule that will allow him to bring his work to completion. In the same way, the successful student will first assess what is required to complete his training, then logically plan, step by step, a schedule that will allow him to bring his work to completion. Part of that planning in the *High School of Your Dreams* consists of looking over texts and course requirements before school begins and then developing a schedule to allot the time necessary for completion of required reading and assignments. Additionally, the student on an Apprenticeship Track will need to make contacts for 'field work,' or hands-on experience in the field of his choice.

That field work will then also be included, for credit, in the scheduling.

Your first assignment then, is to develop a preliminary schedule of your course and field work for the year, class by class, and submit the schedule to your teacher for consultation and approval.

Stepping Up to the Plan

1. Make two copies of the *Class Lesson Plan Form* [see Table of Contents for *Forms and Charts*] for each course that you are taking this year.

2. Turn to the page on which the first course you have chosen is listed in this volume.

3. Using the sample page of the *Apprenticeship Track: Class Lesson Plan Form* as a model, list chosen text and material titles on the form.

4. Count the total number of pages in the text you plan to use.

5. Divide the total number of pages by the 36 weeks of a standard school year.

6. The resulting number of pages represents the *approximate* number of pages to be read from the text in a week's time. Enter that number on the *Class Lesson Plan Form*. [The 36 weeks is not a mandatory figure, but is simply a standard number of weeks around which to begin scheduling. The highly motivated student may complete the course in less than 36 weeks, or perhaps follow a family schooling schedule outside the given number of weeks. Another option is to note the number of chapters in a text and equitably distribute them over the weeks of the school year.]

If you are using a video series in place of a text, similarly divide the number of lessons or units for distribution throughout the school year.

7. Now look over your remaining supplemental materials. Find like topics that focus on the same material covered in chapter or lesson headings from the texts that you listed. It is best to schedule supplemental materials with 'core' text or video chapters that address similar topics.

8. Add these supplemental materials to the schedule.

9. At first glance, one might think that writing skills are unnecessary, for example, to a building contractor. However, the ability to present ideas in written form is useful in every field. [Each time a contractor writes up an estimate or a proposed contract, he relies on composition skills.]

Drawing either from suggested topics or ideas of your own, add to your year's schedule, at minimum, one short essay [1-2 pages] for each elective course. Plan one longer [3-4 pages] essay or research paper for your favorite class.

On the lines provided under 'Supplemental Materials and Essay Topics,' enter the tentative topics on which you will write.

In time, you may find that one particular aspect of the subject catches your interest, and you'd like to learn more about that topic. If so, you may certainly substitute a topic of your choice, replacing a previously scheduled topic for the papers.

[For English Composition, students should follow a writing schedule as suggested by the English Composition program they are using.]

10. Hands-on projects, daily journals recording field experiences, or tests may be substituted for some essays, at the discretion of the teacher.

11. Is this course essential to your chosen field of study? Would you like hands-on experience in this field? If so, which of the *Experiential Learning/ Career and Vocational Bridge* activities catch your eye? [See list under each course heading and also complete listing in Table of Contents.] List them, and any others that might come to mind, on your form. Make note to locate and contact professionals in this field. You may use hours amassed in the field for course credit or as volunteer hours.

12. When you have completed filling out this form, attach it to the second blank copy. Fill out the blank copy week by week throughout the year, making changes in assignments where appropriate.

13. In the same way, fill out forms for the rest of your courses.

As you progress through the year and are exposed to the riches of new discovery, you will likely wish to modify topics, readings, and other portions of your schedule. You are welcome to make modifications, tailoring the class to fit your interests and educational goals; this is the *High School of Your Dreams.* Beginning the year with a *Class Lesson Plan Form* for each course, however, gives you a framework on which to build.

Finally, keep in mind that your ability to grasp similar subjects at a post-high school level is related directly to the degree to which you challenged yourself to gain knowledge of the subject in high school. After thoughtful and prayerful consideration, submit a completed *Class Lesson Plan Form* for each course to your teacher for consultation and approval.

> *Teaching a child of six to drive an automobile would be inappropriate; it would be equally inappropriate not to provide instruction in safe driving skills to a young adult. In a similar fashion, good parenting and teaching include first guiding the student, and then releasing him, wisely prepared and armed with the armor of God, into a secular world.*

Core Subjects
and Electives

AERONAUTICS

Science Labs:

Labs essentially provide students an opportunity to test theories against reality, i.e., allow students to apply what they have learned from their texts in hands-on settings.

Most colleges don't require documented science labs as part of a high school science course. In fact, there is no national standard or definition of what exactly constitutes a high school science lab. However, since some colleges do require documented science lab work, it is best to include at least 20 hours of lab work in each science course that your student takes.

Keeping in mind that 'lab' means hands-on learning that applies book-learning to reality, credit for a Geology lab might be earned by visiting a fossil bed and searching for fossils. Students might photograph the rock formations where the fossils were found, identify the type of rock in which the fossils were found, and identify the types of fossils therein. Brief descriptions or notations about why and how fossils were found in this type of geological structure might be included. All of this information would then be assembled into a lab report.

An Environmental Science lab might include similar notations about discoveries made in a pond ecosystem, including a description and photographs of the pond, plant and animal aquatic life, and conclusions as to how and why those particular plants and animals live in that environment.

In essence, no matter which science courses are chosen, students will devote at least 20 hours of class time to lab work—that is, hands-on projects, exploration, and conclusions about what the student learned—which will be documented in a hard-copy notebook or portfolio.

Parents might also double-check with colleges to which students might apply to determine whether or not there are lab requirements.

Please also note that students who enroll in science classes at local colleges gain those lab credits while simultaneously earning both high school and college credit.

Book List:

S=*Aerodynamics for Naval Aviators,* Hugh Hurt

S=*Aviation: The First 100 Years*—Barron's

S, B=Aviation: Boy Scout Merit Badge Handbook

S=*Introduction to Aeronautics: A Design Perspective*, 2nd Edition [Aiaa Education Series] by R. Stiles, and J. Bertin, United States Air Force Academy S. Brandt, Cranfield Institute of Technology, and R. Whitford

S=https://store.im.tamu.edu—Instructional Materials Service, curricula: aircraft maintenance services

S=*Rod Machado's Private Pilot Handbook,* Rod Machado

S, B=Space Exploration: Boy Scout Merit Badge Handbook

Supplemental Reading:

Aviation History magazine—www.historynet.com/magazines/aviation_history/

[see **Famous Names Related to Aeronautics** for biographical reading]

Links:

www.cadets.ca/air/—Royal Canadian Air Cadets

www.aopa.org/—Aircraft Owners and Pilots Association

www.aviationweek.com—aviation news

http://gocivilairpatrol.com—Civil Air Patrol

www.cato.org/—enter 'science and space' in search box

www.doleta.gov/oa/brochure/
aerospace_fact_sheet.pdf—aerospace
apprenticeship information

www.eaa.org/—Experimental Aircraft
Association

www.faa.gov/—Federal Aviation

www.erau.edu—Embry-Riddle
Aeronautical University—aviation,
aerospace

www.getofftheground.com/books.
html—piloting, other books

www.nasa.gov/offices/education/
about/index.html—NASA; aeronautics
education, design, more

www.jpl.nasa.gov—Jet Propulsion
Laboratory

www.khake.com/page41.html—aviation
and aerospace career descriptions,
requirements

www.landings.com—aviation
information, links

www.mercyairlift.org—airborne
disaster assistance

www.nasa.gov/centers/glenn/
education/index.html—student
opportunities, education, interactive

http://science.nasa.gov

www.rocketcontest.org—Team America
Rocketry Contest

www.popularmechanics.com—Popular
Mechanics magazine: automotive,
aviation, computers, home improvement, robotics, woodworking, more

www.priestpilots.org—National
Association of Priest Pilots

www.quest.arc.nasa.gov

http://www.discoveryeducation.com/
teachers/free-lesson-plans/flight.cfm

http://spaceflight.nasa.gov/home/

www.historynet.com/aviation-history—
Aviation History magazine

http://virtualskies.arc.nasa.
gov—aeronautics, aviation research,
navigation, and more

http://www.ipl.org/div/subject/
—Internet Public Library

Church Teaching:

Laborem exercens: On Human Work, Papal
Document John Paul II [www.catholic-pages.
com/documents/]

Possible Essay Topics:

• Discuss the role of weather as it relates to
aeronautics. In the case of piloting winged
aircraft, list at least three weather conditions
that might reduce flight safety. Present the
means available for being aware of, and
avoiding, those conditions. What corrective
action might be taken if those conditions were
encountered unexpectedly?

• Read Laborem exercens, Section 25, Work
as a Sharing in the Activity of the Creator.
We are called, even in our secular activities
and employment, 'to assist one another to live
holier lives.' In what ways might those working
in aeronautics, whether through personal
example or public service, fulfill this calling?
Elaborate and discuss.

• Research and read about defects and design
flaws that have caused calamity in the U.S.
Space Program. How were those defects
discovered? In what way did their discovery
affect the advancement of the space program?
How were they corrected?

• In the 1970's, Russian Cosmonauts returned
from space and reportedly commented that
they had been in the heavens but had not
found evidence of God there. Read Psalm 139:
7-10. In your studies of aeronautics, how have
you encountered the Creator of the Heavens?

In what ways does your Faith influence your interest in, or grasp of, aeronautics?
• Given the opportunity, what dreams do you have for a future in aeronautics? List your dreams, plans, and goals. Arrange them in order of 'attack.' Outline steps toward their achievement. Write about your dream.

Research:

You may, in conjunction with your text and field work, wish to investigate the following topics in greater depth. Credit may be obtained through reading and hands-on, experiential learning including field trips, volunteering, and apprenticeships. Learning is demonstrated through the production of projects, experiments, essays or reports. Reports may be based on note-taking and observation and might include graphs, charts, illustrations and diagrams.

To aid in research, ask and answer, "Who, what, where, when and why?" [For example: *What* law of motion produces lift? *Who* was instrumental in developing the earliest models of aircraft? *How* does airflow produce lift?]

Aircraft:
• lift
    angle of attack
    high-lift devices
• drag
    friction drag
    form drag
    induced drag
• describe differences
    ground speed
    true air speed
    indicated air speed
• Wing design: describe differences and function
    delta wing
    swept-back wing
    swept-forward wing
    straight wing

• tail function
    fin
    rudder
    stabilizer
    elevator
    stabilator
• tail design: describe differences and function
    anhedral assembly
    right-angle assembly
    swept-back assembly
    T assembly
    twin assembly
    V assembly
• propeller design: describe differences and function
    two-bladed, three-bladed, four-bladed
• describe differences and function, particularly in speed and power
    reciprocating engine
    jet engine
    rocket engine
• navigation
    pilotage
    dead reckoning
    radio navigation

Rocket types: describe differences and function
    solid-propellant
    liquid-propellant
    electric-powered
    nuclear-powered

Famous Names Related to Aeronautics: Read and Report

In what ways did the Catholic Church aid in discoveries/inventions/advancement?

How did the person's faith [or lack thereof] influence his/her work?

What might have motivated the person to become involved in the field?

In what ways did his/her discoveries/inventions/advancement change the field of study?

In what ways did his/her discoveries/inventions/advancement ultimately change society?

Sir George Cayley

Leonardo da Vinci

Sir Isaac Newton

Ferdinand von Zepplin

Roger Bacon [Franciscan Monk]

Otto Lillienthal

Samuel Langley

Orville and Wilbur Wright [homeschooled]

Charles Lindbergh

Amelia Earhart

James Doolittle

Charles Yaeger

William Lear [homeschooled]

Experiential Learning/Career and Vocational Bridge:

[See Table of Contents for *Experiential Learning: Discovery Centers* with focus on aeronautic sites]

[See Table of Contents for *Process Project Outline* and *Following in Their Footsteps* projects]

Aeronautics Projects:

• Research, design, and construct a rocket. Change design; document changes and note how the alterations affected flight patterns and range.

• Research, design, and construct a remote control airplane. Change design; document changes and note how the alterations affected flight patterns.

• Participate in Civil Air Patrol Cadet program [Civil Air Patrol is an U.S. Air Force Auxiliary; http://gocivilairpatrol.com, check for local group. Each year CAP awards more than $200,000 in scholarships; about 10% of each year's freshman class at the U.S. Air Force Academy participated in the Air Cadet program.]

• Join a flying club.

• Volunteer at a local airport.

AGRICULTURAL SCIENCE

Science Labs:

Labs essentially provide students an opportunity to test theories against reality, i.e., allow students to apply what they have learned from their texts in hands-on settings.

Most colleges don't require documented science labs as part of a high school science course. In fact, there is no national standard or definition of what exactly constitutes a high school science lab. However, since some colleges do require documented science lab work, it is best to include at least 20 hours of lab work in each science course that your student takes.

Keeping in mind that 'lab' means hands-on learning that applies book-learning to reality, credit for a Geology lab might be earned by visiting a fossil bed and searching for fossils. Students might photograph the rock formations where the fossils were found, identify the type of rock in which the fossils were found, and identify the types of fossils therein. Brief descriptions or notations about why and how fossils were found in this type of geological structure might be included. All of this information would then be assembled into a lab report.

An Environmental Science lab might include similar notations about discoveries made in a pond ecosystem, including a description and photographs of the pond, plant and animal aquatic life, and conclusions as to how and why those particular plants and animals live in that environment.

In essence, no matter which science courses are chosen, students will devote at least 20 hours of class time to lab work—that is, hands-on projects, exploration, and conclusions about what the student learned—which will be documented in a hard-copy notebook or portfolio.

Parents might also double-check with colleges to which students might apply to determine whether or not there are lab requirements.

Please also note that students who enroll in science classes at local colleges gain those lab credits while simultaneously earning both high school and college credit.

Resource List:

http://store.im.tamu.edu—agricultural science curricula including animal science, horses, livestock, agribusiness, science technology engineering, environmental and natural resource systems and more

Supplemental Reading:

S, B=Animal Science: Merit Badge Series

S, B=Dog Care: Merit Badge Series

S, B=Farm Mechanics: Merit Badge Series

S, B=Gardening: Merit Badge Series

S, B=Horsemanship: Merit Badge Series

S=In Farmers and Ranchers Do We Trust? [http://perc.org/articles/farmers-and-ranchers-do-we-trust] curriculum in economics and environment

S, B=Veterinary Medicine: Merit Badge Series

Links:

www.4-h-canada.ca/—4-H Canada

www.4-h.org/—4-H

www.cfact.org—Committee for a Constructive Tomorrow, agriculture, environment

www.extension.umn.edu/projects/yardandgarden/ygbriefs/h462deer-coping.html—deer damage control

www.ffa.org—Future Farmers of America

www.invasivespeciesinfo.gov—invasive plants, animals, microbes, control

www.khake.com/page58.html—apprenticeship info, training resources

www.khake.com/page39.html—agriculture, aquaculture, forestry career guide www.khake.com/page81.html—free lessons and lesson plans: agriculture, animal science, horticulture

www.martindalecenter.com/Vet.html— veterinary resources

www.nal.usda.gov—National Agricultural Library

http://netvet.wustl.edu/vet.htm— veterinary resources

www.nrcs.usda.gov—Natural Resources Conservation Service—land use, soil erosion, water quality, wetlands, conservation, natural resources.

http://ohioline.osu.edu/w-fact/pdf/0005.pdf—deer damage control

www.ou.edu/cas/botany-micro/www-vl/—botany, agriculture, biosciences, biology, forestry; university contacts

www.dtnprogressivefarmer.com—'ask the vet,' livestock, magazine

http://rurallivingcanada.4t.com—Rural Living in Canada

www.discoveryeducation.com/teachers/free-lesson-plans/index.cfm—free lessons and lesson plans life science, animals, plants

http://www.ipl.org/div/subject/—Internet Public Library

Supplemental Reading:

A wealth of information relating to the care/raising of animals from guinea pigs to rabbits to beef cattle is available from websites listed above, FFA, 4-H, the county extension, and the public library, e.g., *A Guide to Raising Pigs* by Kelly Klober; *Profitable Beef Production*, by M. Mc Cooper; *Raising Milk Goats the Modern Way*, by Jerry Belanger.

Church Teaching:

C=www.newadvent.org/cathen—Catholic encyclopedia

C=www.catholic-pages.com/—Catholic documents and teaching, current events, more

C=www.zenit.org/en—Vatican news; recent and archived Papal/Church statements

C=*Laborem exercens: On Human Work,* Papal Document John Paul II [www.catholic-pages.com/documents/]

CCC #339 & 342; #2415-2418

Possible Essay Topics:

• Read *Laborem exercens: On Human Work, Sections #5, #21, and #27.* According to Section #21, what type of work is considered by the Church to be of 'fundamental importance'? In Section #5, the Church teaches that agricultural labor fulfills Gen. 1:26 and 28 in what ways? Section #27 indicates that agricultural work can actually be a 'collaboration with the Son of God' toward what end? Using the ideas in these three sections, write an essay about the dignity and place of agriculture in serving humanity.

• Read *CCC #339, 342, & 2417.* What might be some examples of the 'disordered use' of Creation mentioned in #339? Note the comparative value of men and sheep in #342. Can there be extremes of 'disordered use' on both ends of the scale? How does Church teaching [#2417] wisely balance any extremes?

• Keep a detailed journal of an agricultural project selected from **Experiential Learning** suggestions. At the completion of your project, outline all steps and results. Using your outline, write an account of your project.

• What state or federal regulations impact your land/water/pesticide/fertilizer use? Find out more about these regulations through your county extension, Soil and Water Conservation District, or on the internet. List both the negative and positive impact of these regulations on land use, crops, or livestock. Which three points are the most critical to your agricultural venture? Outline those points, then write an essay explaining your support for, or concerns about, those regulations. You may wish to send the finished essay to your congressional/provincial representatives.

• List, outline, and discuss the advantages and disadvantages of mixed farming vs. specialized farming. Include weather, disease, and market factors.

• Given the opportunity, what dreams do you have for a future in agriculture? List your dreams, plans, and goals. Arrange them in order of 'attack.' Outline steps toward their achievement. Write about your dream.

Research:

You may, in conjunction with your text and field work, wish to investigate the following topics in greater depth. Credit may be obtained by reading and hands-on, experiential learning including field trips, volunteering, and apprenticeships, or through breeding/raising, observing, and marketing of animals or plant crops. Reports on production may draw from daily journals and include graphs, charts, illustrations and diagrams.

Following are topics that may be investigated for an introduction to this course. To aid in research and writing, ask and answer, "Who, what, where, when and why?" [For example: *Where* did the breed/plant strain originate? *What* desirable traits have been bred into this breed/plant strain? *Who* was instrumental in developing the breed? *How* are diseases treated/prevented? *Why* is this the most suitable feed?]

Livestock:
• feed
    commercial feeds/home-mixed feeds
    maintenance feeding
    finishing feeds
    mineral supplements/deficiencies
    feeding/watering stations
• housing
• means of containment [fencing, pens]
• breeding
    optimum age
    heat cycle
    gestation
    improving the breed
    special housing requirements
    potential problems with delivery
• young, special care for
    feed
    housing
    growth and development
• diseases unique to the animal and prevention
• immunizations
• health care [e.g., mastitis, abscesses, internal and external parasites, scours]
• differences in and selection of breeds
• showing the animal
• marketing the animal
• home butchering

Agricultural Crops:
• properties of soil
    classifying
    nutrients and deficiencies
    organic matter
• erosion
    causes
    control
• fertilizers
    inorganic
    organic
• local crop production
    plant diseases and control

post-harvest management
- crop rotation

Famous Names Related to Agricultural Science: Read and Report

In what ways did the Catholic Church aid in discoveries/inventions/advancement?

How did the person's faith [or lack thereof] influence his/her work?

What might have motivated the person to become involved in the field?

In what ways did his/her discoveries/inventions/advancement change the field of study?

In what ways did his/her discoveries/inventions/advancement ultimately change society?

Robert Bakewell—selective breeding

Luther Burbank—plants

George Washington Carver—plants

John Deere—farm machinery

Cyrus McCormick—farm machinery

Fr. Gregor Mendel—genetics/hybrids

Charles Townshend—crop rotation

Experiential Learning/Career and Vocational Bridge:

[See Table of Contents for *Process Project Outline* and *Following in Their Footsteps* projects.]

Agricultural Science Projects:

- Collect soil samples from various points. Classify; develop and put into practice a method for improving soil fertility. Plant small, experimental plots in amended and non-amended soils. Use exactly the same seed, fertilizer, irrigation, and disease control products on each plot, so that the only variable is soil quality. Carefully record all details of your project, including dates, amounts, and all applicable measurements. Record and compare production between improved and non-improved soils.
- Plant two small, experimental plots with identical seed, soil, fertilizer application, and irrigation. Use only chemical pest control on the first plot, and organic pest control on the second. Record and compare production between the two plots.
- Create a plant hybrid.
- Contact/join your local chapter of Future Farmers of America or 4-H.
- Grow a plant or raise an animal to show in the county fair.
- Raise an animal for market.
- Participate in a guide dog puppy training program.

  www.assistancedogsinternational.org/standards/training-programs/

  www.guidedogs.com/site/PageServer?pagename=help_volunteer_puppy

  www.guidedogs.org

- Cross-breed a small animal [e.g., rabbits, cavies] for select traits such as coat, color, or meat production.
- Visit a college that has a strong agricultural program; arrange a tour. Find out about agricultural research and development conducted at their facilities. What discoveries have been made at this college/university that have directly impacted agriculture in your state/province and elsewhere?
- Find out about agricultural research and development conducted both currently and in the past at the agricultural research facilities listed below. What discoveries have been

made at these colleges/universities that have directly impacted agriculture in your state/province and elsewhere? [For facilities not listed, websearch by typing 'agricultural research college' or 'agricultural research facility' in your search engine.]

http://bio.albertainnovates.ca/library/alberta's-bio-sectors/—Alberta Agricultural Research Institute; links to Canadian agricultural colleges and other research programs

http://agsci.oregonstate.edu/research/—Oregon State

www.ag.purdue.edu/arp/Pages/default.aspx—Purdue

www.ars.wisc.edu—Wisconsin

www.ifas.ufl.edu—University of Florida

www.dal.ca/faculty/agriculture.htm—Nova Scotia Agricultural College

http://illinois.edu—University of Illinois

> *Some students may lack the ability to pursue college studies; far more are perfectly capable of college-level work, but have true gifts and career goals in non-academic fields.*

APOLOGETICS

For this course:
Please select, at minimum, four books from the listings below. At least one of the four books should be selected from starred entries. It is further recommended that some type of concordance of the Holy Bible, preferably Catholic, be purchased/borrowed for this course.

*C=*Beginning Apologetics*—Catholic Answers

C=*Catechism of the Catholic Church*

C=*YOUCAT: Youth Catechism of the Catholic Church* [CHC]

*C=*Catholicism and Fundamentalism,* Karl Keating

C,TM, T/AK=*Didache High School Religion Series* [CHC]

> *Introduction to Catholicism* [9th gr.]
>
> *Understanding the Scriptures* [10th gr.]
>
> *The History of the Church* [11th gr.]
>
> *Our Moral Life in Christ* [12th gr.]

C=*Handbook of Christian Apologetics,* Peter Kreeft

C=*One, Holy, Catholic and Apostolic,* Kenneth Whitehead

*C=*Protestant Fundamentalism and the Born Again Catholic,* Fr. Robert J. Fox

C=*Search & Rescue,* Patrick Madrid

C=*The Belief of Catholics,* Ronald Knox

C=*The Bible and the Qur'an,* Jacques Jomier, O.P.

C=*The Question and Answer Catechism,* Fr. John Hardon

C=*Theology and Sanity,* Frank Sheed

C=*The Path to Rome,* Hilaire Belloc

*C=*Where is That in the Bible?,* Patrick Madrid

*C=*Where is That in Tradition?,* Patrick Madrid

C=*The Truth Is Out There* [CHC]

C=*Yours Is the Church,* Mike Aquilina [CHC]

Links:

C=www.adoremus.org—Church documents

C=www.catholic.com—Catholic Answers: apologetics resources and Catholic radio

C=www.catholiceducation.org— orthodox Catholic writers; excellent resource for apologetics articles

C=www.catholicfirst.com—Catholic Information Center—search the Catechism, Early Church Fathers

C=www.catholic-pages.com/—Catholic documents and teaching, current events, more

C=www.envoymagazine.com

C=www.ewtn.com

C=www.steveraysstore.com—videos: Peter, Keeper of the Keys, Apostolic Fathers: Handing on the Faith

C=www.legionofmary.org

C=www.newadvent.org/cathen— Catholic encyclopedia

C=Parish Visitors of Mary Immaculate, www.parishvisitorsisters.org

C=http://scripturecatholic.com/— scriptural answers for apologists

C=www.vatican.va—Vatican website

C=www.zenit.org/en—Vatican news; recent and archived Papal/Church statements

http://www.ipl.org/div/subject/ —Internet Public Library

Church Teaching:

C=www.catholicapologetics.org— invaluable apologetics aid; Scriptural citations, Early Church Fathers

C=www.catholic-pages.com/—Catholic documents and teaching, current events, more

CCC #848, 856

Documents of Vatican II, Vol. 2

Possible Essay Topics:

• Read *CCC* #856. What must be the attitude of the apologist toward 'those who do not yet accept the Gospel'? What approach does the Church recommend for discussion with non-Catholics, and why? Read *Evangelization in the Modern World, #41,* Vatican II, Vol.2. What 'is the primary organ of evangelization'? Explain the wisdom of the Church's approach.

• How do you answer those who deny the necessity of the Sacrament of Penance? Using a Catholic Bible concordance, *Catholicism and Fundamentalism,* or www.catholic.com as resources, research scriptural and early Church teaching. List and outline responses, then write an essay in support of this life-giving, holy Sacrament, instituted by a forgiving Father through His Son.

• Some denominations limit baptism to adults only; other denominations allow baptism only for those who have reached the age of reason, but never for infants. Using a

Catholic Bible concordance, *Catholicism and Fundamentalism*, or www.catholic.com as resources, find at least four scriptural citations in support of infant baptism. Can you find any scriptural admonition *against* infant baptism? Find at least four references from the Early Church Fathers demonstrating the practice of infant baptism. Using these citations, outline a presentation explaining why Holy Mother Church has always welcomed her youngest members to the Sacrament of Baptism.

• St. Ignatius of Antioch was taught, in part, by St. John the Apostle. From St. Ignatius' *Letter to the Smyrnaeans*, we read an admonition against those who don't believe in the Real Presence: "They abstain from the Eucharist... because they do not confess that the Eucharist is the Flesh of Our Saviour Jesus Christ...". St. Justin Martyr, who was born at about the time of St. John's death, wrote in his *First Apology*, "For not as common bread nor common drink do we receive these;...the Eucharist...is both the flesh and the blood...of that incarnated Jesus." In light of these statements, from the earliest years of the Church, how would one answer those who do not believe in the Real Presence, thinking that the doctrine 'crept into' Church teaching centuries after the Ascension of Our Lord? Compose a response that demonstrates the true, consistent teaching of Holy Mother Church: Jesus is indeed present to us, Body, Blood, Soul, and Divinity, in the Sacrament of Holy Eucharist. Use at least three citations each from scriptural evidence and writings of the early Church Fathers.

Research:

Credit may be obtained by researching topics below. Learning may be demonstrated through the production of projects, papers, or reports.

Find evidence on these topics, both from Holy Scripture and early Church Fathers, proving the truths of our Holy Faith.

• God the Father, Son, and Holy Spirit
  Jesus, God the Son and Equal to the Father
  Jesus, Alpha and Omega [and therefore eternal]
  Jesus, *only* Son of Mary
  'Brothers' of Jesus
  Jesus, worshiped as God
• Holy Spirit
  Holy Spirit is a *Person* [Third Person of the Holy Trinity, not just the 'breath' of God]
  Holy Trinity, Biblical evidence
• Mary
  Assumption, precedent in Enoch, Elijah
  Immaculate Conception
  Ever-Virgin
  Mother of God [Jesus is God; Mary is His Mother; Mary is the Mother of God the Son]
  'Hail Mary,' scriptural basis for
• Apostolic Succession and Church Hierarchy, Biblical Evidence
  bishops, deacons, priests [presbyters]
  priests, 'call no man father' [or teacher or rabbi]
• Bible, Origins of
  canon
• 'Born Again,' comes through Holy Baptism
• Hell, Reality of
• Mass, Holy Sacrifice
• Pope
  primacy
  papacy established by Jesus
• Priesthood, male
• Purgatory
  scriptural evidence
  early Church Fathers
• Sacraments 'in dispute'
  Holy Baptism
    of infants
    means of being 'Born Again'
  Holy Eucharist
    established by Jesus

scriptural references to the Body and Blood of Christ
Sacrament of Penance
   confess your sins—scriptural
   instituted by Christ—'whose sins you forgive'
Holy Orders
   celibacy
   male priesthood
   scriptural evidence for a Church with Holy Orders

- Saints
   alive in heaven
   prayers of saints
   relics [cite scriptural evidence of their use]
- Salvation
   not by faith alone
   can be lost
- Statues, Images, and Sacramentals
   scriptural use [see cherubim on Ark, Moses' 'fiery serpent,' Temple decorations]
- Sunday as Lord's Day
- Tradition itself is scriptural

Experiential Learning/Career and Vocational Bridge:

[See Table of Contents for *Process Project Outline* and *Following in Their Footsteps* projects]

Apologetics Projects:
- Join and participate in Legion of Mary. [house to house and other apologetic works] www.legionofmary.org
- Visit religious communities whose apostolate is evangelization.
- Start a youth apologetics discussion/study group.
- Not infrequently, misconceptions and inaccuracies about the Catholic Faith find their way into local newspapers. Carefully monitor your paper for articles on religion [often published on Saturdays and Sundays], and also for religious-themed letters to the editor. ['Always be prepared to make a defense to any one who calls you to account for the hope that is in you, yet do it with gentleness and reverence...' 1 Pet. 3:15] Write charitable rebuttals and explanations and submit them as letters to the editor.
- Create an active game that can be used to teach the primary truths of the Catholic Faith to young children.
- Create a card game that can be used to teach the primary truths of the Catholic Faith to young children.
- Volunteer as an aide in a religious education class or Bible School at your parish.
- With other Catholic homeschoolers, organize a 'Mom's Day Out.' Set a time and location, then provide an afternoon of activities for children from ages 3-8. [This might be done in conjunction with a parish mission or retreat to provide babysitting; students seeking Family Management or Psychology credit could provide care while observing the under-3 age group.] Create art or craft projects, music/songs, physical activities and games, cooking, or hobby demonstrations that can be used to teach the Faith to young children.

ART

S, B=Art: Merit Badge Series

S=*Art in Focus,* McGraw-Hill-Ryerson

C=*Artfully Teaching the Faith,* Steven Kellmeyer

S,V/DVD=*From Monet to Van Gogh: A History of Impressionism*—The Great Courses

S, B=Graphic Arts: Merit Badge Series

S, B=Painting: Merit Badge Series

S, B=Photography: Merit Badge Series

S, B=Pottery: Merit Badge Series

S, B=Sculpture: Merit Badge Series

S, B=Wood Carving: Merit Badge Series

[*See public library for video resources*]

Links:

www.americanillustration.org

C=http://smallpax.blogspot.com—The Catholic Illustrator's Guild

C=www.newliturgicalmovement.org— New Liturgical Movement

C=http://thesacredarts.org/index. html—The Foundation for the Sacred Arts

C=http://thewayofbeauty.org—The Way of Beauty

C=www.thomasmorecollege.edu/ summerprogram—summer art programs

C=www.catholiceducation.org— orthodox Catholic writers; excellent resource for articles on the Arts

www.chipchats.org—National Wood Carvers' Association; magazine

www.khake.com/page27.html—graphic arts career guide, requirements

C=http://mv.vatican.va— Vatican Museums/art

www.nga.gov—National Gallery of Art, collections, virtual tours

www.renaissanceconnection.org/main. cfm

http://www.ipl.org/div/subject/ —Internet Public Library

C=www.studiobrien—respected Catholic artist and author, Michael O'Brien

www.theartgallery.com.au/index.html— The Worldwide Art Gallery—index of paintings, artists, art education

Church Teaching:

C=www.newadvent.org/cathen— Catholic encyclopedia

C=www.catholic-pages.com/—Catholic documents and teaching, current events, more

C=www.zenit.org/en—Vatican news; recent and archived Papal/Church statements

Message to Artists—Pope Paul VI, Second Vatican Council

The Function of Art—Pope Pius XII

To Artists—ecclesial pronouncement, Pope John Paul II

Sacrosanctum Concilium, Documents of Vatican II, Vol. 1, Chapter VII

CCC #2500-2503, 2513

Possible Essay Topics:

• Read *CCC* #2503. Think of art—whether Stations of the Cross, a crucifix, or other works—that you have seen that is not in

conformity with this directive. Contrast its effect with 'the authentic beauty of sacred art' as described in this passage. Draw/sketch/ paint/sculpt pieces that might replace those works whose effect falls outside the directives.
• Research the life and work of Fra Angelico. How did his approach usher in a new era in sacred art? [See www.catholicartists.org/ about/archives/links/—Catholic Artists; info on Fra Angelico]
• Read *CCC* #2501. If 'the ultimate end of man' is joyful unity with Our Lord in Heaven, and 'art is not an absolute end in itself,' what motives should drive artistic expression? Outline the main ideas in #2501, then re-write in your own words.
• Write about a work that has influenced your vision of art. In what ways did the artist or his work change your perspective?
• Research sculpture produced by the Aztecs, with religious themes, from the 12th to the 16th century. Research European art, with religious themes, from the same time period. Compare and contrast form, images, and themes. How do they compare in light of *CCC* #2502?
• Given the opportunity, what dreams do you have for a future in art? List your dreams, plans, and goals. Arrange them in order of 'attack.' Outline steps toward their achievement. Write about your dream.

Research:

You may, in conjunction with your text and field work, wish to investigate the following topics in greater depth. Credit may be obtained through reading and hands-on, experiential learning including field trips, volunteering, and apprenticeships. Learning is demonstrated through the production of projects, experiments, essays or reports. Reports may be based on note-taking and observation and might include graphs, charts, illustrations and diagrams.

You may wish to create a notebook exhibiting varieties of artistic expression by culture or epoch, or a portfolio demonstrating some or all of the techniques listed.

• Art History
  African
  Asian
  Aztec, Native Peoples
  East Indian
  Greek
  Roman

• Technique
  Illustration
    background, foreground
    composition
    foreshortening
    perspective
    proportion
    shading and shadows, direction of light
  Sculpting
    suggestion of movement
    use of texture

Famous Names Related to Art: Read and Report

In what ways did the Catholic Church aid in the artist's work?

How did the person's faith [or lack thereof] influence his/her work?

What might have motivated the person to produce his work?

In what ways did his/her methods change commonly used artistic approaches?

In what ways did his/her work impact or change society?

Michelangelo

Raphael

Fra Angelico

Sandro Botticelli

Giotto

Caravaggio

Hokusai

Diego Rivera

Leonardo DaVinci

El Greco

Rembrandt

Frederic Remington

Van Gogh

William Blake [homeschooled]

Andrew Wyeth [homeschooled]

Experiential Learning/Career and Vocational Bridge:

[See Table of Contents for *Experiential Learning: Art Museums*]
[See Table of Contents for *Process Project Outline* and *Following in Their Footsteps* projects]

Art Projects:

Photograph and/or photocopy your creations for use in portfolios.

• Locate an art museum in your area; volunteer.

• Compose a sketch, painting, or sculpture based on *CCC* #2250.

• With other Catholic homeschoolers, organize a 'Mom's Day Out.' Set a time and location, then provide an afternoon of activities for children from ages 3-8. [This might be done in conjunction with a parish mission or retreat to provide babysitting; students seeking Family Management or Psychology credit could provide care while observing the under-3 age group.] Create art or craft projects, music/songs, physical activities and games, cooking, or hobby demonstrations that can be used to teach the Faith to young children.

• Create a set of Stations of the Cross.

• Create a design to be used on liturgical vestments.

• Create a mosaic for a baptistry.

• Sculpt a set of holy water fonts.

• Design a mural for the 'Cry Room' or nursery in your parish. Show your design to your pastor and volunteer to paint the mural.

• Arrange a still life. Render in pencil, chalk, charcoal, pastels, pen and ink, marking pens, watercolor, wood or linoleum block, and oil. Which medium is your favorite?

• Create a portrait. Render in pencil, chalk, charcoal, pastels, pen and ink, marking pens, watercolor, wood or linoleum block, and oil. Which medium is your favorite?

• Inspired by the 'Guardian Angel Prayer,' draw/paint a picture, based on the prayer, suitable for a child. Create a work that might be hung on a wall, or reduced to holy-card size for slipping into a pocket.

• Inspired by the 'Guardian Angel Prayer,' draw/paint a picture, based on the prayer, suitable for a member of the armed forces. Create a work that might be hung on a wall, or reduced to holy-card size for slipping into a pocket.

• Illustrate the Luminous Mysteries of the Holy Rosary.

• Carve a crucifix in wood.

• Create clip-art for the liturgical year and scan to CD for parish or diocesan use.

• Volunteer your services with set design and painting at a local theater.

ASTRONOMY

Science Labs:

Labs essentially provide students an opportunity to test theories against reality, i.e., allow students to apply what they have learned from their texts in hands-on settings.

Most colleges don't require documented science labs as part of a high school science course. In fact, there is no national standard or definition of what exactly constitutes a high school science lab. However, since some colleges do require documented science lab work, it is best to include at least 20 hours of lab work in each science course that your student takes.

Keeping in mind that 'lab' means hands-on learning that applies book-learning to reality, credit for a Geology lab might be earned by visiting a fossil bed and searching for fossils. Students might photograph the rock formations where the fossils were found, identify the type of rock in which the fossils were found, and identify the types of fossils therein. Brief descriptions or notations about why and how fossils were found in this type of geological structure might be included. All of this information would then be assembled into a lab report.

An Environmental Science lab might include similar notations about discoveries made in a pond ecosystem, including a description and photographs of the pond, plant and animal aquatic life, and conclusions as to how and why those particular plants and animals live in that environment.

In essence, no matter which science courses are chosen, students will devote at least 20 hours of class time to lab work—that is, hands-on projects, exploration, and conclusions about what the student learned—which will be documented in a hard-copy notebook or portfolio.

Parents might also double-check with colleges to which students might apply to determine whether or not there are lab requirements.

Please also note that students who enroll in science classes at local colleges gain those lab credits while simultaneously earning both high school and college credit.

Book List:

S, T/AK=*Astronomy*—Cliff's

S, B=*Astronomy: Merit Badge Series*

S=*Astronomy: A Self-Teaching Guide* [Wiley Self-Teaching Guides], Dinah L. Moche

S, T/AK=*Astronomy the Easy Way*—Barron's

S, R, T/AKA=*Astronomy Today,* Eric Chaisson

S, AK=*Essential Atlas of Astronomy*—Barron's

S=*Stars and Planets*—Barron's

Supplemental Reading

S=*Astronomy*—Standard Deviants

S=*The Book of Constellations*—Barron's

C=*Brother Astronomer: Adventures of a Vatican Scientist,* Guy Consolmagno

S, CP, T/AKA=*The Cosmic Perspective*—Pearson Prentice Hall

C=*The Limits of a Limitless Science,* Fr. Stanley Jaki, O.S.B.

C=*Planets and Planetarians: A History of Theories of the Origin of Planetary Systems,* Fr. Stanley Jaki, O.S.B.

S, V/DVD=*Understanding the Universe: An Introduction to Astronomy*—The Great Courses Lecture Series

Links

1,200 page, free science supplies catalog!—www.wardsci.com—Ward's Natural Science—1-800-962-2660

www.aiaa.org—American Institute of Aeronautics and Astronautics http://aas.org/education/—American Astronomical Society

www.aavso.org/—American Association of Variable Star Observers

C=www.catholiceducation.org—orthodox Catholic writers; excellent resource for articles on science

www.cato.org/—type 'science and space' into search box

http://vaticanobservatory.org—Vatican Observatory, Tucson

http://saturn.jpl.nasa.gov

http://101science.com/space.htm

www.eaaa.net/—Escambia Amateur Astronomers' Association

www.earthobservatory.nasa.gov

www.enchantedlearning.com/Home.html—printables: maps, geology, anatomy, astronomy, botany, more

http://www.aavso.org/education/vsa/—Hands-On Astrophysics

www.hubblesite.org/newscenter

www.astromax.org/aao1001.htm

www.nrao.edu/—National Radio Astronomy Observatory

http://solarsystem.nasa.gov/planets/

http://pds.jpl.nasa.gov/planets

www.rasc.ca—Royal Astronomical Society of Canada

www.discoveryeducation.com/search/page/-/-/lesson-plan/space/index.cfm—astronomy lesson plans

http://seds.org—Students for the Exploration and Development of Space

www.skyandtelescope.com/community/organizations/—find an astronomy club/observatory near you

http://skyandtelescope.com/—Sky & Telescope—magazine and info

www.space.com/news—space news, more

http://spaceflight.nasa.gov/home/index.html

www.usno.navy.mil/USNO—U.S. Naval Observatory

http://www.ipl.org/div/subject/—Internet Public Library

Church Teaching:

C=www.newadvent.org/cathen—Catholic encyclopedia

C=www.catholic-pages.com/—Catholic documents and teaching, current events, more

C=www.zenit.org/en—Vatican news; recent and archived Papal/Church statements

CCC #282-286; #2500

Possible Essay Topics:

• Read CCC #282-286. 'The question about the origins of the world and of man has been the object of many scientific studies which have splendidly enriched our knowledge of the age and dimensions of the cosmos...' How do these readings from the Catechism answer the five questions posed in #282? How should the study of astronomy be approached in light of #286? Underline the phrases that seem to answer the five questions, then outline and write a response.

• Astrophysicist Fr. Georges Lemaitre proposed the 'Big Bang' theory of Creation, with astronomers Edwin Hubble, George Gamow, Robert Wilson, and Arno Penzias following his theoretical lead. Is. 42:5 speaks of a 'stretching out' of the heavens that is in harmony with the 'stretching out' that would be associated with an expanding universe. Research. Citing at least four sources, write about your discoveries relating to the 'Big Bang' theory of Creation. [To get you started: see www.catholiceducation.org/articles/science/sco022.html—Fr. Georges Lemaitre and the 'Big Bang.']

• Read CCC # 2500. 'God reveals himself... through the universal language of creation... the order and harmony of the cosmos...' In your study of astronomy, what have you discovered that reveals to you God's unmistakable handiwork? Describe in detail what you have found, including specifics of design that reveal an Intelligent Designer.

• Using at least three references [see Hubble websites listed in **Links**] note at least three significant astronomical discoveries revealed by the Hubble Space Telescope. How have these discoveries advanced the field of astronomy? Discuss.

• Given the opportunity, what dreams do you have for a future in astronomy? Research steps leading to a career in astronomy. [See http://aas.org/learn/careers-astronomy] List your dreams, plans, and goals. Arrange them in order of 'attack.' Outline steps toward their achievement. Write about your dream.

Research

You may, in conjunction with your text and field work, wish to investigate the following topics in greater depth. Credit may be obtained through reading and hands-on, experiential learning including field trips, volunteering, and apprenticeships. Learning is demonstrated through the production of projects, experiments, essays or reports. Reports may be based on note-taking and observation and might include graphs, charts, illustrations and diagrams.

To aid in research, ask and answer, "Who, what, where, when and why?" [For example: *Where* are black holes found? *What* is their makeup? *Who* discovered.....? *When* do meteorites....? *Why* does the atmosphere...?]

• sun
    sunspots
    solar flares
• planets
    orbits
    day/night time differences in rotation [Jupiter vs. Pluto, for example]
    'years'/orbit
• gravity differences on various planets
• moons of various planets
    lunar calendars [Hebrew]
• eclipses
• stars
    nebulae
    black holes
    constellations
    Milky Way
    supernovas
    white dwarves
    neutrons
    variable stars
    binary stars
    eclipsing binary stars
• natural satellites
    comets, meteors

Famous Names Related to the Science of Astronomy: Read and Report

In what ways did the Catholic Church aid in discoveries/inventions/advancement?

How did the person's faith [or lack thereof] influence his/her work?

What might have motivated the person to become involved in the field?

In what ways did his/her discoveries/inventions/advancement change the field of study?

In what ways did his/her discoveries/inventions/advancement ultimately change society?

St. Albert the Great

Benjamin Banneker

Nicolaus Copernicus

Edmond Halley

Fr. Stanley Jaki, O.S.B.

Georges Lemaitre, S.J.

Maria Mitchell

Experiential Learning/Career and Vocational Bridge:

[See Table of Contents for *Experiential Learning: Discovery Centers*]

[See Table of Contents for *Process Project Outline* and *Following in Their Footsteps* projects]

Astronomy Projects:

• Find planetariums and observatories in your area. Visit and volunteer. [www.skyandtelescope.com/community/organizations—check also with colleges/community colleges.]

• Join an astronomy club.

• Build a solar system model and give a presentation to a homeschooling group. [See www.noao.edu/education/peppercorn/pcmain.html and www.exploratorium.edu/ronh/solar_system/]

• Amateur astronomers have made significant contributions to our understanding of God's creative, heavenly handiwork. In past decades, amateurs have discovered a significant number of comets. [Snyder-Murakami Comet; Shoemaker-Levy 9 Comet, which crashed spectacularly onto Jupiter's surface; two comets first sighted by Yuji Hyakutake; and finds by Canadian Vance Petriew, to

name a few.] Set up a telescope in your yard or other suitable place. Journal your findings on a regular basis.

• Research. Using graphs, charts, and photographs, name and display stages of star evolution. Present your display to a homeschooling group.

Books, videos, and websites listed as references for the courses in this volume are not 'recommended' or 'preferred,' but rather widely used options from which to choose, depending on the intended field of study, educational goals, and the mental and spiritual maturity of the student.

BIOLOGY

Science Labs:

Labs essentially provide students an opportunity to test theories against reality, i.e., allow students to apply what they have learned from their texts in hands-on settings.

Most colleges don't require documented science labs as part of a high school science course. In fact, there is no national standard or definition of what exactly constitutes a high school science lab. However, since some colleges do require documented science lab work, it is best to include at least 20 hours of lab work in each science course that your student takes.

Keeping in mind that 'lab' means hands-on learning that applies book-learning to reality, credit for a Geology lab might be earned by visiting a fossil bed and searching for fossils. Students might photograph the rock formations where the fossils were found, identify the type of rock in which the fossils were found, and identify the types of fossils therein. Brief descriptions or notations about why and how fossils were found in this type of geological structure might be included. All of this information would then be assembled into a lab report.

An Environmental Science lab might include similar notations about discoveries made in a pond ecosystem, including a description and photographs of the pond, plant and animal aquatic life, and conclusions as to how and why those particular plants and animals live in that environment.

In essence, no matter which science courses are chosen, students will devote at least 20 hours of class time to lab work—that is, hands-on projects, exploration, and conclusions about what the student learned—which will be documented in a hard-copy notebook or portfolio.

Parents might also double-check with colleges to which students might apply to determine whether or not there are lab requirements.

Please also note that students who enroll in science classes at local colleges gain those lab credits while simultaneously earning both high school and college credit.

Note: Catholic texts and materials are listed where available, but students on a college track should be aware that college courses invariably present a secular view. For example, the student will be exposed to evolutionary theory in college biology courses. Even orthodox Catholic colleges will discuss the evolutionary viewpoint, yet at the same time present Church teaching on the subject. Thus, during the high school years when parents are available for guidance, and for the student to be fully prepared for college courses, it is not necessarily imprudent to study secular materials alongside those that present Catholic teaching.

Book List:

Please also see Science, General *for more titles.*

S=*The Anatomy Student's Self-Test Coloring Book*, Dr. Kurt Albertine

S, CP, T/AK, CD=*Biology*, Miller and Levine [CHC]

S, CP, T/AKA, CD=*Biology*, Campbell [for AP]—Pearson Prentice Hall

S, V/DVD=*Biology*, Standard Deviants

S=*Biology: A Self-Teaching Guide* [Wiley Self-Teaching Guides], Steven Daniel Garber

S, T/AK=*Biology: Cliff's Study Solver*—Cliff's

S, T/AK=*E-Z Biology*—Barron's

S=*Illustrated Guide to Home Biology Experiments*, Robert Thompson [CHC]

S, CP, T/AKA, Interactive CD= *Essentials of Human Anatomy and Physiology*—Pearson Prentice Hall

Experiences in Biology, Kathleen Julicher—Homeschool Science Press [biology lab for homeschool]

S, CP,T/AK=*AP Biology*—Barron's

S, B=Insect Study: Merit Badge Series

S, B=Mammal Study: Merit Badge Series

S, B=Medicine: Merit Badge Series

S=*Oceanography: An Invitation to Marine Science*, Tom S. Garrison

S, T/AK, B=*Pacemaker Biology*, Globe Fearon—basic concepts

S, B=Reptile and Amphibian Study: Merit Badge Series

NCC=*Science Shepherd Biology*, Scott Hardin [2008 edition]

S, B=Veterinary Medicine: Merit Badge Series

S=*Zoology Coloring Book*, Lawrence Elson [www.coloringconcepts.com—This is often used in college classrooms, but can benefit those at lower academic levels as well.]

For those who desire a comprehensive lab experience, community colleges often offer lab without requiring the student to be enrolled in the Biology class itself.

Supplemental Reading:

S, T/AK=*Anatomy*—Cliff's

S=*Anatomy Coloring Book*, www.coloringconcepts.com

S=*Anatomy*, Standard Deviants video

S, AK=*Anatomy and Physiology the Easy Way*, Edward Alcamo—Barron's

S=*Biology Coloring Book*, www.coloringconcepts.com

C=*Catholic Bioethics and the Gift of Human Life*, William May

C=*Communicating the Catholic Vision of Life*, Russell Smith

S, CP, T/AKA=*Concepts of Genetics*—Pearson, Prentice Hall

S, AK=*Essential Atlas of Anatomy*—Barron's

S, AK=*Essential Atlas of Biology*—Barron's

Experiments in Plant-Hybridization, Fr. Gregor Mendel

Explore the World Using Protozoa, Roger Anderson

C=*Fabre's Book of Insects*, John Henri Fabre

S, CP, T/AKA, Interactive CD=*Essentials of Human Anatomy and Physiology*—Pearson Prentice Hall

NCC=*Ethics for Doctors, Nurses and Patients*, H.P. Dunn

S=*Start Exploring: Gray's Anatomy: A Fact-Filled Coloring Book*, Freddy Stark

C=*The Human Person: Dignity Beyond Compare*, Sr. Terese Auer, O.P. [CHC]

C=*Called to Happiness: Guiding Ethical Principles*, Sr. Terese Auer, O.P. [CHC]

C=*Life is a Blessing: A Biography of Jerome Lejeune: Geneticist, Doctor, Father*— Clara Lejeune

C=*Science of Today and the Problems of Genesis*, Fr. O'Connell [archaeological/origin of man]

C=*The Life of the Fly*, John Henri Fabre

C=*The Life of the Spider*, John Henri Fabre

C=*The Shroud of Turin: The Most Up-to-Date Analysis of All the Facts*, Bernard Ruffin

S, V/DVD=*Understanding the Human Body: An Intro to Anatomy and Physiology*—The Great Courses

Links:

1,200 page, free science supplies catalog!—www.wardsci.com—Ward's Natural Science—1-800-962-2660

C=www.all.org—American Life League, topical index, end of life care, euthanasia, eugenics, fetal development, stem cell research

www.ansp.org—Academy of Natural Sciences

www.audubon.org—Audubon Society

www.biochemweb.org—virtual library of biochemistry and cell biology

C=www.cathmed.org—Catholic Medical Association, medicine and ethics

C=www.cathmed.org/students/—Catholic Medical Students' Association, articles on medicine, ethics

C=www.catholiceducation.org—orthodox Catholic writers; excellent resource for articles on science

www.commtechlab.msu.edu/sites/dlc-me/zoo/—microbes

http://brainconnection.positscience.com

www.enchantedlearning.com/Home.html—printables: maps, geology, anatomy, astronomy, botany, more

www.eyeofscience.de—scientific photography; microscopic world: botany, zoology, etc.

www.hhmi.org/biointeractive/—Howard Hughes Medical Institute, animations, virtual labs

http://socrates58.blogspot.com/2006/11/philosophy-christianity-index-page.html

http://education.usgs.gov/secondary.html—animals, plants

www.invasivespeciesinfo.gov—invasive plants, animals, microbes, control

www.khake.com/page39.html—agriculture, aquaculture, forestry career guide

www.khake.com/page22.html—medical, health career guide, requirements

www.khake.com/page77.html—free lessons and lesson plans: health, nursing, biology

C=www.lifeissues.net—excellent site for current issues in the news; site in association with OMI

C=www.lifesite.net—daily news, current events; Canada, U.S., world

www.martindalecenter.com/Vet.html—veterinary resources

www.micro.magnet.fsu.edu/index.html—cells, DNA, microscopic views of much more

C=www.ncbcenter.org—National Catholic Bioethics Center, articles on current medical/moral controversies

C=One More Soul—http://onemoresoul.com—life issues

www.ou.edu/cas/botany-micro/www-vl/—botany, agriculture, biosciences, biology, forestry; university contacts

www.discoveryeducation.com/teachers/—free lessons and lesson plans for astronomy, space, earth science, forensics science, geography, health, history, life science, animals, ecology, human body, microscopic world, plants, physical science, technology, weather

http://frog.edschool.virginia.edu—virtual frog dissection

www.mnh.si.edu/mna/—Smithsonian data on mammals

C=www.wf-f.org/MedicalMoral.html— Women for Faith and Family—medical and moral issues

http://www.ipl.org/div/subject/ —Internet Public Library

Church Teaching:

C=www.newadvent.org/cathen— Catholic encyclopedia

C=www.catholic-pages.com/—Catholic documents and teaching, current events, more

C=www.zenit.org/en—Vatican news; recent and archived Papal/Church statements

Declaration on Euthanasia [Iura et Bona], Congregation for the Doctrine of the Faith

Declaration on Procured Abortion [Quaestio de abortu], Documents of Vatican II, Vol. 2

Instructions on the Respect for Human Life in its Origin and on the Dignity of Procreation [Donum Vitae], Congregation for the Doctrine of the Faith

Humani Generis, Pope Pius XII

Of Human Life [Humanae Vitae], Pope Paul VI

The Gospel of Life [Evangelium Vitae], Pope John Paul II

CCC #2295, 2296, 2270, 2274, 2277, 2279, 2237, 2417, 1932

Possible Essay Topics

• In what ways was Pope Paul VI's *Humanae Vitae* prophetic? List and expound on the predicted societal changes that have come to pass.

• Read *CCC* #2270, 2274. In what ways does a lack of respect for human life degrade society? In what ways does Church teaching on the sanctity of life uplift and improve society? Compare and contrast.

• Read *Declaration on Procured Abortion,* Paragraph 17, Documents of Vatican II, Vol. 2. In what ways does devaluing the sanctity of life alter the focus of biological studies? How does respect for human life foster true scientific progress in the life sciences? Compare and contrast.

• How might the medical use of adult stem cells prove superior to fetal stem cells, from both medical and ethical standpoints? [See www.all.org and www.lifeissues.net] How does the use of fetal stem cell lines violate Church teaching that 'it is never right to do evil that good may come of it'?

• In what ways have the lives of animals been extended and their health improved through the administration of vaccines, surgery, and other modern medical advances? How does animal experimentation benefit not only humans, but animals as well? Can humane animal experimentation be justified in view of Gen. 1:26? See also CCC #2417.

• Given the opportunity, what dreams do you have for a future in biological sciences? List your dreams, plans, and goals. Arrange them in order of 'attack.' Outline steps toward their achievement. Write about your dream.

Biology: Anatomy

• Research and describe in detail the anatomical and biological evidence that the Shroud of Turin is not a 'painted forgery,' but truly a burial cloth. [see www.shroud.com/menu. htm] In what ways is a knowledge of anatomy inextricably linked with our Faith?

Biology: Fetology

• "Prenatal diagnosis is morally licit, 'if it respects the life and integrity of the embryo and the human fetus and is directed toward its safeguarding or healing as an individual...It is gravely opposed to the moral law when this is done with the thought of possibly inducing an abortion, depending upon the results: *a diagnosis must not be the equivalent of a death sentence.' "* [CCC #2274] Compare and contrast the positive and negative effects of amniocentesis, CVS, and ultrasound testing. Include information about maternal and fetal risks and benefits, and false positive readings for nonexistent birth defects. What should be the Catholic response if 'birth defects' are found?

• Read *CCC # 456-459*. How did Jesus' Incarnation identify him with, and sanctify, the life of the unborn? In what ways might prenatal care recommended by a Catholic doctor differ from that prescribed by an unbeliever?

• Research and discuss the effects of previous abortion on later pregnancies, including sterility, ectopic pregnancy, miscarriage, and premature birth.

• How are abortion and breast cancer linked? [one possible informational source— www.lifeissues.net]

Famous Names Related to the Science of Biology: Read and Report

In what ways did the Catholic Church aid in discoveries/inventions/advancement?

How did the person's faith [or lack thereof] influence his/her work?

What might have motivated the person to become involved in the field?

In what ways did his/her discoveries/inventions/advancement change the field of study?

In what ways did his/her discoveries/inventions/advancement ultimately change society?

St. Albert the Great

Baron Cuvier

Alexander Fleming

Edward Jenner

Robert Koch

Shibasaburo Kitasato

Anton van Leeuwenhoek

Dr. Jerome Lejeune [devout Catholic, noted geneticist and fetologist, proposed for beatification]

Carolus Linnaeus

Joseph Lister

Fr. Gregor Mendel

Marshall Nirenberg

Louis Pasteur [devout Catholic]

Helen Brooke Taussig

Andreas Vesalius

Research:

Biology Topics: Anatomy

You may, in conjunction with your text and field work, wish to investigate the following topics in greater depth. Credit may be obtained through reading and hands-on, experiential learning including field trips, volunteering, and apprenticeships. Learning is demonstrated through the production of projects, experiments, essays or reports. Reports may be based on note-taking and observation and might include graphs, charts, illustrations and diagrams.

To aid in research, ask and answer, "Who, what, where, when and why?" [For example: *What* caused the spread of the disease? *Who* discovered.....? *When* do animals....? *Why* does blood...?]

• skeleton
• muscles
• skin

- heart and circulation
- blood and lymphatic systems
- immune system
- lungs and respiratory system
- endocrine system
- digestive system
- urinary system
- brain
- nervous system
- auditory system
- smell and taste
- reproduction
- life of the unborn child

Supplementary materials/activities:
   science videos [library]
   anatomy coloring books
   dissect/examine bones, heart and various
      organs that may be obtained from a
      butcher

Biology Topics: Zoology

You may, in conjunction with your text and field work, wish to investigate the following topics in greater depth. Credit may be obtained through reading and hands-on, experiential learning including field trips, volunteering, and apprenticeships. Learning is demonstrated through the production of projects, experiments, essays or reports. Reports may be based on note-taking and observation and might include graphs, charts, illustrations and diagrams.

To aid in research, ask and answer, "Who, what, where, when and why?" [For example, "Which animals estivate and why?" "How do amphibian methods of caring for offspring differ from methods followed by mammals?"]

- animal cells
- hibernation
- estivation
- migration
- vertebrates
   mammals on land and in the sea

[habitat and habits for each animal
  researched]
anatomy
  circulatory system
  respiratory system
  gestation and methods of caring for
  offspring
  skeletal
fish
  [habitat and habits for each]
  anatomy
   circulatory system
   respiratory system
   gestation and methods of caring for
   offspring
   skeletal
amphibians
  [habitat/habits for each]
  anatomy
   circulatory system
   respiratory system
   gestation and methods of caring for
   offspring
   skeletal
birds
  [habitat/habits for each]
  anatomy
   circulatory system
   respiratory system
   gestation and methods of caring for
   offspring
   skeletal

rodents
  [habitat/habits for each]
  anatomy
   circulatory system
   respiratory system
   gestation and methods of caring for
   offspring
   skeletal
reptiles
  [habitat/habits for each]
  anatomy
   circulatory system

respiratory system
gestation and methods of caring for offspring
skeletal
- invertebrates
  [habitat/habits]
  anatomy
    circulatory system
    respiratory system
    gestation and methods of caring for offspring
    exoskeletons
  protozoans
  annelids
  mollusks
  crustaceans
  insects
    metamorphosis
  arachnids
- genetics
  mutations and selective breeding

Biology Topics: Fetology

You may, in conjunction with your text and field work, wish to investigate the following topics in greater depth. Credit may be obtained through reading and hands-on, experiential learning including field trips, volunteering, and apprenticeships. Learning is demonstrated through the production of projects, experiments, essays or reports. Reports may be based on note-taking and observation and might include graphs, charts, illustrations and diagrams.

To aid in research, ask and answer, "Who, what, where, when and why?"

- conception
  fraternal twins
  identical twins
- implantation
- research developmental stages, week by week
- placenta

- mechanics of fetal nutrition
- maternal illness and possible effect on unborn child
- maternal diet
- effects of smoking, drugs on fetal development
- miscarriage, causes of
- Rh factor

- diagnosis of congenital birth defects and compassionate care
  amniocentesis
  chorionic villi sampling [CVS]
  ultrasound
  Down's Syndrome
  hydrocephalus
  spina bifida
  intrauterine fetal surgery

- prenatal awareness and response of baby to:
  sound, including voices of parents and siblings
  light
  taste
  touch & pain

Suggested Reading:
C=*Redeemer in the Womb: Jesus Living in Mary,* John Saward

Links:

www.gentlebirth.com

http://fetus.ucsfmedicalcenter.org

www.gentlebirth.org—infomation on ultrasound, risks

www.sfuhl.org—Science for Unborn Human Life—learning in the womb

www.nrlc.org—National Right to Life

www.physiciansforlife.org/content/view/258/43/—fetal surgery

Experiential Learning/Career and Vocational Bridge:

[See Table of Contents for *Process Project Outline* and *Following in Their Footsteps* projects]

Biology Projects:
- Right to Life:
    Study stages of fetal development.
    Borrow fetal models and give a presentation to a youth group.
- veterinary clinic
- animal shelter
- wildlife rehab or refuge
- plant nursery
- nursing home
- hospital [investigate CNA license]
- crisis pregnancy center
- newborn nursery
- Church-connected bio-ethics or pro-life outreach
- One More Soul
- American Cancer Society
- American Red Cross

See also: Animal Husbandry, Botany

BOTANY

Science Labs:

Labs essentially provide students an opportunity to test theories against reality, i.e., allow students to apply what they have learned from their texts in hands-on settings.

Most colleges don't require documented science labs as part of a high school science course. In fact, there is no national standard or definition of what exactly constitutes a high school science lab. However, since some colleges do require documented science lab work, it is best to include at least 20 hours of lab work in each science course that your student takes.

Keeping in mind that 'lab' means hands-on learning that applies book-learning to reality, credit for a Geology lab might be earned by visiting a fossil bed and searching for fossils. Students might photograph the rock formations where the fossils were found, identify the type of rock in which the fossils were found, and identify the types of fossils therein. Brief descriptions or notations about why and how fossils were found in this type of geological structure might be included. All of this information would then be assembled into a lab report.

An Environmental Science lab might include similar notations about discoveries made in a pond ecosystem, including a description and photographs of the pond, plant and animal aquatic life, and conclusions as to how and why those particular plants and animals live in that environment.

In essence, no matter which science courses are chosen, students will devote at least 20 hours of class time to lab work—that is, hands-on projects, exploration, and conclusions about what the student learned—which will be documented in a hard-copy notebook or portfolio.

Parents might also double-check with colleges to which students might apply to determine whether or not there are lab requirements.

Please also note that students who enroll in science classes at local colleges gain those lab credits while simultaneously earning both high school and college credit.

Book List:

Please also see Science, General, *for more titles*

S, B=Plant Science: Merit Badge Series

S, AK=*Essential Atlas of Botany*—Barron's

S=*Botany For Dummies*, René Fester Kratz

S=*Botany for Gardeners*, Brian Capon

S, B=Landscape Architecture: Merit Badge Series

S, CP, T/AKA=*Plant Biology*—Pearson Prentice Hall

S=http://store.im.tamu.edu—Plant Science courses/texts with focus on agriculture

Supplemental Reading:

http://store.im.tamu.edu—curricula: horticulture, greenhouse and nursery

S=*Botany Coloring Book,* www.coloringconcepts.com

S=*Common Weeds of the United States,* U.S. Dept. of Agriculture—Dover Publications

C=*Experiments in Plant-Hybridization,* Fr. Gregor Mendel

S=*National Audubon Society Field Guide to North American Wildflowers*

Links:

1,200 page, free science supplies catalog!—www.wardsci.com—Ward's Natural Science—1-800-962-2660

www.ansp.org—Academy of Natural Sciences online tours

http://botit.botany.wisc.edu/—UW-Madison Department of Botany—virtual botany

www.enchantedlearning.com/Home.html—printables: maps, geology, anatomy, astronomy, botany, more

www.invasivespeciesinfo.gov—invasive plants, animals, control

www.khake.com/page21.html—horticulture, landscape career guide, requirements

www.khake.com/page81.html—free lessons and lesson plans: horticulture

www.micro.magnet.fsu.edu/index.html—cells, microscopic views

www.niagaraparks.com/school-of-horticulture/index.html—Niagara Parks Botanical Gardens and School of Horticulture; three-year institute; Niagara Falls, Ontario, Canada

http://ohioline.osu.edu—Ohio State University Extension—food, agricultural, and environmental information

www.ou.edu/cas/botany-micro/www-vl/—botany, agriculture, biosciences, biology, forestry; university contacts

http://www.dtnprogressivefarmer.com/dtnag/—agriculture, etc. and magazine

www.discoveryeducation.com/teachers/—free lessons and lesson plans for astronomy, space, earth science, forensics science, geography, health, history, life science, animals, ecology, human body, microscopic world, plants, physical science, technology, weather

www.usna.usda.gov/—U.S. National Arboretum

http://www.ipl.org/div/subject/—Internet Public Library

Church Teaching:

C=www.newadvent.org/cathen—Catholic encyclopedia

C=www.catholic-pages.com/—Catholic documents and teaching, current events, more

C=www.zenit.org/en—Vatican news; recent and archived Papal/Church statements

CCC # 2293-2294

Possible Essay Topics:

• Traces of which plants were discovered on the Shroud of Turin? How was pollen identification used to trace the origins and history of the Shroud? What type of chemical analysis of plants was used to help date the Shroud? Describe process and methods used. [See research by Dr. Avinoam Danin, Hebrew University of Jerusalem, and by Dr. Raymond Rogers, chemist from Los Alamos National Laboratory. See also www.shroud.com/menu.htm]

• Read CCC #2293-2294. 'It is an illusion to claim moral neutrality in scientific research and its applications...[Science] must be at the service of the human person, of his inalienable rights, of his true and integral good, in conformity with the plan and the will of God.' Think of and then research ways that the Catholic botanist can 'be at the service of the human person.' [E.g., plant hybrids that might flourish in desertified Third World countries, plant development for medical applications.] List several possibilities, then discuss how these uses might fulfill the above quote. [Cite the CCC quote, above, in your essay.]

• Websearch current developments in the medicinal uses of yew and black elderberry, and antibiotic properties/health benefits of lavender, onions, rosemary, and other herbs. Cite researchers' names and laboratory titles where indicated. Tie your conclusions to 1 Tim. 4:4.

Research

You may, in conjunction with your text and field work, wish to investigate the following topics in greater depth. Credit may be obtained through reading and hands-on, experiential learning including field trips, volunteering, and apprenticeships. Learning is demonstrated through the production of projects, experiments, essays or reports. Reports may be based on note-taking and observation and might include graphs, charts, illustrations and diagrams.

To aid in research, ask and answer, "Who, what, where, when and why?" [For example: *Where* are mosses found? *What* caused the spread of the disease? *Who* discovered.....? *When* do seeds....? *Why* does pollen...?]

• kingdoms and classification
• photosynthesis
• structure of a flower
• plant cells
• flowering plants
    seeds
    monocotyledons
    dicotyledons
• non-flowering plants
    mosses
    ferns
    fungi
    conifers
• herbs, medicinal

Famous Names Related to the Science of Botany: Read and Report

In what ways did the Catholic Church aid in discoveries/inventions/advancement?

How did the person's faith [or lack thereof] influence his/her work?

What might have motivated the person to become involved in the field?

In what ways did his/her discoveries/inventions/advancement change the field of study?

In what ways did his/her discoveries/inventions/advancement ultimately change society?

George Washington Carver [homeschooled]

Carolus Linnaeus

Fr. Gregor Mendel

Experiential Learning/Career and Vocational Bridge:

[See Table of Contents for *Experiential Learning: Discovery Centers*]

[See Table of Contents for *Process Project Outline* and *Following in Their Footsteps* projects]

Botany Projects:
• Collect, photograph or sketch: evergreens or wildflowers, classify and identify by scientific name. Press and place specimens in album. How are these plants used? To which diseases and insect damage are they prone? What means are used in their control? [Use **Links** and also websearch plants' attributes by name, e.g, cedar beneficial uses; cedar diseases.]
• Plant several varieties of one vegetable or flower. Chart germination, days to bloom, days to harvest, productivity, disease resistance of each variety.
• Locate an arborist; meet, and explain your interest. Ask permission to 'shadow' the arborist for a day/week.
• Start an herb garden, planting herbs beneficial to health. Press and dry samples of each herb in a notebook. Label herbs by scientific name and common name; list health benefits of each herb.
• Volunteer your landscape services, particularly for a parish or an elderly neighbor.
• Collect, photograph, or sketch: common weeds. Classify and identify by scientific name, press and place specimens in album. Note invasive weeds and their origins. How and/or why were the invasive plants introduced to North America? How has their presence been detrimental? What means are used in their control? Despite their 'common-ness,' research reveals that our Creator designed many 'common' weeds' with beneficial uses. List those uses alongside their respective plants. [See *Common Weeds of the United States*. Use **Links** and also websearch plants' attributes by name, e.g, dandelion beneficial uses; dandelion control.]
• Work part-time at a commercial or state nursery.
• Investigate possible markets for flower and vegetable seedlings, including farmers' markets and small grocers. Grow and market plants wholesale.
• Visit a college that has a strong botany program; arrange a visit. Find out about botanical research and development conducted at their facilities. What botanical discoveries have been made at this college/university?

BUILDING AND CONSTRUCTION

S, B=Architecture: Merit Badge Series

S=*Big Book of How To,* Better Homes and Gardens [wiring, plumbing, carpentry, etc.]

S=*Home Maintenance for Dummies,* www.dummies.com [plumbing, heating, roofing, etc.]

S, B=Home Repairs: Boy Scout Merit Badge Handbook

S, B=Plumbing: Boy Scout Merit Badge Handbook

S=*The Very Efficient Carpenter: Basic Training for Residential Construction*

S=*Wiring,* Creative Homeowners

S=*Wiring a House,* Cauldwell

www.cengagesites.com/academic/?site=4389—some titles referenced at this link may be purchased used through amazon.com

http://store.im.tamu.edu/Construction-Maintenance-C46aspx—Instructional Materials Service, curricula: construction, electronics

www.nccer.org/—construction related curricula

Supplemental Reading:

www.buildingtrades.com

www.sedelmeier.com/magazines_construction.htm

Building Repair & Maintenance (construction trade magazine)

Links:

www.doityourself.com—basic electrical wiring, installing faucets, sinks, much more; interactive

www.tcu.gov.on.ca/eng/employmentontario/training/—Ontario Canada, apprenticeship training

www.ipl.org/div/subject/—Internet Public Library

www.habitat.org—Habitat for Humanity International

www.khake.com/page14.html—carpentry and construction career guide, requirements

www.khake.com/page58.html—apprenticeship info, training resources, U.S. and Canada

www.khake.com/page82.html—free lessons and lesson plans: construction, electricity, masonry, carpentry

www.doleta.gov—apprenticeships by state, county, and occupation

www.popularmechanics.com—Popular Mechanics magazine: automotive, aviation, computers, home improvement, robotics, woodworking, more

http://technicaljobsearch.com/job-banks/apprenticeships.htm—apprenticeships U.S. and Canada

Church Teaching:

C=www.newadvent.org/cathen—Catholic encyclopedia

C=www.catholic-pages.com/—Catholic documents and teaching, current events, more

C=www.zenit.org/en—Vatican news; recent and archived Papal/Church statements

CCC #1913, 2288

Possible Essay Topics:

• Keep a daily journal of your building construction activities. Note skills learned, including names of equipment on which you have trained. Note errors, how they were corrected, and why. Record names and contact information of those for and with whom you worked. All of this information may be used in job resumes for future employment.

• Read *CCC* #1913 and 2288. Copy the two sentences from these two readings in which 'the common good' is mentioned. Think of ways that volunteering your skills to repair or construct housing for the underprivileged answers the call that all participate in promoting 'the common good.'

• Given the opportunity, what dreams do you have for a future in building and construction? List your dreams, plans, and goals. Arrange them in order of 'attack.' Outline steps toward their achievement. Write about your dream.

• If you volunteer with Habitat for Humanity or some other home-repair or construction outreach, keep a daily record of your activities. What was the end result of your volunteer experience? How did it fulfill *CCC* # 1913 and 2288?

Experiential Learning/Career and Vocational Bridge:

[See Table of Contents for *Process Project Outline* and *Following in Their Footsteps* projects]

Building and Construction Projects:

Note: Take step-by-step photographs of volunteer, part-time, and apprenticeship experience whenever possible for use in portfolios.

• Seek part-time employment [or volunteer] on clean-up with a local contractor. Proving a strong work ethic may open the door to an apprenticeship.

• Volunteer with your parish/parish school maintenance employee/s, particularly on construction and repair jobs.

• Contact and interview local contractors in person, particularly those within your parish. Ask what preparation and training they would recommend for a career in building construction.

• Contact your diocesan offices. Many dioceses have youth summer programs that provide ministry opportunities in home repair for the underprivileged.

• Volunteer with Habitat for Humanity. See above web address; volunteer opportunities in construction of housing for the poor in U.S., Canada, more. Keep a daily journal and take photographs. When your work is completed, compile an album of the experience.

• Find out about alternative construction, e.g, hay bale construction, building with old tires, packed dirt. If feasible, construct a small storage building, play house, or animal shelter using one of these methods.

BUSINESS CLUSTER

S, AK=*Accounting the Easy Way*—Barron's typing, computer, accounting

S, D/DVD=*Accounting*—Standard Deviants

S, B=American Business: Merit Badge Series

S=*Basic Economics: A Common Sense Guide to the Economy,* Thomas Sowell

S, AK=*Bookkeeping the Easy Way,* Wallace Kravitz—Barron's

C=*Apostles and Markets*—free online Catholic economics course—www.acanthuseducation.org/apostles_and_markets/

S, T/AK=*Business in Action,* Courtland Bovee—Pearson Prentice Hall [economics, management, marketing]

S, B=Entrepreneurship: Merit Badge Series

S, V/DVD=*Finance*—Standard Deviants

S, B=Personal Finance: Merit Badge Series

S, B=Salesmanship: Merit Badge Series

S=*The Complete Idiot's Guide to Economics,* Tom Gorman

S=*The Price Waterhouse Personal Tax Adviser,* Donna Carpenter

S, T/AK=*Typing the Easy Way*—Barron's

S=*Typing for Everyone,* Nathan Levine

C=Virtue Based Management—www.stantoninus.net

Links:

www.bbc.co.uk/schools/typing/—free online typing program

www.cybf.ca/—Canadian Youth Business Foundation

http://www.businessinsider.com/10-awesome-business-ideas-for-the-teen-entrepreneur-2011-2?op=1

www.epionline.org—Employment Policies Institute

www.ja.org—Junior Achievement—hands-on business and economics

http://studentcenter.ja.org/Learn/Pages/default.aspx

http://studentcenter.ja.org—Junior Achievement—ideas for your starting your own business, career and college planning, scholarships

http://lessonplans.btskinner.com—Tonya Skinner's Lesson Plans—business, accounting, career prep computer concepts, keyboarding, business math, more

C=www.stantoninus.net—St. Antoninus Institute for Catholic Education in Business

www.toastmasters.org—Toastmasters International—public speaking for leadership, business

http://www.ipl.org/div/subject/—Internet Public Library

Church Teaching:

Centesimus Annus—Pope John Paul II's Encyclical On the 100th Anniversary of *Rerum Novarum*

CCC #2409-2410, 2432, 2434

Possible Essay Topics:

• Read *CCC* #2432. In what ways are those responsible for business enterprise responsible to society? How do profits benefit not only a company, but ultimately benefit employees as well? List points, outline, and expound.

• Read *CCC #2434* and/or *Centesimus Annus* – Pope John Paul II's Encyclical On the 100th Anniversary of *Rerum Novarum*. What is the attitude of the Church toward fair wages? Explain the difference between a 'fair wage' and 'minimum wage.' Compare and contrast. [See www.cato.org—enter 'minimum wage' in Search box.]

• Given the opportunity, what dreams do you have for a future in business? List your dreams, plans, and goals. Arrange them in order of 'attack.' Outline steps toward their achievement. Write about your dream.

Experiential Learning/Career and Vocational Bridge:

[See Table of Contents for *Process Project Outline* and *Following in Their Footsteps* projects]

Business Cluster Projects:

• Perhaps the best way to learn office skills, including filing and computer applications, is to work in an office! Parish offices are often grateful for volunteer help when preparing mailings and handouts for fund drives, missions, Bible School, and RCIA programs.

- office aide in parochial school
- office aide in parish or diocesan office
- office aide to parish Director of Religious Education
- office aide in Catholic radio station

• Start a business, e.g., lawn-mowing, yard care, babysitting, provide animal care during owners' vacation. Blow leaves, shovel snow, clean gutters, become a personal shopper for harried women who work outside the home; hang outdoor Christmas lights for a fee. Give music lessons; tutor public-schooled children in your home. If your location and

zoning permit, build a small kennel on your property and pet-sit. [See http://studentcenter. ja.org/Learn/Pages/default.aspx—click on 'Resources.'] Record *all* your expenses and profits, clients' names, contact information, and dates of service. Remember that each contact is an opportunity to 'be Christ to the world.' Be sure to tithe!

• Become involved in Future Business Leaders of America or Junior Achievement; start a chapter in your area.

Each [student] is a precious and unrepeatable miracle, not because of what he does, but because of who he is: a child of God. Those who use their God-given gifts to the best of their ability, in whatever capacity, give glory to God not according to man's measure, but according to God's.

CAREER DEVELOPMENT AND COLLEGE PREP

Online Resources:

Type in search box: 'online courses _____ degree'

Book List:

S=*300 Best Jobs Without a Four-Year Degree*, Michael Farr

S, DVD=*Career Enhancement—* Standard Deviants

S, T/AK=*Cliff's Study Guides for AP, SAT, ACT—*Cliff's

S=*College Exploration on the Internet,* Andrew Morkess

C, T/video=*LifeWork: Finding Your Purpose in Life,* Rick Sarkisian, Ph.D. [CHC]

C=*Pilgrims of the Holy Family,* Kerry and Nancy MacArthur [CHC]

S=Princeton Review series—numerous titles for college test and course prep

S, B=Scholarship: Merit Badge Series

S=*Student Success Secrets,* Eric Jensen—study strategies and note-taking

S=*The Princeton Review: America's Elite Colleges: The Smart Applicant's Guide to Ivy League,* Dave Berry

College Prep Writing Workshop [E-book], Sandra Garant [CHC]

See also Table of Contents: Selecting a College: Catholic Colleges that Love Homeschoolers

Links:

www.bls.gov/ooh/home.htm—U.S. Department of Labor Statistics' Occupational Outlook

http://breyerstate.com, 208-935-0233; Breyer State University; online, distance education offering associates, bachelor's, master's and doctorates in fields such as Criminal Justice, Equine Studies, Journalism, Marketing, Early Child Care, Business Management, Medical Office Assistant, Nursing, Psychology, Pre-Med and more

www.collegeandcareerpress.com—college prep newsletter, free info

www.collegeboard.org—college board practice tests

www.varsitytutors.com/practice-tests—practice tests for standardized tests

www.cybf.ca—Canadian Youth Business Foundation

www.fastweb.com—free; excellent, comprehensive scholarship search

www.hslda.org/docs/nche/000002/00000240.asp—homeschoolers admitted to military

www.hslda.org/highschool/military.asp—homeschoolers admitted to military

www.kaplan.com—PSAT/SAT description and information, test prep books

www.kaptest.com—college board practice tests

www.khake.com—educational links for every imaginable career; see sampling below

www.khake.com/page18.html—electrical occupations

www.khake.com/page19.html—electronics career

www.khake.com/page20.html—engine technology

www.khake.com/page46.html—environmental, biology

www.khake.com/page27.html—graphic arts

www.khake.com/page21.html—horticulture, landscape

www.khake.com/page28.html—law enforcement, security, investigative

www.khake.com/page22.html—medical, health

www.khake.com/page29.html—metalworking and welding

www.khake.com/page33.html—military

www.khake.com/page48.html—performing arts

www.princetonreview.com—college prep info, free practice tests

www.studyguidezone.com—free test preparation for PSAT, SAT, ACT, GED

http://technicaljobsearch.com/job-banks/apprenticeships.htm—apprenticeships U.S. and Canada

http://www.ipl.org/div/subject/—Internet Public Library

Curricula/text/video Resources:

www.khake.com/page58.html—apprenticeship info, training resources

www.khake.com/page93.html—career curriculum resources

www.khake.com/page94.html—career development interactive lessons/activities

www.khake.com/page60.html—vocational curriculum resources

http://store.im.tamu.edu/Construction-Maintenane-C46.aspx

http://store.im.tamu.edu/Trade-Industrial-Education-Materials-C386.aspx

www.nccer.org/—construction related curricula

Study Skills and Test Preparation:

A Word to Those Who are Vocational School or College-Bound

Due to class size and lack of constant, individualized student-teacher interaction, public and private schools rely on frequent test-taking to assess student progress. Conversely, homeschoolers not infrequently eliminate most test-taking from their school routine, because the immediate, daily feedback makes obvious a student's performance.

However, homeschoolers can find themselves at a disadvantage when faced with testing, often for the first time, in post-high school education. In addition, students accustomed to test-taking have generally developed the study skills requisite to testing success. Again, those homeschooling students who lack test-taking experiences also tend to be deficient in study skills.

Therefore, it is recommended that, beginning in the freshman year of high school, timed tests should be periodically administered to students in courses such as history and science. At the same time, students should begin taking practice tests offered both online and in 'Preparing for the SATS/ACTS' workbooks.

In addition to test-taking proficiency, another study skill necessary for post-high school success is the ability to take good notes. One approach that fits a homeschool setting employs the use of lecture videos such as those available from The Great Courses [www.thegreatcourses.com]. Viewing video lectures with historical or literary topics provides note-taking practice while simultaneously earning credit for those subjects. Students may also wish to incorporate note-taking suggestions from one of the books listed below.

Note-Taking and Study Skills:

S=*Learning to Learn*, Gloria Frender

S=*Student Success Secrets*, Eric Jensen—study strategies and note-taking

S=*Test Smart! Ready-to-Use Test-taking Strategies and Activities*, Gary Abbamont

College Boards:

NOTE: When purchasing SAT study materials, make certain that they are for the current test format.

Information on college testing and GED preparation, including practice tests and online courses:

www.petersons.com

www.princetonreview.com

For the most current SAT and ACT test preparation materials, go to www.amazon.com and enter 'SAT Preparation Barron's,' 'ACT Preparation Barrons,' or 'Master the SAT Peterson's.'

Church Teaching:

CCC #2230

Possible Essay Topics:

• Read *CCC #2230*. Who might be your first source of guidance in choosing a profession? After seeking the Holy Spirit's light, who might be your second source of guidance? Ask your parents' observations about your God-given aptitudes. Draw up a list of activities in which you have participated in the past four or five years. Which seemed most to capture your interest? Based on your findings, write about what your aptitudes might be.

Experiential Learning/Career and Vocational Bridge:

• If you are college-bound or have a training program in mind, check into visiting the institution. Most Catholic colleges offer a free overnight in dorms, guided tours of the campus, and 'sampling' of classroom lectures.

Catholic homeschoolers for years have been accepted without accredited diplomas, not only at noted institutions like Franciscan University of Steubenville and Thomas Aquinas College, but in secular colleges across the United States and Canada.

CHEMISTRY

Science Labs:

Labs essentially provide students an opportunity to test theories against reality, i.e., allow students to apply what they have learned from their texts in hands-on settings.

Most colleges don't require documented science labs as part of a high school science course. In fact, there is no national standard or definition of what exactly constitutes a high school science lab. However, since some colleges do require documented science lab work, it is best to include at least 20 hours of lab work in each science course that your student takes.

Keeping in mind that 'lab' means hands-on learning that applies book-learning to reality, credit for a Geology lab might be earned by visiting a fossil bed and searching for fossils. Students might photograph the rock formations where the fossils were found, identify the type of rock in which the fossils were found, and identify the types of fossils therein. Brief descriptions or notations about why and how fossils were found in this type of geological structure might be included. All of this information would then be assembled into a lab report.

An Environmental Science lab might include similar notations about discoveries made in a pond ecosystem, including a description and photographs of the pond, plant and animal aquatic life, and conclusions as to how and why those particular plants and animals live in that environment.

In essence, no matter which science courses are chosen, students will devote at least 20 hours of class time to lab work—that is, hands-on projects, exploration, and conclusions about what the student learned—which will be documented in a hard-copy notebook or portfolio.

Parents might also double-check with colleges to which students might apply to determine whether or not there are lab requirements.

Please also note that students who enroll in science classes at local colleges gain those lab credits while simultaneously earning both high school and college credit.

Book List:

Please also see Science, General, for more titles

S=*Basic Chemistry*, Karen Timberlake [CHC]

S, T/AK=*Chemistry*—Cliff's

S, T/AK=*E-Z Chemistry*—Barron's

S=*Chemistry: Concepts and Problems: A Self-Teaching Guide* [Wiley Self-Teaching Guides], Clifford C. Houk

S=*Chemistry for Everyone: A Helpful Primer for High School or College Chemistry*, Suzanne Lahl

S=*Chemistry: Concepts and Problems: A Self-Teaching Guide*, Clifford Houk

S=*Illustrated Guide to Home Chemistry Experiments*, Robert Thompson [CHC]

Experiences in Chemistry, Kathleen Julicher—Homeschool Science Press [chemistry lab for homeschool]

Supplemental Reading:

S, CP, T/AKA, CD Virtual Lab=*Chemistry*—Pearson Prentice Hall

S, B=Chemistry: Merit Badge Series

S, V/DVD=*Chemistry*—Standard Deviants

S, V/DVD=*Chemistry*—The Great Courses [with workbook]

S=*CRC Handbook of Chemistry and Physics*, David Lide

S, T/AK=*AP Chemistry*—Barron's

S=*Radioactive Substances*, Marie Curie

S=*The Chemical Tree: A History of Chemistry*, William Brock

Links:

www.rsc.org/periodic-table

1,200 page, free science supplies catalog!—www.wardsci.com—Ward's Natural Science—1-800-962-2660

www.bls.gov/ooh/architecture-and-engineering/chemical-engineers.htm

www.chm.davidson.edu/vce/index.html—virtual chemistry

http://csee.lbl.gov/—Center for Science and Engineering Education interactive site and links

http://education.jlab.org/indexpages/index.html—all about elements and atoms, games and puzzles

www.fas.org/—Federation of American Scientists

http://ie.lbl.gov/xray—X-ray spectrum of elements

www.lbl.gov/MicroWorlds/—interactive materials sciences

www.martindalecenter.com

www.micro.magnet.fsu.edu

http://www.101science.com/chemJAVA.htm#Chemistry

http://www.ipl.org/div/subject/—Internet Public Library

Church Teaching:

C=www.newadvent.org/cathen—Catholic encyclopedia

C=www.catholic-pages.com/—Catholic documents and teaching, current events, more

C=www.zenit.org/en—Vatican news; recent and archived Papal/Church statements

CCC #159, 2293-2294

Possible Essay Topics:

• Read *CCC* #2293-2294. 'It is an illusion to claim moral neutrality in scientific research and its applications...[Science] must be at the service of the human person, of his inalienable rights, of his true and integral good, in conformity with the plan and the will of God.' Think of and then research ways that the Catholic chemist can 'be at the service of the human person.' [E.g., pharmacological research in the development of new drugs to treat previously untreatable illness.] List several possibilities, then discuss how these uses might fulfill the above quote. [Cite the *CCC* quote, above, in your essay.]

• '...methodical research in all branches of knowledge, provided it is carried out in a truly scientific manner and does not override moral laws, can never conflict with the faith, because the things of the world and the things of faith derive from the same God.' [*CCC* #159] How is chemistry part of the study of an ordered universe, revealing the hand of its Creator? List four examples of the order and logical structure that you find in chemistry. Read paragraph #159 in its entirety and refer to it in your essay.

• Given the opportunity, what dreams do you have that necessitate the study of chemistry? List your dreams, plans, and goals. Arrange them in order of 'attack.' Outline steps toward their achievement. Write about your dream.

Research:

You may, in conjunction with your text and field work, wish to investigate the following chemistry-related careers in greater depth. Credit may be obtained through reading and hands-on, experiential learning including field trips to labs and science museums, and volunteering. Learning is demonstrated through the production of projects, experiments, essays or reports. Reports may be based on note-taking and observation and might include graphs, charts, illustrations and diagrams. Find out more about these professions:

• anesthesiologist
• biochemist
• chemical engineer

- agricultural chemist
- forensic chemist
- pharmaceutical chemist
- criminologist
- dietician
- Food and Drug Inspector
- geneticist
- laboratory analyst
- medical technician
- nuclear scientist
- pharmacist
- pharmacologist
- physician
- soil scientist
- toxicologist
- veterinarian

Famous Names Related to the Science of Chemistry: Read and Report

In what ways did the Catholic Church aid in discoveries/inventions/advancement?

How did the person's faith [or lack thereof] influence his/her work?

What might have motivated the person to become involved in the field?

In what ways did his/her discoveries/inventions/advancement change the field of study?

In what ways did his/her discoveries/inventions/advancement ultimately change society?

St. Albert the Great

Antoine Henri Becquerel

Robert Boyle

Pierre and Marie Curie [both homeschooled]

Michael Farady

Antoine Lavoisier [devout Catholic]

Louis Pasteur [devout Catholic]

Linus Pauling [homeschooled]

COMMUNICATIONS

S, B=Communications: Merit Badge Series

S, T=*Media and Culture: An Introduction to Mass Communication*, Richard Campbell

S=*Writing and Reporting News: A Coaching Method*, Carole Rich

Links:

www.aim.org/—Accuracy in Media

C=http://canadiancatholicradio.wordpress.com—Catholic radio in Canada

C=www.catholicculture.org/news—Catholic World News, Catholic journalists

C=www.catholiceducation.org—orthodox Catholic writers; excellent resource for art cles on the media

C=www.catholicnews.com/—Catholic News Service

C=www.catholic-pages.com/dir/culture_wars.asp—articles about anti-Christian bias in today's culture

C=www.catholicpress.org—Catholic Press Association of U.S. and Canada

C=www.cctn.org—Catholic Community Television Network

C=www.ewtn.com—lists of affiliated Catholic radio stations across the United States and Canada

C=www.franciscanmedia.org

C=http://ihradio.com—Immaculate Heart Radio

http://www.khake.com/page43.html—journalism, communications career guide, requirements www.mrc.org—Media Research Center for bias in journalism

C=http://nccbuscc.org/ccc/—Catholic Communications Campaign

C=www.paxcc.org—Archdiocese of Miami radio

C=www.radiomaria.us—Radio Maria

C=www.saintjosephradio.net

http://townhall.com—communications, journalism

C=http://usccb.org/media/index. cfm—U.S. Conference of Catholic Bishops: movies, TV, radio

C=www.vatican.va/news_services/ —Vatican News Services

http://www.ipl.org/div/subject/ —Internet Public Library

Church Teaching:

C=www.newadvent.org/cathen— Catholic encyclopedia

C=www.catholic-pages.com/—Catholic documents and teaching, current events, more

C=www.zenit.org/en—Vatican news; recent and archived Papal/Church statements

Dawn of a New Era [Aetatis Novae], Pontifical Council for Social Communications

Decree on the Media and Social Communication [Inter Mirifica], Second Vatican Council

Ethics in Advertising, Pontifical Council for Social Communications

Ethics in Communication, Pontifical Council for Social Communications

Pastoral Instruction on the Means of Social Communication [Communio et Progressio], ibid

CCC #2493-2498, 2286

Possible Essay Topics:

• *CCC* #2493-2498. #2498 states, 'Nothing can justify recourse to disinformation for manipulating public opinion through the media.' While this quote addresses the use of media for propaganda purposes, it also calls to mind the manipulation that originates within the media itself. Media bias is demonstrated in two ways: in the *way* a story is reported, and by not reporting it at all. In the first instance, a story might be slanted to the point that what is finally reported is untrue. E.g., a pro-life demonstration is attended by 500,000 pro-lifers and 180 pro-aborts; reporters film and interview only the pro-aborts, giving the appearance that the pro-aborts were in the majority. In the second instance, the news media simply ignore the demonstration altogether, with the result that the country is unaware that a demonstration has occurred. Objective reporting, in contrast, would present the facts of the demonstration and leave the viewer/listener/reader to draw his own conclusions. Compare and contrast the implications of these three approaches to reporting.

• Research and write about anti-Catholic/ Christian bias in the media. [See www. catholiceducation.org]

• '...they are guilty of scandal who establish... social structures leading to the decline of morals...This is also true of...manipulators of public opinion who turn it away from moral values.' In what ways are the television and motion picture industry guilty of scandal, according to this statement? How might television and film be used to positively impact society? [Include Catholic examples where possible.] Read and quote from *CCC* #2286-2287.

• Read *Decree on the Media and Social Communication [Inter Mirifica]*, from the documents of the Second Vatican Council, Vol.1. What does the Church teach about the responsibilities of those working in communications? In what ways might Catholic journalists provide a positive influence on society through their work? In your essay, include at least two references to *Inter Mirifica*.

• In the 1990's, the Catholic country of East Timor sought its independence from Indonesia. The response from the Muslim government was a bloody, decade-long attack on the Catholic population, which was largely ignored by the secular news media. Similarly, the Muslim Sudanese government had for decades, continuing into the 21st century, brutalized the Catholic population of Sudan, bombing churches, slaughtering more than 2 million people, and forcing countless others into slavery. Again, the secular news media was silent. Had you been involved in the communications field at the time of these atrocities, how might you have reported? Research the Timorese and Sudanese conflicts and write news articles on each. [Note: in the 21st century, the Sudanese government has extended their atrocities to include non-Catholic tribesmen, atrocities which the secular media has covered to a limited degree. For these articles, focus on the anti-Catholic abuses that went uncovered.]

• Given the opportunity, what dreams do you have for a future in communications? List your dreams, plans, and goals. Arrange them in order of 'attack.' Outline steps toward their achievement. Write about your dream.

Research:

You may, in conjunction with your text and field work, wish to learn more about the following communication organizations. Credit may be obtained through reading and hands-on, experiential learning including field trips, volunteering, and apprenticeships. Learning is demonstrated through the production of projects, experiments, essays or reports. Reports may be based on note-taking and observation and might include graphs, charts, illustrations and diagrams.

"Who, what, where, when and why?"

• Vatican Radio
• EWTN
• Catholic News Service
• Catholic Press Association of U.S. and Canada
• Canadian Catholic Radio
• Catholic Community Television Network
• Catholic World News
• Catholic Communications Campaign
• International Catholic Union of the Press [UCIP] and International Network of Young Journalists

Famous Names Related to Communications: Read and Report

How did the person's faith influence his/her work?

What might have motivated the person to become involved in Catholic broadcasting?

In what ways did his/her contribution to Catholic communications ultimately change society?

Mother Angelica

Archbishop Fulton Sheen, 'Life is Worth Living'

Experiential Learning/Career and Vocational Bridge:

[See Table of Contents for *Process Project Outline* and *Following in Their Footsteps* projects]

Communications Projects:

• Produce a video documentary of a day in the life of a Catholic homeschooling family. [Begin the day with Holy Mass!]
• Produce a video documentary of a day in the life of a Catholic priest or sister.
• Produce a video documentary of a parish or diocesan outreach to the disadvantaged.
• Interview, in person or over the telephone, someone in Catholic radio or television.
• Volunteer with:

    Catholic radio and television stations
        [See 'Communications' in diocesan
        directory; some dioceses produce
        television and radio programs.]
    diocesan communications office
    diocesan newspaper

COMPUTER SCIENCE

Science Labs:

Labs essentially provide students an opportunity to test theories against reality, i.e., allow students to apply what they have learned from their texts in hands-on settings.

Most colleges don't require documented science labs as part of a high school science course. In fact, there is no national standard or definition of what exactly constitutes a high school science lab. However, since some colleges do require documented science lab work, it is best to include at least 20 hours of lab work in each science course that your student takes.

Keeping in mind that 'lab' means hands-on learning that applies book-learning to reality, credit for a Geology lab might be earned by visiting a fossil bed and searching for fossils. Students might photograph the rock formations where the fossils were found, identify the type of rock in which the fossils were found, and identify the types of fossils therein. Brief descriptions or notations about why and how fossils were found in this type of geological structure might be included. All of this information would then be assembled into a lab report.

An Environmental Science lab might include similar notations about discoveries made in a pond ecosystem, including a description and photographs of the pond, plant and animal aquatic life, and conclusions as to how and why those particular plants and animals live in that environment.

In essence, no matter which science courses are chosen, students will devote at least 20 hours of class time to lab work—that is, hands-on projects, exploration, and conclusions about what the student learned—which will be documented in a hard-copy notebook or portfolio.

Parents might also double-check with colleges to which students might apply to determine whether or not there are lab requirements.

Please also note that students who enroll in science classes at local colleges gain those lab credits while simultaneously earning both high school and college credit.

Note:
*Due to rapid and ever-changing developments in computer science, texts can become outdated within six months time. For the most up-to-date training, it is suggested that students refer to computer science magazines and websites for current trends and instruction. See also **Links**, below.*

A word about credit awarded for Computer Science: remember that the majority of classes will have 'overlapping' credit possibilities. For example, researching and writing a report on earthquakes for Earth Science might include three hours of reading the text and supplementary materials, two hours of internet research, two hours creating a computer-generated PowerPoint presentation of earthquake data, and two hours of composition on the computer, for a total of nine hours. All nine hours may be used for Earth Science credit. However, note that six of these hours are expended on computer use. Those hours, if desired, could be subtracted from Earth Science credit—if you already have plenty of Earth Science hours—and used instead for Computer Science. [Note that the *same* hours can't be used twice, for two different courses. Rather, 'banked' hours are hours in excess of the 180 gained in one class and assigned to another.]

Resources List:

Ol=www.onlineschoolclassroom.com—classes in computer programming languages; online instructors

S=*PC World* Magazine

S=*Mastering Computer Typing: A Painless Course for Beginners and Professionals,* Sheryl Roberts

Supplemental Reading:

C=*Brain, Mind, and Computers,* Fr. Stanley Jaki, O.S.B.

Links:

www.doleta.gov—apprenticeships by state, county, and occupation

http://computer.howstuffworks.com—answering your questions about computers

www.computer.org—Institute of Electrical and Electronics Engineers: computer science, magazines, education

www.tcu.gov.on.ca/eng/employmentontario/training/—Ontario, Canada apprenticeship training

www.informationweek.com—latest in computer developments

www.khake.com/page17.html—computer science career guide, requirements

www.khake.com/page58.html—apprenticeship info, training resources, U.S. and Canada

www.khake.com/page65.html—free lessons and lesson plans: computer technology, computer tutorials, web design

http://lessonplans.btskinner.com/computercon.html—Tonya Skinner's Lesson Plans, computers

www.microsoft.com

www.networkcomputing.com—latest computer news and downloads

http://www.ipl.org/div/subject/—Internet Public Library

Church Teaching:

C=www.newadvent.org/cathen—Catholic encyclopedia

C=www.catholic-pages.com/—Catholic documents and teaching, current events, more

C=www.zenit.org/en—Vatican news; recent and archived Papal/Church statements

CCC #2293-94

Possible Essay Topics:

• Read *CCC* #2293-2294; throughout the passage, substitute the word 'computer' for the words, 'science' and 'scientific.' In what ways do these two paragraphs offer guidance for the use of computer technology? What are some negative uses of computer technology? And positive uses? [E.g., violent computer games vs. computer software that teaches our Holy Faith through games, or computer applications that track natural disasters for more efficient delivery of relief.] List examples of each, then compare and contrast the end results of each.

• " 'Lord, when did we see thee hungry and feed thee, or thirsty and give thee drink?...And when did we see thee sick...?' And the King will answer them, 'Truly, I say to you , as you did it to one of the least of these my brethren, you did it to me.' " [Matt. 25:35-40] Websearch human-computer interfaces for medical purposes and rehabilitation for the disabled, e.g., eye-tracking systems, virtual reality, computer-assisted rehabilitation therapy. Write about your discoveries from the standpoint of the scriptural quote.

• Given the opportunity, what dreams do you have for a future in computer technology? List your dreams, plans, and goals. Arrange them in order of 'attack.' Outline steps toward their achievement. Write about your dream.

Famous Names Related to Computer Science: Read and Report

How did the person's faith [or lack thereof] influence his/her work?

What might have motivated the person to become involved in the field?

In what ways did his/her discoveries/inventions/advancement change the field of study?

In what ways did his/her discoveries/inventions/advancement ultimately change society?

Bill Gates

Lawrence Page and Sergey Brin, inventors of 'Google'

Experiential Learning/Career and Vocational Bridge:

[See Table of Contents for *Process Project Outline* and *Following in Their Footsteps* projects]

Computer Science Projects:
• Design and maintain a website for:
  your parish or a parish ministry
  local Crisis Pregnancy Center
  St. Vincent de Paul
  local Catholic homeschool group [include
    contact people and resources]
• Design an interactive computer game to
    teach the Faith to young children.
• Volunteer to enter data for:
  your parish
  religious education program/DRE
  local Crisis Pregnancy Center
  St. Vincent de Paul
• Teach a one-session class in computer
    basics to a homeschool group.

CRIMINAL JUSTICE/ FORENSIC SCIENCE

S, B=Crime Prevention: Merit Badge Series

S, AK=*Criminal Justice*—Cliff's

S=*Criminal Justice: A Brief Introduction,* Frank Schmalleger

S, T, AKA=*Criminalistics: An Introduction to Forensic Science*— Pearson Prentice Hall

S, B=Fingerprinting: Merit Badge Series

S=*Great Jobs for Criminal Justice Majors,* Stephen Lambert

S=www-ims.tamu.edu/—Instructional Materials Service: Fundamentals of Criminal Law, Law Enforcement Training, Introduction to Criminal Justice

S, B=Law: Merit Badge Series

S=*Introduction to Criminal Justice,* Larry Siegel

Links:

http://exploring.learningforlife. org/services/career-exploring/ law-enforcement/

http://store.im.tamu.edu/Personal-Protective-Services-C50.aspx

www.atf.gov—Bureau of Alcohol, Tobacco, Firearms, and Explosives

http://canada.justice.gc.ca/eng/index. html—Canadian Department of Justice

C=www.catholiceducation.org— orthodox Catholic writers; excellent resource for articles on capital punishment

www.fbi.gov/

www.fletc.gov/—Federal Law Enforcement Training Center and U.S. Dept. of Homeland Security

www.govspot.com/categories/ crimeandjustice.htm

www.heritage.org/—The Heritage Foundation, current issues, including crime

www.khake.com/page28.html—law enforcement, investigative career guide, requirements

www.khake.com/page77.html—free lessons and lesson plans: law

www.rcmp-grc.gc.ca/index-eng.htm— Royal Canadian Mounted Police

http://exploring.learningforlife. org/services/career-exploring/ law-enforcement/43821

www.justice.gov—U.S. Department of Justice

http://www.ipl.org/div/subject/ —Internet Public Library

Church Teaching:

C=www.newadvent.org/cathen— Catholic encyclopedia

C=www.catholic-pages.com/—Catholic documents and teaching, current events, more

C=www.zenit.org/en—Vatican news; recent and archived Papal/Church statements

Jubilee in Prisons, [homily] Pope John Paul II, July, 2000

CCC #1897-1898, 1909-10, 2266

Possible Essay Topics:

• Read *CCC* #1897-1898. "Human society can be neither well-ordered nor prosperous unless it has some people invested with legitimate authority to preserve its institutions and to devote themselves as far as is necessary to work and care for the good of all.' Using traffic laws as an example, write about the benefits of order in society. Explain what might happen without those same laws. Compare the effects of anarchy, or the absence of law, with those of a society whose laws 'work and care for the good of all.' Quote *CCC* #1897-1898 in your paper.

• For the common good, should drug testing in the workplace be mandated by law? Or would such testing infringe on the right to privacy? Testing for grocery store clerks may seem an invasion, but what about airline pilots or surgeons? Think of examples; reference the Bill of Rights or other legal precedent. Present both sides, but make your case for one.

• Research and describe in detail the physical evidence demonstrating that the Shroud of Turin is no ordinary piece of cloth [see www.shroud.com/menu.htm]. In what ways might a knowledge of forensics be used to witness to our Holy Faith?

• What landmark ruling originated with Miranda vs. Arizona? Research. Do you think Miranda should be overturned? Why or why not? Give examples, and attach a copy of the 'rights' to your essay.

• Given the opportunity, what dreams do you have for a future in criminal justice? List your dreams, plans, and goals. Arrange them in order of 'attack.' Outline steps toward their achievement. Write about your dream.

Research:

You may, in conjunction with your text and field work, wish to investigate in greater depth the following topics and fields related to Criminal Justice. Credit may be obtained through reading and hands-on, experiential learning including field trips, volunteering, and apprenticeships. Learning is demonstrated through the production of projects, experiments, essays or reports. Reports may be based on note-taking and observation and might include graphs, charts, illustrations and diagrams describing history or current operations.

• Bureau of Alcohol, Tobacco, Firearms, and Explosives
• CIA
• FBI
• Drug Enforcement Agency
• Federal Air Marshall program
• juvenile corrections
• criminal court system
• cybercrime
• Customs and Border Patrol programs
• criminology
• Homeland Security
• Royal Canadian Mounted Police
• parole and probation
• forensic chemistry
• DNA fingerprinting
• Secret Service
• forensic chemistry
• Study the Bill of Rights [first ten amendments to the Constitution].

Experiential Learning/Career and Vocational Bridge:

[See Table of Contents for *Process Project Outline* and *Following in Their Footsteps* projects]

Criminal Justice Projects:

- Check for police cadet programs in your locale. Rural counties often have mounted sheriff's posse volunteer opportunities; state patrols frequently have Explorer cadet programs.
  - city police
  - county sheriff
  - state police
- Contact an attorney from your parish; spend a day in his office. [Remember that attorneys have different specialties; not all specialize in criminal law.]
- Contact your county courthouse; find out when and where criminal court trials are held. Attend a trial; go early for pre-trial hearings.
- Attend a juvenile court hearing. If you are able to attend a criminal court trial, contrast the two experiences.

DRAMA

[See public library for video resources]

S, B=Cinematography: Merit Badge Series

C=*Collected Plays and Chesterton on Shaw [Vol. XI],* G.K.Chesterton—Ignatius

C=*Praise Him with Your Very Life,* Mother Mary Francis—Catholic Heritage Curricula [CHC]

S, V/DVD=*Shakespeare*—Standard Deviants

S, V/DVD=*Shakespeare: Comedies, Histories, and Tragedies*—The Great Courses

C=*It's a Mystery: The Perfect Personality,* Sandra Garant—Catholic Heritage Curricula [CHC], directing children in theatrical presentations

C=St. Luke Productions [video and audio by Catholic artist Leonardo Defilippis, www.stlukeproductions.com]:
  - St. Francis: Troubadour of God's Peace
  - The Gift of Peace
  - Maximilian: Saint of Auschwitz
  - Therese: The Story of a Soul
  - The Passion According to Luke
  - St. John of the Cross
  - The Confessions of St. Augustine
  - The Song of Songs
  - The Gospel of John

S, B=Theater: Merit Badge Series

C=*The Jeweler's Shop,* Karol Wojtyla

S, V/DVD=*Understanding Literature and Life: Drama, Poety and Narrative*—The Great Courses

C=*Witness to Hope: The Biography of John Paul II,* George Weigel

Mandatory Reading:

C=*Decree on the Means of Social Communication [Inter Mirifica]*, Documents of Vatican II, Vol. I

Links:

C=www.catholiceducation.org— orthodox Catholic writers; articles on the arts

C=www.epiphanystudio.com/home— Catholic theater

C=www.stlukeproductions.com— Catholic dramatic production

http://www.ipl.org/div/subject/ —Internet Public Library

Church Teaching:

C=www.newadvent.org/cathen— Catholic encyclopedia

C=www.catholic-pages.com/—Catholic documents and teaching, current events, more

C=www.zenit.org/en—Vatican news; recent and archived Papal/Church statements

Decree on the Means of Social Communication [Inter Mirifica], Documents of Vatican II, Vol. 1

Pastoral Instruction on the Means of Social Communication [Communio et Progressio], Vatican II, Vol.1

Possible Essay Topics:

• Pope John Paul II, as a young man, wrote and participated in theatrical productions. Research his involvement in drama. What was his purpose in participating? [See *Witness to Hope: The Biography of Pope John Paul II*, pp. 33-38 and 62-66.] Weigel states, '... Karol Wojtyla deliberately chose the power of resistance through culture, through the power of the word, in the conviction that the 'word' [and in Christian terms, the Word] is that on which the world turns.' If all of Hollywood held this conviction, in what ways might our society be different? Give examples to support your conclusion.

• 'The noble and ancient art of the theatre has been widely popularized by the means of social communication. One should take steps to ensure that it contributes to the human and moral formation of its audiences.' Read *Inter Mirifica*, Chapter II. In what ways do most secular theatrical productions 'contribute to the...moral formation' of their audiences? Watch 'The Jeweler's Shop' or Mel Gibson's 'The Passion of the Christ.' How do these productions 'contribute to the...moral formation' of their audiences? Compare and contrast the end results of these two productions with Hollywood's usual fare.

• Read *Inter Mirifica* in its entirety. Write a brief essay on this teaching of the Church.

• Watch a Leonardo Defilippis production of your choice. Write a brief essay explaining how this playwright and actor fulfills the following quote from *Communio et Progressio*. 'The Church has always shown considerable interest in the theater which, in its origins, was closely connected with manifestations of religion. This ancient interest in the theater should be maintained by Christians today and full use be made of its possibilities. Playwrights should be encouraged and helped to set man's religious preoccupations on the platform of the public stage.'

• Given the opportunity, what dreams do you have for a future in drama? List your dreams, plans, and goals. Arrange them in order of 'attack.' Outline steps toward their achievement. Write about your dream.

Experiential Learning/Career and Vocational Bridge:

[See Table of Contents for *Process Project Outline* and *Following in Their Footsteps* projects]

Drama Projects:
Note: Catholic homeschoolers in some areas have had positive, wholesome experiences participating in community theater. However, standards and atmosphere are only as good as the director's. Do your homework; view a few productions and visit before making commitments.

• Organize other homeschoolers and
    produce a skit for presentation at:
    homeschool group
    nursing or retirement home
    home for retired religious
    religious education program
    'Bible School'
• Research 'morality plays' from the Middle
    Ages. Write a modern 'morality play.'

DRIVER'S ED

S=*Drive Right: You are the Driver,* Margaret Johnson

S=*Driver Ed in a Box*—interactive software that includes videos, textbook, student workbook, parent companion and training mirrors—www. driveredinabox.com

S=*Responsible Driving,* McGraw-Hill

S, B=Traffic Safety: Boy Scout Merit Badge Handbook

www.americandrivingacademy.com— homestudy driving academy, reduced insurance rates in most states for graduates of this homestudy program. Check website to see if your state is included.

Church Teaching:

Yes, there is a Church teaching applicable to Driver's Ed! At dinner tonight, read *CCC* #2290 to your parents and family.

Books, videos, and websites listed as references for the courses in this volume are not 'recommended' or 'preferred,' but rather widely used options from which to choose, depending on the intended field of study, educational goals, and the mental and spiritual maturity of the student.

EARTH SCIENCE

Science Labs:

Labs essentially provide students an opportunity to test theories against reality, i.e., allow students to apply what they have learned from their texts in hands-on settings.

Most colleges don't require documented science labs as part of a high school science course. In fact, there is no national standard or definition of what exactly constitutes a high school science lab. However, since some colleges do require documented science lab work, it is best to include at least 20 hours of lab work in each science course that your student takes.

Keeping in mind that 'lab' means hands-on learning that applies book-learning to reality, credit for a Geology lab might be earned by visiting a fossil bed and searching for fossils. Students might photograph the rock formations where the fossils were found, identify the type of rock in which the fossils were found, and identify the types of fossils therein. Brief descriptions or notations about why and how fossils were found in this type of geological structure might be included. All of this information would then be assembled into a lab report.

An Environmental Science lab might include similar notations about discoveries made in a pond ecosystem, including a description and photographs of the pond, plant and animal aquatic life, and conclusions as to how and why those particular plants and animals live in that environment.

In essence, no matter which science courses are chosen, students will devote at least 20 hours of class time to lab work—that is, hands-on projects, exploration, and conclusions about what the student learned—which will be documented in a hard-copy notebook or portfolio.

Parents might also double-check with colleges to which students might apply to determine whether or not there are lab requirements.

Please also note that students who enroll in science classes at local colleges gain those lab credits while simultaneously earning both high school and college credit.

Book List:

Please also see Science, General, *for more titles*

S, CP, T/AKA=*Earth Science*—Pearson Prentice Hall

S, T/AK=*E-Z Earth Science*— Barron's

S, B=Geology: Merit Badge Series

S, B=Soil and Water Conservation: Merit Badge Series

http://store.im.tamu.edu—vocational curriculum resources: environmental science, forestry

Supplemental Reading:

S=*Beneath Our Feet: The Rocks of Planet Earth*, R. H. Vernon

C=*Origin of the Human Species*, Dennis Bonnette

S=*Eco-Scam: The False Prophets of Ecological Apocalypse*, Ronald Bailey

C=*Science of Today and the Problems of Genesis*, Fr. Patrick O'Connell [Archaeological/origin of man]

NCC=*The Flood*, Alfred Rehwinkel—the Flood, archaeological and Biblical evidence

S=*The Practical Geologist*, Dougal Dixon

S=*Trashing the Planet*, Dixie Lee Ray

S=*The True State of the Planet*, Ronald Bailey

Links:

1,200 page, free science supplies catalog!—www.wardsci.com—Ward's Natural Science—1-800-962-2660

C=www.catholiceducation.org— orthodox Catholic writers; excellent resource for articles on science www.cato.org/research—environment, climate, energy and conservation, global warming, water policy, pollution

http://earthquake.usgs.gov/earthquakes/eqinthenews/—current earthquake tracker

http://earthquake.usgs.gov/earthquakes/—current earthquake tracker

http://education.jlab.org/indexpages/index.html—all about elements and atoms, games and puzzles

www.education.noaa.gov—National Oceanic and Atmospheric Association

www.enchantedlearning.com/Home.html—printables: maps, geology, anatomy, astronomy, botany, more

www.epa.gov—Environmental Protection Agency

www.nrcan.gc.ca/earth-sciences/home—Geological Survey of Canada, earth sciences, natural resources, geoscience

www.globalwarming.org

www.iris.edu/seismon/

http://spaceplace.nasa.gov—interactive views of earth and more

www.nasa.gov/audience/forstudents/9-12/index.html

http://nesarc.org—Endangered Species Act information

http://scienceandpublicpolicy.org

www.worldclimatereport.com

www.noaa.gov—weather, climate, oceans, research

www.noaa.gov/charts.html—ocean charting, navigation, aerial photography

www.noaa.gov/ocean.html—ocean research

www.oar.noaa.gov—ocean and coastal research

http://oceanexplorer.noaa.gov—ocean exploration

www.swpc.noaa.gov—space weather research

www.science.gov—earth, oceans, natural resources, more

www.usgs.gov/—U.S. Geological Survey—geography, geology, geospatial information, water and more

http://volcano.oregonstate.edu/—volcano watch and more

http://volcanoes.usgs.gov—volcano information

http://www.ipl.org/div/subject/—Internet Public Library

Church Teaching:

C=www.newadvent.org/cathen—Catholic encyclopedia

C=www.catholic-pages.com/—Catholic documents and teaching, current events, more

C=www.zenit.org/english—Vatican news; recent and archived Papal/Church statements

C=*Statement on Evolution*, Pope John Paul II, Address to Pontifical Academy of Sciences, 1997

CCC #282-289

Possible Essay Topics:

• Track earthquake activity for three months. [See http://earthquake.usgs.gov/earthquakes/eqarchives/epic/—or http://earthquake.usgs.gov/earthquakes/eqinthenews/] Record date of occurrence. Find out which plates or fault lines are involved; record. Look for patterns of activity. Write a short report about your discoveries, including areas of greatest activity and any apparent connection between events.

See also:

> www.extremescience.com/plate-tectonics.htm
>
> www.platetectonics.com/—plate tectonics
>
> www.pbs.org/wgbh/aso/tryit/tectonics/intro.html—plate tectonics

• Read *CCC* #282-286. 'The existence of God the Creator can be known with certainty through his works, by the light of human reason, even if this knowledge is often obscured and disfigured by error. This is why faith comes to confirm and enlighten reason ...' By studying the earth, one also learns of Him Who created it.

Human understanding of earth's origins is necessarily limited, because 'proof' in science requires replication and observation of an event. Since man is unable to create from nothing to replicate and observe the Creation event, even science relies on faith to believe scientific theory.

For example, scientists for years believed that the coelacanth, an 'ancient fish,' appeared in the fossil records before dinosaurs, and became extinct about 65 million years ago. Imagine their surprise when coelacanths were discovered, alive and flourishing, off the coasts of Africa and Asia in the 20th century. Additionally, no one had told the coelacanth that, in the past 65 million years, he should by all scientific reasoning have evolved considerably; the unmutated fish was easily recognized from the 65 million-year-old fossilized images of his forebears. [See www.dinofish.com or http://unmuseum.mus.pa.us/

coelacan.htm] Research and write about the coelacanth. Think: science helps us to learn of God's creative intelligence; science also has its limitations. Refer to *CCC* #282-286 in your essay.

Research

You may, in conjunction with your text and field work, wish to investigate the following topics in greater depth. Credit may be obtained through reading and hands-on, experiential learning including field trips, volunteering, and apprenticeships. Learning is demonstrated through the production of projects, experiments, essays or reports. Reports may be based on note-taking and observation and might include graphs, charts, illustrations and diagrams.

To aid in research, ask and answer, "Who, what, where, when and why?" [For example: *Where* is the 'Ring of Fire'? *What* is the relationship between plate tectonics and earthquakes? *Who* discovered.....? *When* does erosion....? *Why* does conservation..?]

• environments and habitats
  tundra
  deserts
  coniferous forest
  tropical rain forest
  grasslands
  aquatic environments
  swamps
  rivers
  oceans
  food webs/chains
• conservation and management of God's gifts/wise use
  erosion
  agriculture and stewarding farm land
  land reclamation
  reforestation

- ocean
    - tides
    - tidal waves
    - currents
    - water cycle
    - coral reef
- weather
- climate
- Earth's structure
    - plate tectonics
    - continents
    - continental drift
    - volcanoes
    - earthquakes
        - faults
    - rock
        - sedimentary
        - igneous
        - metamorphic
    - caves/caverns
    - weathering
    - soil formation
    - mountains
    - glaciers
    - poles and magnetic fields

Experiential Learning/Career and Vocational Bridge:

[See Table of Contents for *Process Project Outline* projects.]

Earth Science Projects:

See also Hands-on Science Sites, U.S. And Canada *in* Table of Contents.

- Set up a weather station. Record and journal. Find annual records for precipitation and temperature. How do your records compare?

    http://ols.nndc.noaa.gov/
    plolstore/plsql/olstore.
    prodspecific?prodnum=C00095-PUB-

A0001#TABLES—climatological data by city, region

- Volunteer as a weather spotter with a local television station.
- Track volcanic activity for three months. Note whether the activity is from a shield, composite, or cinder cone volcano. How does volcanic action differ amongst the different types of volcanoes? Chart or graph activity.

    www.volcano.si.edu/weekly_report.cfm

- Track earthquake activity. Select three specific countries/regions to track; chart or graph activity.

    http://earthquake.usgs.gov/
    earthquakes/eqarchives/epic/

    http://www.iris.ecu/seismon/—track recent earthquake activity

- Visit fossil sites.
- Visit mineral and gem sites.
- Visit caverns/caves.
- Visit an oceanographic institute.

...an accredited diploma alone is no guarantee that a student will be accepted by a college; conversely, the student with solid SAT scores and a portfolio brimming with evidence of a motivated young adult will likely be welcomed at university, diploma or not.

ELECTRICAL SCIENCE

Science Labs:

Labs essentially provide students an opportunity to test theories against reality, i.e., allow students to apply what they have learned from their texts in hands-on settings.

Most colleges don't require documented science labs as part of a high school science course. In fact, there is no national standard or definition of what exactly constitutes a high school science lab. However, since some colleges do require documented science lab work, it is best to include at least 20 hours of lab work in each science course that your student takes.

Keeping in mind that 'lab' means hands-on learning that applies book-learning to reality, credit for a Geology lab might be earned by visiting a fossil bed and searching for fossils. Students might photograph the rock formations where the fossils were found, identify the type of rock in which the fossils were found, and identify the types of fossils therein. Brief descriptions or notations about why and how fossils were found in this type of geological structure might be included. All of this information would then be assembled into a lab report.

An Environmental Science lab might include similar notations about discoveries made in a pond ecosystem, including a description and photographs of the pond, plant and animal aquatic life, and conclusions as to how and why those particular plants and animals live in that environment.

In essence, no matter which science courses are chosen, students will devote at least 20 hours of class time to lab work—that is, hands-on projects, exploration, and conclusions about what the student learned—which will be documented in a hard-copy notebook or portfolio.

Parents might also double-check with colleges to which students might apply to determine whether or not there are lab requirements.

Please also note that students who enroll in science classes at local colleges gain those lab credits while simultaneously earning both high school and college credit.

Book List:

S=*Complete Electronics Self-Teaching Guide with Projects*, Harry Kybett

S, B=Electricity: Merit Badge Series

S, B=Electronics: Merit Badge Series

S=*Electronics for Dummies,* Gordon McComb

S, T/AK=*Electronics the Easy Way—*Barron's

S, T/AKA=*Electrical Wiring,* Ralph Duncan

S, T/AK=*Understanding Electricity*

http://store.im.tamu.edu/Search.aspx?c=47

Supplemental Reading:

S=*How Electronic Things Work...and What to Do When They Don't,* Robert Goodman [audio/music systems, CD, TV, PC, VCR, telephones, etc.]

Links:

www.doleta.gov—apprenticeships by state, county, and occupation

www.doityourself.com—basic electrical wiring

www.tcu.gov.on.ca/eng/employmentontario/training/—Ontario, Canada apprenticeship training

http://electronics.howstuffworks.com—how electronic things work

www.habitat.org—Habitat for Humanity International

www.khake.com/page58.html—apprenticeship info, training resources, U.S. and Canada

www.khake.com/page18.html—
electrical occupations career guide,
requirements, more about electricity

www.khake.com/page19.html—
electronics career guide, requirements,
more about electricity

www.khake.com/page82.html—free
lessons and lesson plans: construction,
electricity

www.physics.uoguelph.ca/tutorials/
ohm/index.html—electricity, interactive
lessons

http://technicaljobsearch.com/
job-banks/apprenticeships.htm—
apprenticeships U.S. and Canada

http://www.101science.com/chemJAVA.
htm#Electronics

http://www.ipl.org/div/subject/
—Internet Public Library

Possible Essay Topics:

• Write about the history and development of alternating and direct currents. Compare their uses, including the benefits and disadvantages of each. Why is AC used predominately in the United States and Canada?
• Given the opportunity, what dreams do you have for a future in electronics? List your dreams, plans, and goals. Arrange them in order of 'attack.' Outline steps toward their achievement. Write about your dream.

Research:

You may, in conjunction with your text and field work, wish to investigate the following electronics-related careers in greater depth. Credit may be obtained through reading and hands-on, experiential learning including field trips to labs and science museums, and volunteering. Learning is demonstrated through the production of projects, experiments, essays or reports. Reports may be based on note-taking

and observation and might include graphs, charts, illustrations and diagrams. Find out more about these professions:

• photonics
• robotics
• broadcast technicians
• automotive electrician
• power plant technician
• electronics engineering
• aircraft electronics
• radio mechanics

Famous Names Related to Electronics: Read and Report

In what ways did the Catholic Church aid in discoveries/inventions/advancement?

How did the person's faith [or lack thereof] influence his/her work?

What might have motivated the person to become involved in the field?

In what ways did his/her discoveries/inventions/advancement change the field of study?

In what ways did his/her discoveries/inventions/advancement ultimately change society?

Andre-Marie Ampere—physics [devout Catholic]

Wilhelm Roentgen

Alexander Graham Bell [homeschooled]

John Fleming

Lee DeForest

Guglielmo Marconi [homeschooled]

Experiential Learning/Career and Vocational Bridge:

See also *Career and Vocational Bridge/ Volunteer* section of this volume [See Table of Contents for *Process Project Outline* and *Following in Their Footsteps* projects]

Electronics Projects:
• Build a radio.
• Create/wire a lighting system for a poorly-lit area of your home. [with parental permission]
• Build an intercom system to connect the kitchen with select rooms in the house. [with parental permission]
• Volunteer with Habitat for Humanity: See above web address; volunteer opportunities in construction of housing for the poor in U.S., Canada, more.
• Find an electrician in your parish and ask if you might 'shadow' him for a day.
• Wire a dog house or an outbuilding for lights. [with parental permission]

ENGLISH, COMPOSITION AND GRAMMAR

Four years of English are required for all *High School of Your Dreams* educational 'tracks.' However, credit may be earned through reading, viewing dramatic productions, essays, reports, journals, spelling, and vocabulary programs—anything that involves the use of English! As always, those whose career paths will require the greatest exposure to composition, grammar, and literature should select their materials accordingly. For the college bound, *Jensen's Format Writing* is recommended for its training in crafting logical, clear presentations. Such writing is useful not only in preparation for college-level composition, but also for the SAT essays.

Additionally, English Composition and English Literature may be taught simultaneously or alternately. Possible division might include 1/2 year Lit., followed by 1/2 year Comp., or a monthly rotation.

Grammar:

S, T/AK=*English Grammar,* Cliff's Study Solver [329 pages]—Cliff's

S, T/AK=*E-Z English [Barron's E-Z Series]*—[includes grammar, punctuation, spelling, vocabulary, some writing]

S, T/AK=*English Grammar for Dummies,* www.dummies.com

S, T/AK=*E-Z Grammar*—Barron's

S, T/AK=*Prentice Hall Grammar Workbook*—Pearson Prentice Hall

www.dailygrammar.com/archive. shtml—grammar worksheets

S, B=*Life Skills English,* Student Workbook, [AGS Basic English

Grammar] by AGS Secondary—special ed

S=*How Grammar Works: A Self-Teaching Guide* [Wiley Self-Teaching Guides], Patricia Osborn

Composition:

S, T/AK=*Essentials of Writing*—Barron's [grammar/well written sentence]

NCC, CP=*Jensen's Format Writing,* Frode Jensen [recommended!] [CHC]

C=*Writing Workshops III-IV,* Sandra Garant [CHC]

College Prep Writing Workshop [E-book], Sandra Garant [CHC]

S, T/AK=*Research Papers for Dummies,* www.dummies.com

S, TM, V/DVD=Teaching Writing: Structure and Style, www.excellenceinwriting.com

C=*Creative Communications [Part III: Advanced Projects for Real Writers],* Sandra Garant [CHC]

AP Testing:

S, T/AK, CP=*AP English Literature and Composition*—Barron's

S, T/AK, CP=*AP English Language and Composition*—Barron's

Spelling/Vocabulary:

NCC, CP=*Jensen's Vocabulary,* Frode Jensen [CHC]

S, T/AK=*E-Z Spelling*—Barron's

S, T/AK=*Vocabulary Success*—Barron's

S, AK=*Word Power Made Easy,* Norman Lewis

Supplemental:

C=*The Book of Catholic Quotations,* Chapin [recommended for quotes around which to build essays; excellent for taking along to college as well]

S=*Elements of Style,* Strunk and White

Links:

C=http://blog.catholicwritersguild.com

C=www.wf-f.org—Women for Faith and Family [sponsor annual *Voices* Young Writers' Contest, ages 12-21]

www.essaycompetition.org—annual international essay competition

C=www.studiobrien.com—respected Catholic artist and author, Michael O'Brien

www.tsowell.com/About_Writing.html—advice to aspiring writers, Thomas Sowell

http://www.ipl.org/div/subject/—Internet Public Library

Church Teaching:

C=www.newadvent.org/cathen—Catholic encyclopedia

C=www.catholic-pages.com/—Catholic documents and teaching, current events, more

C=www.zenit.org/en—Vatican news; recent and archived Papal/Church statements

Catholic Schools, Malgre les declarations, Documents of Vatican II, Vol.2

Possible Essay Topics:

What is your chosen field? What are your interests? In addition to essay topics suggested below, writing credit can also be earned for essays on other topics that capture the student's imagination. See 'Possible Essay Topics' listed with elective courses, e.g., Agricultural Science, Art, Environmental Science, Family Management. In addition, Social Problems Today has a number of suggested topics on which to write.

• If you are composing a book report about a book written by a Catholic author, selected from the Literature course:

Is the author's Faith evident in his writing? In what ways? Is there obvious reference to Catholic teaching, or is the message subtle? How is the Faith woven into the story?

• Brainstorm five ways to avoid giving in to temptation. Narrow your list to the three best; write a short essay.

• Brainstorm for an essay comparing the popular 'feminist' attitude vs. Our Lady's attitude of feminine service.

For example:

self-serving vs. serving others: 'Behold, the Handmaid of the Lord'

anti-life vs. pro-life

Think of at least four contrasting attitudes. Pick the best three; compare and contrast.

• Compare and contrast ordinary 'table' bread with Eucharistic Bread from Heaven. Think of at least four points for each. Narrow to the three best examples; write.

• 'Cats make better pets than dogs.' [or vice versa] Think of at least four points for each. Narrow to the three best examples; write.

• Read *CCC* #2266-2267. What is the teaching of the Church regarding the death penalty? Write an essay comparing and contrasting a sentence of life imprisonment with the death penalty. Think of at least four points for each. Narrow to the three best examples; write.

• 'Men should/shouldn't carry purses.' Think of at least four points for each. Narrow to the three best examples; write.

• Refute: 'Abortion is a necessary evil. It is better for a baby not to be born than to be born into a destitute family.' Ideas: If a family is too poor to feed another child, and killing is a legitimate option, why not kill one of their older children, who eats more than a baby would? Is murder ever an acceptable solution to problems? How about adoption? Or helping the father get vocational training and a better job so he can feed not only the new blessing from God, but also raise the standard of living for his entire family? Which is the more compassionate attitude? Think of four points to refute the statement; narrow to three examples, and write.

• 'Animals [including rodents and insects] should/shouldn't have the same rights as people do.' [Should Little Miss Muffet be sued for striking a defenseless spider?] Think of at least four points in support of your position. Narrow to the three best examples; write. [See websites, below, for ideas.]

www.naiaonline.org

www.catholiceducation.org/directory/ Current_Issues/Environment

• 'Reading the book is better than seeing the movie.' Think of at least four points in support of your position. Narrow to the three best examples; write.

• 'The power of choosing good and evil is within the reach of all.' [Origen—3rd century] Think of at least four points in support of your position. Narrow to the three best examples; expound.

• 'Columbus should have just stayed home.' Think of at least four points in support of your position. Narrow to the three best examples; write.

• 'The internet is a valuable tool to help us learn more about our Faith/is a serious danger to our Faith.' Think of at least four points in support of each position. Narrow to the three best examples; compare and contrast.

• Read *Catholic Schools, Malgre les declarations, Documents of Vatican II, Vol. 2,* paragraphs #40 & 43. Argue: 'Only practicing Catholics should be allowed to teach in Catholic schools.' Think of at least four points in support of your position. [Cite *Catholic Schools* in your arguments.] Narrow to the three best examples; write.

• 'Taking out the trash is/isn't bad for your health.' Think of at least four points in support of each position. Narrow to the three best examples; compare and contrast.

• 'The family is more sacred than the State.' [Pope Pius XI] Think of at least four points; narrow to the three best examples; write. [Ideas: Which is supreme: the laws of the land, or the laws of God? Abortion is legal, but is it moral?]

• 'Overpopulation is not a problem.' Think of at least four points; narrow to the three best examples; write. [Ideas: Can people share resources? Didn't God order man to fill the earth and subdue it? Is it possible that God 'forgot' to plan ahead when He created the earth, and now He should change His mind because there 'aren't enough resources' to go around? Does God make mistakes?] See www.pop.org and www.catholiceducation.org for more ideas.

• 'How many more would become saints if they did to please God half of what they do to please men.' [St. Thomas Aquinas] Write about immodest fashions, in light of the quote above. Which is more important to our eternal souls: to please our peers, or to please God? Think of

at least four points; narrow to the three best examples; write.

• 'Girls are smarter than guys/guys are smarter than girls.' Think of at least four points; narrow to the three best examples; write.

• 'Christ and His Church are two in one flesh.' Expound. Refer in your paper to Lk. 10:16 ["He who hears you, hears Me."] and 1 Tim. 3:15. [The Church is the pillar and bulwark of truth; Jesus is the Way, the Truth, and the Life.]

• Write against the error of indifferentism. [First, find out what indifferentism is.] Is it true that all things have equal value? Is one car as good as another? One pizza? One religion? A doctrine is either true, or it isn't, whether we choose to believe it or not. What problems arise from believing in something that is false? [If I believe that gravity will make me fall up when I jump from the roof of a building, does my belief make it so?] Two 'truths' or two systems of belief that contradict one another cannot be equally true and good, particularly where one's eternal soul is concerned. Think of at least four points; narrow to the three best examples; write.

• 'Those who fall into venial sin, however, experiencing their weakness daily, receive through frequent confession the strength to arrive at the full freedom of the children of God...frequent and reverent recourse to this Sacrament, even when only venial sins are in question, is of great value. Frequent confession is not mere ritual repetition, nor is it merely a psychological exercise. Rather is it a constant effort to bring to perfection the grace of our baptism..." [*The New Order of Penance, Documents of Vatican II, Vol. 2*] Compose a 'letter' that you might send to a friend who goes to confession only once a year, pointing out at least three reasons why he should take advantage of this grace-giving Sacrament more frequently. Refer to the quote, above.

• Think of a topic that interests you, particularly in regard to our Holy Faith; see if it is referenced in the *Catechism of the Catholic Church* or the *Documents of Vatican II.* [Check out the **Church Teaching** links.] What does the Church have to say? Write an essay explaining Church teaching on the subject.

More ideas:
• Everyone should/should not have a bedroom of his own.
• Women should/shouldn't be allowed in combat.
• Video games are educational/a waste of time.
• Men should/shouldn't help with housework.
• Motorcycles should/shouldn't be banned.
• All Catholic youth should/shouldn't be required to serve six months in a mission field.
• TV helps us to grow in Faith/is a danger to our Faith.
• Corporal punishment should/shouldn't be allowed.

More ideas for 'Compare and Contrast' essays:
• environmentalism vs. responsible stewardship of nature
• benefits to living in the 19th century vs. the 21st century
• painting with watercolors vs. painting with oils
• Communion in the hand vs. Communion on the tongue
• 19th century muskets vs. 21st century hunting rifles

Experiential Learning:

• Journal, journal, journal—daily, and pencil in the time you spent on each page. This is writing, too! Is Wildlife Science, or Environmental Science, your favorite class? Journal about the beaver family patting mud and grasses on their dam, stumbled upon while you were checking on anadromous fish runs or testing water quality.

Or does Automotive Mechanics consume your every free hour? Write in your journal about the '68 Ford Mustang you're restoring, how hard it was to find the right parts for the transmission, and what happened to your knuckles when you were putting the pieces together. Include what your mother said when she noticed the grease blotches staining the back of your new shirt; be sure to enclose her lively commentary with quotation marks.

ENGLISH, LITERATURE

Four years of English are required for all 'tracks.' However, credit may be earned through reading, listening to audio books, viewing dramatic productions, letter writing, essays, reports, journals, spelling, and vocabulary programs—anything that involves the use of English! As always, those whose career paths will require the greatest exposure to composition, grammar, and literature should select their materials accordingly.

Additionally, English Composition and English Literature may be taught simultaneously or alternately. Possible division might include 1/2 year Lit., followed by 1/2 year Comp., or a monthly rotation. Certainly, the two can be interwoven by writing about literature under study.

Study Guides as 'Teaching Texts': Please note!

Study guides can be a valuable learning tool for those who desire more in-depth study and discussion than reading the text alone might provide. For the homeschooler, a well-written study guide, used in conjunction with the literary work it amplifies, can provide the thought-provoking insight of a literature teacher. For example, most guides include introductory information about, and discussion of, the book's subject and analysis of the book's central characters. This in-depth study and insight can prove beneficial to students preparing for college level courses and also to students who might wish for more explanation of a seemingly incomprehensible piece of literature.

Further, since the student is given the choice of various literary works and their guides, he learns literary analysis based on books that pique his own interest, rather than those that might be assigned by a distant teacher.

Barron's and Cliff offer study guides for numerous classics, e.g., Aeneid, The Odyssey, The Iliad, Don Quixote, the works of Shakespeare, and numerous modern writers.

Barron's study guides—abbreviated versions of numerous classics, with answer keys and tests—www.barronseduc.com

Cliff's Notes—abbreviated versions of numerous classics, with answer keys and tests—www.cliffsnotes.com

The Great Courses—www.thegreatcourses.com, 1-800-832-2412—audio and video courses

C=*Catholic Great Books Study Guides*, Julie Collorafi [CHC]

C=*The Secret Code of Poetry*, RoseMary Johnson [CHC]

S=*Shakespeare for Dummies*, John Doyle

S=*The Complete Idiot's Guide to American Literature*, Laurie Rozakis

www.sparknotes.com—free, downloadable study guides

C=*Ignatius Critical Editions*, Joseph Pearce [CHC]

C=*Catholic DVD Literature Courses* [CHC]

CP, V/DVD=*Aeneid, Virgil*—The Great Courses

S=*Animal Farm*, George Orwell

CP=*Anna Karenina*, Leo Tolstoy

C=*Anthology of Catholic Poets*, Joyce Kilmer

S=*A Tale of Two Cities*, Charles Dickens

S, B=*Beowulf the Warrior*, Ian Serraillier

✓S=*Beowulf* [Dover]

C=*Bread and Wine,* Iznazo Silone

Canterbury Tales, Chaucer

C=*Chesterton on Dickens [Vol. XV],* G.K.Chesterton—Ignatius

C=*Collected Poetry [Vol.X],* G.K. Chesterton—Ignatius

C, CP=*Confessions,* St. Augustine

Death Comes for the Archbishop, Willa Cather

C, CP=*Don Quixote,* Miguel Cervantes

CP=*Faust,* Johann Goethe

C, NCC=*Garlands of Grace,* classic poetry edited by Regis Martin

S, V/DVD=*Greek Tragedy*—The Great Courses

✓S=*Hamlet,* William Shakespeare

S=*House of Seven Gables,* Nathaniel Hawthorne

S, V/DVD=*Iliad, Homer*—The Great Courses

C=*In This House of Brede,* Rumer Godden

S=*Joan of Arc,* Mark Twain

S=*Kidnapped,* Robert Louis Stevenson

S, V/DVD=*King Arthur and Chivalry*—The Great Courses

C, CP=*Kristen Lavransdatter,* Sigrid Undset

C=*Lepanto,* G.K. Chesterton

S=*Les Miserables,* Victor Hugo

S, V/DVD=*Life and Work of Mark Twain*—The Great Courses

S, V/DVD=*Life and Writings of C.S. Lewis*—The Great Courses

S, V/DVD=*Life and Writings of Geoffrey Chaucer*—The Great Courses

✓S=*Little Women,* Louisa May Alcott

✓S=*Macbeth,* William Shakespeare

S=*Man of the Family,* Ralph Moody

C=*Murder in the Cathedral,* T.S. Eliot

C=*The Path to Rome,* Hilaire Belloc

C=*Poetry as Prayer,* Pauline Books

✓S=*Pride and Prejudice,* Jane Austin

C, B=*Reading Comprehension: Stories of the Saints, Vol. III-IV,* Elaine Woodfield—Catholic Heritage Curricula [CHC]

C=*Edmund Campion,* Evelyn Waugh

C=*Set All Afire,* Louis de Wohl [St. Francis Xavier]

C=*Shadowplay: The Hidden Belief and Coded Politics of William Shakespeare,* Clair Asquith

S, V/DVD=*Shakespeare,* Standard Deviants

S, V/DVD=*Shakespeare: Comedies, Histories, and Tragedies*—The Great Courses

S, B=*Tales from Shakespeare,* Charles and Mary Lamb

S=*Tales of O. Henry,* O. Henry

S=*Taming of the Shrew,* William Shakespeare

S=*The Adventures of Huckleberry Finn,* Mark Twain

C=*The Ballad of the White Horse,* G.K. Chesterton

C=*The Catholic Classics,* Dinesh D'Souza

C=*The Collected Works of G.K. Chesterton, Vol. XVIII: Robert Louis Stevenson, Chaucer, Leo Tolstoy*

C=*The Complete Father Brown,* G.K. Chesterton

NCC=*The Death of Ivan Ilich*, Leo Tolstoy

DVD=*Dante's Divine Comedy*—The Great Courses

C, CP=*The Divine Comedy*, Dante

C=*The Everlasting Man*, G.K. Chesterton

C=*The Golden Book of Catholic Poetry*, Noyes

NCC=*The Great Divorce*, C.S. Lewis

C=*The Harp and Laurel Wreath*, Laura Berquist [poetry of Browning, Yeats, Shakespeare, more]—Ignatius

C=*The Hobbit*, J.R.R. Tolkien

C, CP=*The Inferno*, Dante

C=*The Joyful Beggar*, Louis de Wohl

S=*The Last of the Mohicans*, James Fenimore Cooper

C=*The Man Who Was Thursday*, G.K. Chesterton

C=*The Place Within* [Study Guide by Julie Collorafi, analyzing the poetry of Karol Wojtyla]

C=*The Quest for Shakespeare: The Bard of Avon and the Church of Rome*, biography by Joseph Pearce

C=*The Quiet Light*, Louis de Wohl [St. Thomas Aquinas]

C, CP=*The Shakespeares and 'The Old Faith,'* de Groot [evidence of Shakespeare's possibly Catholic training]

C=*The Spear*, Louis de Wohl

C=*The Tom Playfair Series*, Fr. Francis Finn, S.J. [decades-old favorites]

C=*The World's Great Catholic Literature*, George N. Shuster—an anthology of great Catholic literature

C=*Treasury of Catholic Wisdom*, Fr. John Hardon—Ignatius Press

S=*Uncle Tom's Cabin*, Harriet Beecher Stowe

S=*Up From Slavery*, Booker T. Washington

CP=*Walden*, Henry David Thoreau

CP=*War and Peace*, Leo Tolstoy

Short Stories and Poetry:

An education, particularly for the college-bound, isn't complete without some exposure to the following authors. Public libraries are a fine, free resource.

C=Hilaire Belloc

Robert and Elizabeth Browning

Robert Burns

Emily Dickinson

John Donne

Ralph Waldo Emerson

C=Fr. Frederick William Faber

C=Fr. Leonard Feeney

C=Gerard Manley Hopkins, S.J.

John Keats

C=Joyce Kilmer

Rudyard Kipling

Henry Wadsworth Longfellow

C=John Henry Cardinal Newman

C=Coventry Patmore

C=Joseph Plunkett

Edgar Allen Poe

C=Fr. Abram Ryan

Carl Sandburg

C=Fr. John Bannister Tabb

Alfred, Lord Tennyson

C=Francis Thompson

'Lighter' Reading [that nevertheless portrays courageous character or simply offers a glimpse into the humble lives of those who built the U.S. and Canada]. These books also make worthy additions to the family library.

✓*All Things Bright and Beautiful,* James Herriot

Belles on Their Toes, Frank Gilbreth

✓*Cheaper By the Dozen,* Frank Gilbreth

Conversations with Bullwhackers, Muleskinners..., Fred Lockley [true stories of Northwest pioneers]

Conversations with Pioneer Women, Fred Lockley [true stories of Northwest pioneers]

C=*Karen,* Marie Killilea

Little Britches, Ralph Moody [Old West]

Lost in the Barrens, Farley Mowat [Canadian adventure]

Mama's Bank Account, Kathryn Forbes

Man of the Family, Ralph Moody [Old West]

Never Cry Wolf, Farley Mowat

Stories of the Saints, Volumes III-IV, Elaine Woodfield [CHC]

✓C=*The Complete Father Brown,* G.K. Chesterton

The Dog Who Wouldn't Be, Farley Mowat

NCC=*The Family Nobody Wanted,* Helen Doss

NCC=*The Hiding Place,* Corrie ten Boom [WWII Holocaust]

The Rock Within the Sea, Farley Mowat [Canada]

C=*When Hell Was in Session,* Jeremiah Denton [POW, Viet Nam War]

C=*With Love from Karen,* Marie Killilea

Links:

C=www.catholicauthors.com—authors of Catholic literature and their works

C=www.catholiceducation.org— orthodox Catholic writers; excellent resource for articles on the arts & literature

http://www.ipl.org/div/subject/ —Internet Public Library

Possible Essay Topics:

• Following your favorite book report format, write with your college portfolio in mind.
• Write about a work that has influenced your way of thinking or approach to life. In what ways did the author change your perspective?

Experiential Learning/Career and Vocational Bridge:

• Organize a homeschool library 'swap.' Ask each participating family to list books they are willing to lend, then meet, share lists, and swap.
• Sign on as a library volunteer.
• Find and view Shakespearean theater productions near you. [Websearch 'Shakespearean theater festivals.']

ENVIRONMENTAL SCIENCE

Science Labs:

Labs essentially provide students an opportunity to test theories against reality, i.e., allow students to apply what they have learned from their texts in hands-on settings.

Most colleges don't require documented science labs as part of a high school science course. In fact, there is no national standard or definition of what exactly constitutes a high school science lab. However, since some colleges do require documented science lab work, it is best to include at least 20 hours of lab work in each science course that your student takes.

Keeping in mind that 'lab' means hands-on learning that applies book-learning to reality, credit for a Geology lab might be earned by visiting a fossil bed and searching for fossils. Students might photograph the rock formations where the fossils were found, identify the type of rock in which the fossils were found, and identify the types of fossils therein. Brief descriptions or notations about why and how fossils were found in this type of geological structure might be included. All of this information would then be assembled into a lab report.

An Environmental Science lab might include similar notations about discoveries made in a pond ecosystem, including a description and photographs of the pond, plant and animal aquatic life, and conclusions as to how and why those particular plants and animals live in that environment.

In essence, no matter which science courses are chosen, students will devote at least 20 hours of class time to lab work—that is, hands-on projects, exploration, and conclusions about what the student learned—which will be documented in a hard-copy notebook or portfolio.

Parents might also double-check with colleges to which students might apply to determine whether or not there are lab requirements.

Please also note that students who enroll in science classes at local colleges gain those lab credits while simultaneously earning both high school and college credit.

Book List:

Please also see Science, General, *and* Earth Science

Note: *Texts include politically correct environmental teaching to which student will be exposed in college. It is therefore strongly recommended that students using texts also purchase* Environmentalism and its Spiritual Implications, *access articles from the Acton website, and select titles from Supplemental Reading to balance the course, particularly if the student wishes to pursue college studies in this field.*

S, CP, T/AK*A=Environmental Science: Working with the Earth,* G. Tyler Miller

S, B=Environmental Science: Merit Badge Series

C, NCC=*Environmental Stewardship in the Judeo-Christian Tradition: Jewish, Catholic, and Protestant Wisdom on the Environment*—www.acton.org

S, T/AK=*AP Environmental Science*—Barron's

S, T/AK=*Our Environment: A Canadian Perspective,* Thomson Nelson [Canada, Gr. 12]

http://store.im.tamu.edu/Environmental-Natural-Resource-Systems-ESS-C39.aspx

Supplemental Reading:

[researching the other side of politically correct philosophy]

S=Canada: Reaching for Forestry's Holy Grail [available from http://evergreenmagazine.com]

S=*Eco-Scam,* Ronald Bailey

S=*Evergreen Magazine,* http://evergreenmagazine.com—forestry and environmental

S=*Hoodwinking the Nation,* Julian Simon—environment, natural resources

S=In Farmers and Ranchers Do We Trust?—[http://perc.org/articles/farmers-and-ranchers-do-we-trust] economics and environment curriculum

S=*Trashing the Planet,* Dixy Lee Ray

S=*True State of the Planet: Ten of the World's Premier Environmental Researchers in a Major Challenge to the Environmental Movement,* Ronald Bailey

S=*The Ultimate Resource,* Julian Simon—natural resources, 'overpopulation'

C=*The War Against Population,* Dr. Jacqueline Kasun

Links:

www.21stcenturysciencetech.com/Global_Warming.html

C=www.acton.org/public-policy/environmental-stewardship—co-founded by Fr. Robert Sirico

C=www.catholiceducation.org—orthodox writers; excellent resource for articles on environmental science

www.cato.org/research—environment, climate, energy and conservation, global warming, water policy, pollution

www.ec.gc.ca—Environment Canada—meteorology and environmental information

http://scienceandpublicpolicy.org

www.worldclimatereport.com

www.epa.gov/enforcement/criminal/—Environmental Protection Agency, investigative branch

http://evergreenmagazine.com

www.globalwarming.org

www.govspot.com/categories/environment.htm—EPA Forest Service, more

www.nrcan.gc.ca/earth-sciences/home/—Geological Survey of Canada, earth sciences, natural resources, geoscience

www.heritage.org/—The Heritage Foundation

http://junkscience.com—scientific evidence, global warming, etc.

www.khake.com/page46.html—environmental, biology career guide, requirements

www.naiaonline.org—'animal rights'

http://store.im.tamu.edu/B-6227-Managing-the-White-Tailed-Deer-A-Wildlife-Management-Curriculum-for-High-School-P2763.aspx

www.nationaltrappers.com—National Trappers Association, *American Trapper Magazine,* environment

www.nesarc.org/stories.htm—animal rights in the environment

www.niehs.nih.gov/health/scied/—environmental and health science educational resource; opportunities for summer employment or research and more

www.nrcs.usda.gov/wps/portal/nrcs/ main/national/technical/—Natural Resources Conservation Service—land use, soil erosion, water quality, wetlands, conservation, natural resources

http://ohioline.osu.edu—Ohio State University Extension—food, agricultural, and environmental information

http://perc.org—Property and Environment Research Center

www.raptorsinthecity.org

http://www.ipl.org/div/subject/ —Internet Public Library

Church Teaching:

C=www.newadvent.org/cathen—Catholic encyclopedia
C=www.catholic-pages.com/—Catholic documents and teaching, current events, more
C=www.zenit.org/en—Vatican news; recent and archived Papal/Church statements
CCC #339, 342, 2417, 2418

Possible Essay Topics:

• Read CCC #339, 342, & 2417. What might be some examples of the 'disordered use' of Creation mentioned in #339? Note the comparative value of men and sheep in #342. Can there be extremes of 'disordered use' on both ends of the scale? How does Church teaching [#2417] wisely balance any extremes?
• Research and write about the health of various forests. Reference at least three different articles in your essay.
• Read CCC #2415. 'Animals, like plants and inanimate beings, are by nature destined for the common good of past, present, and future humanity. Use of the mineral, vegetable, and animal resources of the universe cannot be divorced from respect for moral imperatives.' List three ways that animals and plants are 'destined for the common good... of humanity.' Now think of three reasons that man has a moral imperative toward wise use of natural resources. Compare and discuss.
• Find out about successful restoration of lands that were strip mined for coal. What were the conditions before restoration? What were the conditions after cleanup? How have animal populations been affected by the change? Does it follow that, if an environment is 'destroyed,' it will always be so? Discuss. [To get you started: websearch 'AEP coal lands,' 'reforestation surface coal mines,' or 'AEP reclaimed coal lands.']
• Read CCC #2418. 'It is contrary to human dignity to cause animals to suffer or die needlessly...One can love animals; one should not direct to them the affection due only to persons.' Research the near extinction of the buffalo in the 19th century due to wanton and unregulated hunting. Then research articles about animal rights activists who vandalize private property and subvert human rights to animal rights. Contrast the two extremes and compare with the balanced guidance of the Church.
• Given the opportunity, what dreams do you have for a future in environmental sciences? List your dreams, plans, and goals. Arrange them in order of 'attack.' Outline steps toward their achievement. Write about your dream.

Research:

You may, in conjunction with your text and field work, wish to investigate the following environmental-related careers in greater depth. Credit may be obtained through reading and hands-on, experiential learning including field trips to labs and science museums, and volunteering. Learning is demonstrated through the production of projects, experiments, essays or reports. Reports may be based on note-taking and observation and might include graphs, charts, illustrations and diagrams. Find out more about these professions:

- agricultural and natural resources
- marine biologist
- park ranger
- environmental scientist
- park naturalist
- wildlife control
- conservation scientist
- soil and water specialist
- environmental analyst
- environmental planner
- plant pathologist
- urban and regional planner

Experiential Learning/Career and Vocational Bridge:

[See Table of Contents for *Process Project Outline* and *Following in Their Footsteps* projects.]

Environmental Science Projects:

- Contact local industries; take an industrial tour. Find out what measures they are taking to protect the environment.
- Visit the local Soil and Water Conservation or Natural Resources offices. Find out just what services they provide. [Most offices have a wealth of free materials describing various aspects of their services.] Arrange a homeschool tour; find out what measures they are taking to protect the environment.
- Purchase a water quality testing kit. [Check the internet for resources.] Test at least three different streams/ponds/waterways in your area. Record differences over a six month period, including times of heavy runoff. Chart/graph/report.

- Visit Fish and Wildlife offices. What services do they provide? Find out about regional concerns with overpopulated or endangered species. What measures are being taken to correct the imbalance? Find out about volunteer opportunities.

Books, videos, and websites listed as references for the courses in this volume are not 'recommended' or 'preferred,' but rather widely used options from which to choose, depending on the intended field of study, educational goals, and the mental and spiritual maturity of the student.

Family Management

C=*Back to the Family,* Dr. Ray Guarendi

S=*Big Book of Home How-To,* Better Homes and Gardens [wiring, plumbing, carpentry, etc.]

C=*By Love Refined,* Alice von Hildebrand

S=*Dare to Repair: A Do-It-Herself Guide to Fixing (Almost) Anything in the Home,* Julie Sussman

S, B=*Family Life: Merit Badge Series*

S, T/AK=*Goals for Living: Managing Your Resources,* Nancy Wehlage—Thomson Nelson Pub. [Canada, Gr. 9–12; childhood development, parenting, financial management, meal and budget management]

S=*Home Maintenance for Dummies,* www.dummies.com [plumbing, heating, roofing, etc.]

S, B=*Home Repairs: Merit Badge Series*

S, AKA, B=*Life School Worktexts*—Fearon

    Consumer Skills

    First Aid and Home Safety

NCC=*Living Well on One Income,* Cynthia Yates

C=*Generation Next: A Catholic Guide to Financial Freedom for Young Adults,* Phil Lenahan [CHC]

S, V/DVD=*No-Brainers: Personal Finance*—Standard Deviants

S, B=*Personal Finance: Merit Badge Series*

C=*The Catholic Answers Guide to Family Finances,* Philip Lenahan

C=*The Catholic Family Handbook,* Rev. Lawrence Lovasik

C=*The Mission of the Catholic Family,* Rick Sarkisian, Ph.D.

S=*The Price Waterhouse Personal Tax Adviser,* Donna Carpenter

S=*Wiring,* Creative Homeowners

Supplemental Reading:

S=*7 Myths of Working Mothers,* Suzanne Venker

C=*Christian Fatherhood,* Steve Wood

C=*Covenant of Love,* Pope John Paul II—Ignatius

NCC=*Day Care Deception: What the Child Care Establishment Isn't Telling Us,* Brian Robertson

C=*Discipline That Lasts a Lifetime,* Dr. Ray Guarendi

C=*Happy Are You Poor: The Simple Life and Spiritual Freedom,* Fr. Thomas Dubay

C=*Head of the Family: Christian Fatherhood in the Modern World,* Clayton Barbeau

C=*Home-Alone America: The Hidden Toll of Day Care,* Mary Eberstadt

C=*If You Really Loved Me: 101 Questions on Dating, Relationships, and Sexual Purity,* Jason Evert

C=*Love and Responsibility,* Pope John Paul II—Ignatius

C= *Marriage: The Mystery of Faithful Love,* Dietrich von Hildebrand

S, V/DVD=*No-Brainers: Auto Care*—Standard Deviants

NCC=*There's No Place Like Work: How Business, Government, and Our Obsession with Work Have Driven Parents from Home,* Brian Robertson

S=*The Toddler's Busy Book,* Trish Kuffner—helpful ideas for entertaining small children

Links:

C=www.catholiceducation.org—excellent, orthodox resource; current topics including marriage, parenting, children's response to media violence, day care, and much more

www.howtocleananything.com

www.housecleaning-tips.com

C=www.dads.org—Catholic men's website

C=www.catholicdadsonline.org

C=www.newmanconnection.com/institute/courses/rich-gift-of-love—Theology of the Body course

www.doityourself.com—basic electrical wiring, installing faucets, sinks, much more; interactive

www.frc.org—Family Research Council

www.livingonadime.com—money-saving ideas

www.heart4home.net—money-saving ideas

www.garysullivanonline.com—home repair, including video tips

www.khake.com/page77.html—free lessons and lesson plans: nutrition, child care, family, meals

www.msuextension.org/store/Departments/Family-and-Community-Topic-Categories/Family-Financial-Management.aspx

http://ohioline.osu.edu/lines/home.html—home financial management

www.stretcher.com/index.cfm—family budgeting tips

www.psnh.com/downloads/Home%20Appliance%20Usage%20Costs.pdf?id=4294968770&dl=t

www.psnh.com/CustomerSupport/Home/Tips-for-Reducing-Your-Bill.aspx

http://www.ipl.org/div/subject/—Internet Public Library

Church Teaching:

C=www.newadvent.org/cathen—Catholic encyclopedia

C=www.catholic-pages.com/—Catholic documents and teaching, current events, more

C=www.zenit.org/en—Vatican news; recent and archived Papal/Church statements

Enchiridion on the Family: A Compendium of Church Teaching on Family and Life Issues from Vatican II to the Present, Pontifical Council for the Family

Christian Marriage [Casti Conubii], Pope Pius XI

Family, Marriage and 'De Facto' Unions, Pontifical Council for the Family

Letter to the Bishops of the Catholic Church on the Collaboration of Men and Women in the Church and in the World

Letter to Families from Pope John Paul II

On the Dignity and Vocation of Women [Mulieris Dignitatem], Pope John Paul II

On Mixed Marriages....[Matrimonia Mixta], Pope Paul VI—NCCB

Preparation for the Sacrament of Marriage, Pontifical Council for the Family

The Role of the Christian Family in the Modern World [Familiaris Consortio], Pope John Paul II

The Theology of the Body, Pope John Paul II

The Truth and Meaning of Human Sexuality: Guidelines for Education within the Family, Pontifical Council for the Family

CCC #2196-2233

Possible Essay Topics:

• Read *The Role of the Christian Family in the Modern World [Familiaris Consortio],* by Pope John Paul II. [Pay particular attention to paragraphs 29-30.] In what ways does devaluing the sanctity of life alter the focus of marriage? Think of four ways; pick the best three and write. Reference the document in your essay.

• How does the careful stewardship of family finances, including tithing and sharing our goods with the poor, reflect our Holy Faith and trust in God's providence? Think of four ways; pick the best three and write.

• Compare and contrast the negative and positive impacts of a two-parent family with a mother who is employed outside the home with a two-parent family with a mother who stays at home to nurture her children. Research the cost of child care, the need for a second vehicle, insurance and fuel, an increase in prepared meal consumption and meals eaten out, and cost of work-appropriate clothing. Based on a $10 an hour wage, and factoring the previously mentioned expenses, what is the approximate financial gain of a second income? If the family income appears to be insufficient without the additional income,

is there an alternate way to budget within a single income? [E.g., move to a less expensive home to lower housing costs, purchase a less expensive vehicle to reduce car payments, eliminate fast food.]

• What are the effects of television viewing on the mental and social development of young children? [Web search studies by Dr. Dimitri Christakis and Dr. Jane Healy of TV's effects on the developing brain.]

• What are the effects of day care on the mental and social development of young children? Select three significant effects; expound. [See *Supplemental Reading.*]

Research:

You may, in conjunction with your text and field work, wish to investigate the following topics in greater depth. Credit may be obtained through reading and hands-on, experiential learning including field trips, volunteering, and apprenticeships. Learning is demonstrated through the production of projects, experiments, essays or reports. Reports may be based on note-taking and observation and might include graphs, charts, illustrations and diagrams.

Find out about early childhood development. Websearch 'developmental milestones children' or log on to:

www.ldonline.org/article/6313

www.firstsigns.org/healthydev/milestones.htm

• You may wish to arrange your findings in chronological order and/or chart, then compose age-appropriate tests based on your findings. Contact parents with children in those age groups and ask permission to test and observe. Find out how many hours of television children in your test group are allowed to watch each day. Find out how frequently children are read to, and for what length of time. Remember that not all children reach every milestone at the same time!

• Find out, based on your research, methods to enrich a child's learning environment.

At what age should a child be able to:
— speak in three to five word sentences
— walk alone
— drink from a cup
— recognize pictures of objects and respond appropriately, e.g., 'moo' at a picture of a cow
— wave good-bye
— put two blocks in a 'stack'
— reach for and grasp objects
— point to eyes, nose, ears, mouth, and hair on command
— identify circles, squares, and triangles
— identify at least one color
— recite simple rhymes and say the blessing before meals
— tell his first and last name
— sit alone
— count to five
— say three or four individual words
— respond to her name
— follow simple commands like 'Please bring me the spoon.'
— lift his head and chest when lying on his stomach
— speak in two-word sentences like 'want down' or 'more milk.'
— understand simple prepositions like 'under,' 'over,' 'behind,' 'on'
— babble
— pull himself up to a standing position on furniture

Experiential Learning/Career and Vocational Bridge:

[See Table of Contents for *Process Project Outline* and *Following in Their Footsteps* projects.]

Family Management Projects:

• Volunteer as Mother's Helper [volunteer babysitting service to new mothers]

• Find and record the prices of: sweater, blouse, skirt, man's shirt, and man's slacks at a department store and again at a second-hand clothing store. Total prices from the department store and second-hand clothing store and compare. You may wish to document your findings by attractively drawing the garments in a booklet, labeling by price and source of purchase, and writing a few paragraphs about your findings.

• What can you repair? You might begin with learning how to repair a leaking faucet.

• Using weekly grocery ads, plan dinner menus for your family for one month, including sale items wherever possible. No mixes of any sort are allowed; fresh and canned fruits and vegetables are acceptable. [Do not purchase or prepare the foods, just plan the menus.] Each week, visit the grocery store and record prices for all menu ingredients and items. Save all menus. At the end of the month, using the same menus, visit the grocery store and record non-sale prices of all items when the sales have ended. Total menu costs for the month at sale and non-sale prices. How much money was saved by centering menus around sale items?

• Plan a month's worth of dinner menus for your family based on foods that they enjoy. [Do not purchase or prepare the foods, just plan the menus.] Include prepared frozen dishes and prepared boxed meals. Visit the grocery store and record the prices of all ingredients and items listed on the menus.

How did the month's grocery bill differ from the menus based on sale prices and cooking 'from scratch'?

• Find out about the differences between formula feeding and breast feeding. What are the health advantages or disadvantages for both baby and mother? Chart or graph and compare your findings.
[One resource: http://ohioline.osu.edu/lines/food.html]

• Using weekly grocery ads, plan dinner menus for your family for two weeks, including sale items wherever possible. No mixes of any sort are allowed; fresh and canned fruits and vegetables are acceptable. Prepare the meals for your family.

• Learn how to repair a toilet that won't stop running.

• Calculate a budget for a month: rent, utilities [electric/gas/heating] telephone, water, garbage, food, car payments and maintenance, fuel; medical, dental, and car insurance, clothing. Include in your budget an 'emergency' savings fund for car repair and unexpected dental and medical costs. Find and compare: rent cost for furnished and unfurnished apartments. How might the use of public transit compare with car payments, fuel, insurance and maintenance? What wage will you need to earn to live within this budget? Remember to subtract taxes in figuring your income. Organize and compile your figures in a notebook, neatly labeling each category.

• Learn how to free a clogged sink and a clogged toilet.

• With other Catholic homeschoolers, organize a 'Mom's Day Out.' Set a time and location, then provide an afternoon of activities for children from ages 3-8. [This might be done in conjunction with a parish mission or retreat to provide babysitting; students seeking Family Management or Psychology credit could provide care while observing the under-3 age group.] Create art or craft projects, music/ songs, physical activities and games, cooking, or hobby demonstrations that can be used to teach the Faith to young children.

• Check a car's oil level and change oil.

• Volunteer with a Catholic summer camp. www.mysummercamps.com/camps/Religious_Camps/Catholic/

• Change a car's flat tire.

• Learn to use a fire extinguisher and install a smoke alarm.

• Get a 1040 Tax Form and fill it out based on a $28,000 annual income for a family of five.

GEOGRAPHY

C=*1001 Facts for Your Catholic Geography Bee, Level 3,* Kerry and Nancy MacArthur—Catholic Heritage Curricula [CHC]

S=*The Usborne Geography Encyclopedia with Complete World Atlas,* Gillian Doherty

S=*Regional Geography of the United States and Canada,* Tom McKnight

S=*Across This Land: A Regional Geography of the United States and Canada (Creating the North American Landscape),* John Hudson

S=*The World Today: Concepts and Regions in Geography,* Harm de Blij

C=*Persecuted and Forgotten,* Aid to the Church in Need [available for a small donation]—details current political and social conditions that culminate in persecution of Catholics/Christians around the world, in a few brief pages for each country

NCC=*Persecuted: The Global Assault on Christians,* Paul Marshall [2013]

S=*Geography,* Standard Deviants video

S=*Physical Geography: A Self-Teaching Guide* [Wiley Self-Teaching Guides], Michael Craghan

S, T/AK=*World Geography: Building a Global Perspective,* Thomas Baerwald

Strongly recommended:

Recent edition of *The Catholic Almanac*—very inexpensive through used book dealers

Supplemental Reading:

C=*2000 Years of Christianity in Africa,* John Baur

S=*Fewer: How the New Demography of Depopulation Will Shape the Future,* Ben Wattenberg

S=*Migrations and Cultures: A World View,* Thomas Sowell

http://makingmaps.owu.edu/

Links:

C=www.catholicculture.org/news/

C=www.catholiceducation.org—orthodox Catholic writers; excellent resource, see history articles

C=www.catholicnet.com—country-by-country statistics

www.yourchildlearns.com/map-puzzles.htm—numerous free interactive maps puzzles for all computers and devices

www.directionsmag.com

http://education.usgs.gov/secondary.html—topographic maps, online maps, satellite imagery, more

www.factmonster.com/ipka/A0770414.html

http://geographyworldonline.com/

www.enchantedlearning.com/Home.html—printables: maps, geology, anatomy, astronomy, botany, more

C=www.steveraysstore.com—10+ video series, Steve Ray—Holy Land tour, apostles, early Church

http://geography.howstuffworks.com/

www.govspot.com/categories/worldgovernment.htm—information on world governments, leaders, UN, more

www.discoveryeducation.com/teachers/—free lessons and lesson plans for geography

www.usgs.gov/climate_landuse/—U.S. Geological Survey, geography

www.wunderground.com/satellite/
vis/1k/US.html—U.S. and international
satellite images, updated every 20 min.

http://www.ipl.org/div/subject/
—Internet Public Library

Church Teaching:

*Decree on the Catholic Churches
of the Eastern Rite [Orientalium
Ecclesiarum]*, Second Vatican Council

*The Light of the East [Orientale
Lumen]*, Pope John Paul II

Toward a Pastoral Approach to Culture,
Pontifical Council for Culture

CCC #1921-23, 2313, 2425

Possible Essay Topics:

• Read *CCC* #2313. In the 1990's, the Catholic country of East Timor sought its independence from Indonesia. The response from the Muslim government was a bloody, decade-long attack on the Catholic population. Similarly, the Muslim Sudanese government had for decades, continuing into the 21st century, brutalized the Catholic population of Sudan, bombing churches, slaughtering more than 2 million people, and forcing countless others into slavery. Research the Timorese and Sudanese conflicts. Report; reference *CCC* #2313 and include maps of both countries.

> C=www.catholicnet.com—country-by-country statistics
>
> C=www.catholicculture.org/news/
>
> C=www.catholiceducation.org—see 'Persecution of Christians' pages

• Research and write about the changing European culture as influenced by the expanding Muslim population in France, Germany, and Great Britain. Include in your essay information about the Moorish Muslim occupation of Spain from the 8th to the 15th century.

• " 'The Church has rejected the totalitarian and atheistic ideologies associated in modern times with 'communism' or 'socialism.'" [*CCC* #2425] Research and write about the Roman Catholic Church in China. When was China first evangelized? Who are some of the martyrs of China? What is the 'Catholic Patriotic Association' church? How and why was it established? What is the 'underground' Roman Catholic Church, and why is it 'underground'? Who was Cardinal Kung? In light of what you have learned, what do you see as the reasons for the statement in *CCC* #2425?

> C=www.catholiceducation.org—see 'Persecution of Christians' pages
>
> C=www.cardinalkungfoundation.org—wealth of information on the Church in China
>
> C=www.catholicnet.com—country-by-country statistics
>
> C=www.catholicculture.org/news/

• Find out and write about the Church in Nigeria. From which countries did the priests who first evangelized Nigeria come? Is the Church growing or shrinking in Nigeria? Include information on Cardinal Arinze.

> C=www.catholicnet.com—country-by-country statistics
>
> C=www.catholicculture.org/news/

• Read and report on *The Miracle of Hope*, autobiography of Francis Xavier Cardinal Nguyen Van Thuan. Discuss changes in the geographical boundaries of Viet Nam during his lifetime. Take note of and discuss changes in the types of governments that ruled Viet Nam during that same time period. Include in your report possible reasons for the statement, " 'The Church has rejected the totalitarian and atheistic ideologies associated in modern times with 'communism' or 'socialism.'" [*CCC* #2425]

Research:

You may, in conjunction with your text and field work, wish to investigate the following topics in greater depth. Credit may be obtained through reading and hands-on, experiential learning including field trips, volunteering, and apprenticeships. Learning is demonstrated through the production of projects, experiments, essays or reports. Reports may be based on note-taking and observation and might include graphs, charts, illustrations and diagrams.

Investigate these geography-related careers and offices:

- surveyor
- computer mapper
- land developer
- zoning investigator
- geophysics
- soil scientist
- urban planner
- land use planning
- cartographer
- aerial photo interpreter
- oceanographer
- Census Bureau—www.census.gov
- Department of Defense, National Geospatial-Intelligence Agency—www1.nga.mil/Pages/default.aspx
- Department of Housing and Urban Development—http://portal.hud.gov/hudportal/HUD
- Environmental Protection Agency—www.epa.gov
- Federal Emergency Management Agency—www.fema.gov
- U.S. Geological Survey—www.usgs.gov

Canada:

Census of Canada—www.census-online.com/links/Canada/

Geological Survey of Canada—www.nrcan.gc.ca/earth-sciences/home—earth sciences, natural resources, geoscience

Experiential Learning/Career and Vocational Bridge:

[See Table of Contents for *Process Project Outline* and *Following in Their Footsteps* projects.]

Geography Projects:

- Newspaper/magazine project: using one secular magazine/newspaper and one Catholic [e.g., *Catholic World Report*], select four countries in the news, preferably on different continents. Cut out and make a notebook of news stories. Who or what groups are involved? What is the nature or situation in the news? What role does government play? Religion? Climate? History?
- Bl. Teresa of Calcutta [Mother Teresa] was born in at least three different countries. How can this be? Find out, draw maps of the different countries, using different colors for boundaries of each. Briefly explain the circumstances. [If possible, draw on tracing paper or other material that can be superimposed for a view of all countries simultaneously.] An atlas of world history would be helpful in this project.
- Create a map of Israel, at least 24 by 36 inches. [Map may be drawn or sculpted.] Indicate borders, capital, and sites significant in the life of Our Lord and the early Church. On a separate sheet, list sites and their significance.
- What crops are commonly grown and eaten in the following countries? Find out and prepare a meal representing the common cuisine of the country. [You may omit one of Peru's common dishes: guinea pig.]
    —Kenya
    —India
    —Viet Nam
    —Iceland
    —Argentina
    —Poland
    —Peru

• Check out the work of the following communities, the countries and peoples they serve. Find out about religion, economy, housing, education, agriculture, and climate of the countries in which the communities minister.

Food for the Poor, 550 SW 12th Ave., Dept/9662, Deerfield Beach, FL 33442

Missionaries of Charity, 335 E. 145th St., Bronx, NY 10451 [718-292-0019]

Society of Our Lady of the Most Holy Trinity [S.O.L.T.s], 700 W Ave. D, Robstown, TX 78380, [www.societyofourlady.net]

• Create a map of modern Europe, at least 24 by 36 inches. [Map may be drawn or sculpted.] Indicate borders, capitals, and places of pilgrimage. On a separate sheet, list pilgrimage sites and their significance. [Or create a similar map of a country of your choice.]

• From which country/countries does your family originate? What circumstances caused your ancestors to come to this country? Did religious persecution play a role in their decision? Write a brief report on the political situation in the country of their origin at the time of their departure.

• Read about the appearances in Mexico of Our Lady of Guadalupe. Pick one of the following related projects:

—How is her Feast Day celebrated in Mexico? Organize a similar celebration for the Feast of Our Lady of Guadalupe for family, friends, or homeschool group.

—Write and perform a song about Our Lady of Guadalupe.

—Create an artistic depiction of Our Lady of Guadalupe.

—Prepare and serve Mexican foods.

• An ignorance of the physical geography of the Pacific Northwest brought ruin to 19th century wagon trains in the early years of migration. Using a topographical map, plot safe courses through mountain passes and across deserts from St. Louis, Missouri to Portland, Oregon, and Sacramento, California.

• List at least three ways that physical geography determines the settlement of an area. How does physical geography affect population distribution in Japan? In Tibet? In Juneau, Alaska? In Alberta, Canada? In Africa? In China? In Australia? Map each of those cities/provinces/countries/continents, including significant physical features. Mark centers of population. Explain the reasons for each of your findings.

• Arrange a visit to your county urban planning or zoning departments, or county surveyor.

• Watch 'Horatio's Drive.' [PBS video about the first cross-country trip by auto, traveled in 1903— prior to the creation of the national highway system.] Draw or purchase a large map and retrace Horatio's route with a highlighting pen; mark breakdowns in red. How long did his trip take? Using a road atlas or internet route mapping, find out how long the auto trip would take today.

The same young person who slumps into his chair at the appearance of a history text may race to the mailbox for the latest issue of American History magazine. "Education" does not have to look like a textbook.

GEOLOGY

Science Labs:

Labs essentially provide students an opportunity to test theories against reality, i.e., allow students to apply what they have learned from their texts in hands-on settings.

Most colleges don't require documented science labs as part of a high school science course. In fact, there is no national standard or definition of what exactly constitutes a high school science lab. However, since some colleges do require documented science lab work, it is best to include at least 20 hours of lab work in each science course that your student takes.

Keeping in mind that 'lab' means hands-on learning that applies book-learning to reality, credit for a Geology lab might be earned by visiting a fossil bed and searching for fossils. Students might photograph the rock formations where the fossils were found, identify the type of rock in which the fossils were found, and identify the types of fossils therein. Brief descriptions or notations about why and how fossils were found in this type of geological structure might be included. All of this information would then be assembled into a lab report.

An Environmental Science lab might include similar notations about discoveries made in a pond ecosystem, including a description and photographs of the pond, plant and animal aquatic life, and conclusions as to how and why those particular plants and animals live in that environment.

In essence, no matter which science courses are chosen, students will devote at least 20 hours of class time to lab work—that is, hands-on projects, exploration, and conclusions about what the student learned—which will be documented in a hard-copy notebook or portfolio.

Parents might also double-check with colleges to which students might apply to determine whether or not there are lab requirements.

Please also note that students who enroll in science classes at local colleges gain those lab credits while simultaneously earning both high school and college credit.

Book List:

S=*Geology: A Self-Teaching Guide*, Barbara W. Murck

S, AK=*Essential Atlas of Fossils and Minerals*—Barron's

S, CP, T/AKA=*Essentials of Geology*—Pearson Prentice Hall

S, B=Geology: Merit Badge Series

S, T/AK=*Geology*—Cliff's

S, V/DVD=*Geology*— Standard Deviants

Supplemental Reading:

S=*Beneath Our Feet: The Rocks of Planet Earth*, R.H. Vernon

C=*Origin of the Human Species*, Dennis Bonnette

S=*Field Guide to Rocks and Minerals*, Frederick Pough [Peterson Guide]

S=*Geology*, Roberts & Hodsdon [Peterson Guide]

C=*The Genesis Flood*, John Whitcomb—Stella Maris

S=*The Practical Geologist*, Dougal Dixon

Links:

1,200 page, free science supplies catalog!—www.wardsci.com—Ward's Natural Science—1-800-962-2660

C=www.catholiceducation.org—orthodox Catholic writers; excellent resource for articles on science topics

www.cavern.com—National Caves Association, listing of caves and caverns across the U.S.

www.geology.com

http://earthquake.usgs.gov/
earthquakes/eqinthenews/

http://earthquake.usgs.gov/
earthquakes/map/—earthquake
mapping

http://education.usgs.gov/secondary.
html—geologic maps, fossils, minerals;
excellent

www.enchantedlearning.com/Home.
html—printables: maps, geology,
anatomy, astronomy, botany, more

www.eyeofscience.de—scientific
photography; microscopic world:
botany, zoology, etc.

www.fema.gov—Federal Emergency
Management Agency

http://geology.er.usgs.gov/paleo/
eduinfo.shtml—Education Resources for
Paleontology

www.goodearthgraphics.com/
showcave.html—listing of caves and
caverns across the U.S.

www.nrcan.gc.ca/earth-sciences/
home—earth sciences, natural
resources, geoscience—Geological
Survey of Canada

www.nps.gov/getinvolved/volunteer.
htm—volunteer opportunities, National
Park Service

www.stategeologists.org—Association
of American State Geologists

www.science.gov

http://geology.campus.ad.csulb.edu/
VIRTUAL_FIELD/index.htm—virtual
geology

http://geology.usgs.gov—U.S.
Geological Survey, geology

www.virtual-geology.info

www.volunteer.gov—volunteer
opportunities

http://www.ipl.org/div/subject/
—Internet Public Library

Church Teaching:

C=www.newadvent.org/cathen—
Catholic encyclopedia

C=www.catholic-pages.com/—Catholic
documents and teaching, current
events, more

C=www.zenit.org/en—Vatican news;
recent and archived Papal/Church
statements

C=*Statement on Evolution*, Pope John
Paul II, Address to Pontifical Academy
of Sciences, 1997

CCC #282-286

Possible Essay/Report Topics:

• Read *CCC* #282-286. 'The existence of God the Creator can be known with certainty through his works, by the light of human reason, even if this knowledge is often obscured and disfigured by error. This is why faith comes to confirm and enlighten reason ...' By studying the earth, one also learns of Him Who created it.

Human understanding of earth's origins is necessarily limited, because 'proof' in science requires replication and observation of an event. Since man is unable to create from nothing to replicate and observe the Creation event, even science relies on faith to believe scientific theory.

For example, scientists for years believed that the coelacanth, an 'ancient fish,' appeared in the fossil records before dinosaurs, and became extinct about 65 million years ago. Imagine their surprise when coelacanths were discovered, alive and flourishing, off the coasts of Africa and Asia in the 20th century. Additionally, no one had told the coelacanth that, in the past 65 million years, he should by all scientific reasoning have evolved considerably; the unmutated fish was easily recognized from the 65 million-year-old fossilized images of his forebears [see www.dinofish.com or http://unmuseum.mus.pa.us/coelacan.htm]. Research and write about the coelacanth. Think: science helps us to learn of God's creative intelligence; science also has its limitations. Refer to *CCC* #282-286 in your essay.

• Find out and report: What important mineral resources are found in the following states? How are these minerals used? What might be some of the reasons for differences in mineral types found from state to state? What are some of the geological hazards to which the states may be prone? What measures are the states taking to reduce the hazards? If desired, you may gather information from:

> www.stategeologists.org—Association of American State Geologists

Research for the following states [and you may include your own, if you'd like]:
— California
— Colorado
— Florida
— Missouri
— North Dakota
— Ohio
— Oregon
— South Carolina

Research:

You may, in conjunction with your text and field work, wish to investigate the following geology-related careers. Credit may be obtained through reading and hands-on, experiential learning including field trips, volunteering, and apprenticeships. Learning is demonstrated through the production of projects, experiments, essays or reports. Reports may be based on note-taking and observation and might include graphs, charts, illustrations and diagrams.

• mineralogist
• prospector
• consulting geologist
• water remote sensing interpreter
• pollution specialist
• petroleum geologist
• structural geologist
• stratigrapher
• soil scientist
• seismologist
• paleontologist
• hydrologist
• glacial geologist
• geophysical explorer
• petroleum or mining company manager or consultant
• surveyor
• mining engineer
• volcanologist
• sedimentologist

Famous Names Related to the Science of Geology: Read and Report

In what ways did the Catholic Church aid in discoveries/inventions/advancement?

How did the person's faith [or lack thereof] influence his/her work?

What might have motivated the person to become involved in the field?

In what ways did his/her discoveries/inventions/advancement change the field of study?

In what ways did his/her discoveries/inventions/advancement ultimately change society?

Fr. Stanley Jaki, O.S.B.

Nicolaus Steno

Baron Georges Cuvier

Robert Mallet

Louis Agassiz

Experiential Learning/Career and Vocational Bridge:

[See Table of Contents for *Experiential Learning: Discovery Centers*]
[See Table of Contents for *Process Project Outline* and *Following in Their Footsteps* projects.]

Geology Projects:

• Visit caverns, caves, or fossil beds. What processes were involved in the formation of these geological sites?
• Find out about geology-related careers: http://geology.com/jobs.htm
• Visit volcanoes or lava beds. When were these sites formed? Are the volcanoes active, dormant, or extinct?
• Arrange to 'shadow' for a day someone in the careers listed above.
• Visit gemstone or other mining operations.
• Find web listings for natural history museums in your state and visit one. [Colleges often have natural history collections.]

GOVERNMENT, CANADIAN

S, T/AK=*All About Law*—Thomson Nelson [Gr. 11-12]

NCC, AK=*Canadian History & Government,* 12 Lifepacs from ADS, Heritage Resources

S=*Civics Today*—Irwin Publishing, Thomson Nelson [Canada, Gr. 10-12]

Links:

C=www.catholiceducation.org— excellent resource for articles, including Canadian government

C=www.ccrl.ca—Catholic Civil Rights League—current legislation, more

www.collectionscanada.gc.ca/index-e.html—Library and Archives of Canada

C=www.jasonkenney.com—MP Jason Kenney, government info

www.lexum.com/en/—Canadian Supreme Court rulings, news releases, judgements

C=www.lifesitenews.com—Canadian Legislative watch, currents events

www.parl.gc.ca/—Parliament, current debates, bills, members

www.pss.gov.bc.ca/osbc/

www.scc-csc.gc.ca/home-accueil/index-eng.asp—Supreme Court of Canada, justices, current activity

http://www.ipl.org/div/subject/ —Internet Public Library

Church Teaching:

C=www.newadvent.org/cathen— Catholic encyclopedia

C=www.catholic-pages.com/—Catholic documents and teaching, current events, more

C=www.zenit.org/en—Vatican news; recent and archived Papal/Church statements

[Church documents, below, available at www.americancatholiclawyers.org]

Diuturnum, Pope Leo XIII—Church teaching on liberty and the source of governmental authority

Vehementer Nos, Pope Pius X—role of state in the salvation of souls

Declaration on Euthanasia [Iura et Bona], Congregation for the Doctrine of the Faith

CCC #1902-1903

CCC #342, 2270, 2273

CCC #2477-2479

CCC #1902-1903 and #2242

Possible Essay Topics:

• Research efforts by the 'Right to Die Society of Canada' to legalize assisted suicide and/or euthanasia. If such efforts are successful, what Canadian law must be ignored? Read *CCC* #2273, which states, in part, 'When the state does not place its power at the service of the rights of each citizen, and in particular of the more vulnerable, the very foundations of a state based on law are undermined...' Infants, children, the elderly, the physically and mentally handicapped, even those who are temporarily disabled by unconsciousness during or following surgery—*all of us*—at one time or another in our lives, are vulnerable, weak members of society. Discuss the long-term implications for a society whose legal system fails to protect its weaker members.

[You may also wish to refer to *Declaration on Euthanasia—Iura et Bona*—in your essay.]
• 'Every citizen is expected to play his part in the formation of public opinion. If needs be, he must do this through representatives who reflect his own views.' *Pastoral Instruction on the Means of Social Communication [Communio et Progressio] #28, Documents of Vatican II, Vol. 1.* Read *CCC* #1902-1903. Each day for a month, follow Canadian legislation and current events. [www.lifesitenews.com] Take notes of legislation that is in direct conflict with the moral teachings of Jesus Christ as expressed through His Church. On the same website, use the links to federal and provincial leaders to identify your own representatives. Write a charitable essay explaining your opposition to the legislation. Include in your essay reference to *CCC* #1902-1903.
• How blessed are those who live in countries that protect the freedom to speak, unafraid of governmental censure or repercussions! Read the Canadian Charter of Rights and Freedoms [available online www.ccrl.ca—Catholic Civil Rights League]. Are there any moral or legal limits to the freedom of speech, e.g., libel or slander? [See *CCC* #2477-2479.] If so, name and discuss. Research. [One possible source: websearch www.lifesitenews.com—type 'freedom of speech Canada' in search box.]
• Read *CCC* #342, 2270, and 2273. The federal Species at Risk Act [SARA] grants legal protection to the Oregon Forest Snail, an 'endangered' mollusk found in Southwestern British Columbia—and in large populations in the states of Washington and Oregon. Research SARA [www.sararegistry.gc.ca/default_e.cfm is one possible resource] and the protections it grants. Research also Canadian abortion legislation. [www.lifesitenews.com is one possible resource] Compare and contrast the protections or lack thereof granted by these two pieces of legislation. Refer in your essay to the *Catechism* quotes.

- Read *CCC* #1902-1903 and #2242. Do citizens have an obligation to reject civil authority when law conflicts with eternal moral truths? When might it be proper to engage in 'civil disobedience'? Discuss, quoting from the *Catechism*.
- Freedom of religion, unimaginable still in many countries around the world, is a great gift. Read the Canadian Charter of Rights and Freedoms [available online www.ccrl.ca— Catholic Civil Rights League]. Are there any legal limits to the freedom of conscience and religion? Should there be, under the Charter, legal limits to this right? What current events seem to infringe upon this freedom? Research and discuss. [One possible source: websearch www.lifesitenews.com—type 'freedom of religion Canada' in search box.]
- Read *Pastoral Constitution on the Church in the Modern World [Gaudium et Spes], Documents of Vatican II, Vol. 1,* Section #75. According to this document, what obligation does the Catholic have to vote? What are some ways that the document urges Christians to take a 'specific and proper role in the political community'? According to the document, 'So that all citizens will be able to play their part in political affairs,' what is 'vitally necessary for the population as a whole and for young people in particular'? Discuss, in essay form.
- Given the opportunity, what dreams do you have for a future in Canadian government? List your dreams, plans, and goals. Arrange them in order of 'attack.' Outline steps toward their achievement. Write about your dream.

Catholics in Canadian Government: Read and Report

- Can one person, living his Catholic Faith, make a difference in society? [Could you be that one person?] Research faithful Catholics involved in Canadian government.

    MP Jason Kenney [www.jasonkenney.com]

Experiential Learning/Career and Vocational Bridge:

[See Table of Contents for *Process Project Outline* and *Following in Their Footsteps* projects.]

Government-related Projects:

- Arrange to visit a court session, or meeting of any local governmental body.
- Design and draw, paint, or sculpt a new national seal that includes reference to Canada's rich Catholic heritage. Write a short paper describing the significance of symbols included in the design.
- Investigate/volunteer with local political party organizations [see local telephone directory or www.lifesitenews.com for party contacts].
- Compose a national anthem that reflects Canada's rich Catholic heritage.
- Identify pro-life governmental representatives. Find out what you can do to help their re-election. Volunteer.
- Visit your provincial parliament when in session. Arrange a meeting with your legislators. You may wish to scan current proposed legislation on your province's website and plan to attend during hearings that are of particular interest.

GOVERNMENT, U.S.

NCC*,CP,T/AK, TM=*Declaration Statesmanship: A Course in American Government,* Ferrier & Seeley—*excellent course, written from a Christian viewpoint by devoted Catholics, but not specifically for a Catholic market [CHC]

NCC, OI=Michael Farris' *Constitutional Law* 20 week on-line course—http://conlaw.hslda.org/cms/

Supplemental Reading:

S, V/DVD=*American Government*—Standard Deviants

C=*Charles Carroll of Carrollton, Faithful Revolutionary,* Scott McDermott

S, B=Citizenship in the Community: Merit Badge Series

S, B=Citizenship in the Nation: Merit Badge Series

S=*Clarence Thomas: A Biography,* Andrew Thomas—biography of Catholic Justice Clarence Thomas

S, AK=*AP U.S. Government and Politics*—Barron's

S, AK=*Painless American Government*—Barron's

S, T/AK=*Let's Review: U.S. History and Government*—Barron's

Links:

C=www.americancatholiclawyers.org—Catholic lawyers, legislative/political activists

http://avalon.law.yale.edu/default.asp—historical documents relating to law

www.catholicculture.org/news/—resource for archived articles

www.cato.org/research—civil liberties, privacy, separation of powers, Supreme Court, the American Founders, elections, Congress, and more

www.eagleteens.com—politics and government, current issues

www.enchantedlearning.com/Home.html—printables: maps, geology, anatomy, astronomy, botany, more

www.eppc.org/—Ethics and Public Policy Center, established in 1976 to clarify and reinforce the bond between the Judeo-Christian moral tradition and the public debate over domestic and foreign policy issues

www.ff.org/—Frontiers of Freedom, government

www.heritage.org/—The Heritage Foundation

www.law.ou.edu/hist—historical documents

C=www.lifesitenews.com—Legislative watch, currents events

www.nrlc.org/—National Right to Life—life issues in the news, legislative involvement

www.law.cornell.edu/supct/justices/scalia.dec.html—Justice Scalia decisions

www.law.cornell.edu/supct/justices/thomas.dec.html—Justice Thomas decisions

www.supremecourthistory.org/history-of-the-court/the-current-court/justice-antonin-scalia/

http://antoninscalia.weebly.com/biography.html—info about Justice Antonin Scalia, Catholic Justice

www.supremecourthistory.org/
history-of-the-court/the-current-court/
justice-clarence-thomas/

http://fac-staff.seattleu.edu/Reede/web/
cthomas.html—bio of Catholic Justice
Clarence Thomas

www.supremecourt.gov—U.S. Supreme
Court cases, journals, info

http://townhall.com—government and
more

www.uscourts.gov—federal courts
information, printables

www.uscourts.gov/educational-
resources.aspx—lesson plans

www.whitehouse.gov

http://www.ipl.org/div/subject/
—Internet Public Library

Church Teaching:

C=www.newadvent.org/cathen—
Catholic encyclopedia

C=www.catholic-pages.com/—Catholic
documents and teaching, current
events, more

C=www.zenit.org/en—Vatican news;
recent and archived Papal/Church
statements

[Church documents, below, available at www.
americancatholiclawyers.org]

Diuturnum, Pope Leo XIII—Church
teaching on liberty and the source of
governmental authority

Vehementer Nos, Pope Pius X—role of
state in the salvation of souls

Pastoral Instruction on the Means of
Social Communication [Communio et
Progressio], Documents of Vatican II,
Vol. 1

Pastoral Constitution on the Church in
the Modern World [Gaudium et Spes],
Documents of Vatican II, Vol. 1

CCC #2273

CCC #2477-2479

CCC #1902-1903 and #2242

Possible Essay Topics:

• What effect has environmental legislation had
on the property rights of landowners? In what
ways has such legislation been detrimental to
private property rights? How has the same
legislation been beneficial to the common
good? Discuss, compare and contrast. [See
www.eagleforum.org/topics/property rights
or www.heritage.org/issues; also **Links** listed
with Environmental Science.]

• Research the Terri Schiavo 'Right to Die' case.
In what ways did the Florida and U.S. legal
systems fail to protect Terri Schiavo's right
to life? In what ways did the legal system
actually advocate for Terri's death? Read CCC
#2273, which states, in part, 'When the state
does not place its power at the service of the
rights of each citizen, and in particular of
the more vulnerable, the very foundations
of a state based on law are undermined...'
Infants, children, the elderly, the physically
and mentally handicapped, even those who
are temporarily disabled by unconsciousness
during or following surgery—all of us—at one
time or another in our lives, are vulnerable,
weak members of society. Discuss the long-
term implications for a society whose legal
system fails to protect its weaker members.

• How blessed are those who live in countries
that protect the freedom to speak, unafraid
of governmental censure or repercussions!
Read the Bill of Rights. Are there any moral
or legal limits to the freedom of speech, e.g.,
libel or slander? [Read CCC #2477-2479, and

Schenck vs. United States, 1919.] If so, name and discuss. Research and write.

• Read *CCC* #342, 2270, and 2273. The Endangered Species Act grants legal protection to the Northeastern Beach Tiger Beetle, found in at least six northeastern states. Research the Endangered Species Act [possible resource: hwww.fws.gov/endangered/] and the protections it grants. Research also U.S. abortion laws [www.lifesitenews.com is one possible resource]. Compare and contrast the protections or lack thereof granted by these two pieces of legislation. Refer in your essay to the *Catechism* quotes.

• Freedom of religion, unimaginable still in many countries around the world, is a great gift. Read the Bill of Rights, and the Preamble and first paragraph [Declaration of Rights] in the Declaration of Independence. From whence do all freedoms derive? Are there any legal limits to the freedom of conscience and religion? Should there be, under the Constitution, legal limits to this right? What current events seem to infringe upon this freedom? Research and discuss.

• Read *Pastoral Constitution on the Church in the Modern World [Gaudium et Spes]*, *Documents of Vatican II, Vol. 1*, Section #75. According to this document, what obligation does the Catholic have to vote? What are some ways that the document urges Christians to take a 'specific and proper role in the political community'? According to the document, 'So that all citizens will be able to play their part in political affairs,' what is 'vitally necessary for the population as a whole and for young people in particular'? Discuss, in essay form.

• Read *CCC* #1902-1903 and #2242. While citizens do not have a Constitutional right to "*falsely* shout 'fire' in a crowded theatre" [*Schenck vs. United States*, 1919], do they not have an *obligation* to do so when there is, indeed, a fire? When might it be proper to

engage in 'civil disobedience'? Is there any law higher than the Constitution?

• Given the opportunity, what dreams do you have for a future in government? List your dreams, plans, and goals. Arrange them in order of 'attack.' Outline steps toward their achievement. Write about your dream.

Catholics in U.S. Government: Read and Report

How did the person's faith influence contributions to legal thought?

What might have motivated the person to become involved in government?

In what ways did his contributions to law/government change society?

Antonin Scalia, Catholic Justice of the Supreme Court

Clarence Thomas, Catholic Justice of the Supreme Court

John Carroll

Daniel Carroll

Experiential Learning/Career and Vocational Bridge:

[See Table of Contents for *Process Project Outline* and *Following in Their Footsteps* projects]

Government-related Projects:
NOTE:
Some may plan to include first-hand exposure to historical sites in their governmental and U.S. History studies. Those who wish to tour the White House, Capitol, Supreme Court, and House and Senate Galleries in Washington, D.C., may contact their senators/representatives, well in

advance of a visit, to obtain tickets/passes for these tours.

Locate *Experiential Historical And Cultural Sites* in Table of Contents; see listing for historical sites in Boston, Philadelphia, Washington, D.C.

• Contact your county courthouse; find out when and where criminal and civil court trials are held. Attend a trial in each court; go early for pre-trial hearings in criminal court.
• 'Every citizen is expected to play his part in the formation of public opinion. If needs be, he must do this through representatives who reflect his own views.' *Pastoral Instruction on the Means of Social Communication [Communio et Progressio] #28, Documents of Vatican II, Vol. 1.* Read *CCC* #1902-1903. Each day for a month, follow U.S. legislation and current events [www.lifesitenews.com]. Take notes of legislation that is in direct conflict with the moral teachings of Jesus Christ as expressed through His Church. On the same website, use the links to congressional leaders to identify your own representatives. [Click on 'politics.'] Write a charitable essay explaining your opposition to the legislation. Include in your essay reference to *CCC* #1902-1903.
• Investigate/volunteer with local political party organizations [see local telephone directory for party contacts].
• Design and draw, paint, or sculpt a new national seal that includes reference to the United States' Catholic heritage. Write a short paper describing the significance of symbols included in the design. [For ideas, research the history of Maryland, Florida, Louisiana, and California.]
• Investigate/volunteer with political action groups, e.g., National Right to Life Committee [see **Links**].

• Visit your state capitol when the legislature is in session. Arrange a meeting with your state senators and legislators. You may wish to follow current proposed legislation on your state's website and plan to attend during hearings that are of particular interest.

HEALTH

Science Labs:

Labs essentially provide students an opportunity to test theories against reality, i.e., allow students to apply what they have learned from their texts in hands-on settings.

Most colleges don't require documented science labs as part of a high school science course. In fact, there is no national standard or definition of what exactly constitutes a high school science lab. However, since some colleges do require documented science lab work, it is best to include at least 20 hours of lab work in each science course that your student takes.

Keeping in mind that 'lab' means hands-on learning that applies book-learning to reality, credit for a Geology lab might be earned by visiting a fossil bed and searching for fossils. Students might photograph the rock formations where the fossils were found, identify the type of rock in which the fossils were found, and identify the types of fossils therein. Brief descriptions or notations about why and how fossils were found in this type of geological structure might be included. All of this information would then be assembled into a lab report.

An Environmental Science lab might include similar notations about discoveries made in a pond ecosystem, including a description and photographs of the pond, plant and animal aquatic life, and conclusions as to how and why those particular plants and animals live in that environment.

In essence, no matter which science courses are chosen, students will devote at least 20 hours of class time to lab work—that is, hands-on projects, exploration, and conclusions about what the student learned—which will be documented in a hard-copy notebook or portfolio.

Parents might also double-check with colleges to which students might apply to determine whether or not there are lab requirements.

Please also note that students who enroll in science classes at local colleges gain those lab credits while simultaneously earning both high school and college credit.

Book List:

S=*Health, Safety, and Nutrition for the Young Child*, Lynn Marotz

S=*E-Z Anatomy and Physiology*—Barron's

S=*The American Red Cross First Aid and Safety Handbook*

S, B=First Aid: Boy Scout Merit Badge Handbook

S=*Food for Today*, Helen Kowtaluk, McGraw-Hill—nutrition

S, V/DVD=*Human Nutrition*—Standard Deviants

S, AKA, B=*Life School Worktexts*—Fearon

    First Aid and Home Safety

    Staying Healthy

S=*Nutrition: An Applied Approach*, Janice Thompson

S, B=Public Health: Merit Badge Series

Supplemental Reading:

C=*Catholic Bioethics and the Gift of Human Life*, William May

C=*Communicating the Catholic Vision of Life*, Russell Smith [available through NCBC]

C=*Comfort for the Sick and Dying*, David Greenstock—Sophia Institute Press

C=*Pro-Life: Defending the Culture of Life against the Culture of Death*, Fr. John Pasquini

Ethics for Doctors, Nurses and Patients, H.P. Dunn

C=*Karen*, Marie Killilea

C=*Love and Life: A Christian Sexual Morality Guide for Teens*, Dr. Colleen Kelly Mast—www.sexrespect.com

C=*Theology of the Body for Beginners,* Christopher West

C=*The Splendor of Truth and Health Care,* Russell Smith [National Conference of Catholic Bishops]

C=*With Love From Karen,* Marie Killilea

Links:

www.acsh.org—American Council on Science and Health, current research and health topics in the news

C=www.all.org—American Life League, topical index, end of life care, euthanasia, eugenics, fetal development, stem cell research

C=www.catholiceducation.org— orthodox Catholic writers; excellent resource for articles on abortion, euthanasia, 'wrongful birth,' cloning, in vitro fertilization, medical ethics

C=www.cathmed.org—Catholic Medical Association

C=www.newmanconnection.com/ institute/courses/rich-gift-of-love— Theology of the Body course

www.enchantedlearning.com/Home. html—printables: anatomy, more

www.govspot.com/categories/health. htm—health information

www.khake.com/page22.html —medical, health career guide, requirements

www.khake.com/page77.html —free lessons and lesson plans: health, nursing, biology

http://brainconnection.positscience. com

C=www.lifeissues.net—excellent site for current issues in the news; site in association with OMI

C=www.lifesitenews.com—daily news, current events; Canada, U.S., world

www.medicinenet.com—medical reference for diseases, treatments

www.nacn-usa.org/—National Association of Catholic Nurses

http://ndb.nal.usda.gov—nutrition information by food

C=www.ncbcenter.org—National Catholic Bioethics Center, articles on current medical/moral controversies

www.niehs.nih.gov/health/scied/— environmental and health science educational resource; opportunities for summer employment or research and more

www.nursesforlife.org—Nurses for Life

www.nutrition.gov/

C=http://onemoresoul.com—One More Soul

C=www.orderalhambra.org—Catholic organization to serve mentally handicapped children

www.discoveryeducation.com/ teachers/—free lessons and lesson plans for health

C=www.vatican.va—Church documents

C=www.wf-f.org/MedicalMoral.html —Women for Faith and Family

http://www.ipl.org/div/subject/ —Internet Public Library

Church Teaching:

C=www.newadvent.org/cathen— Catholic encyclopedia

C=www.catholic.org

C=www.catholic-pages.com/—Catholic documents and teaching, current events, more

C=www.zenit.org/en—Vatican news; recent and archived Papal/Church statements

[Medical-related documents may be found on Catholic medical websites, above]

Enchiridion on the Family: A Compendium of Church Teaching on Family and Life Issues from Vatican II to the Present, Pontifical Council for the Family

Charter for Health Care Workers, Pontifical Council for Pastoral Assistance to Health Care Workers

Declaration on Euthanasia [Iura et Bona], Congregation for the Doctrine of the Faith

Instructions on the Respect for Human Life in its Origin and on the Dignity of Procreation [Donum Vitae], Congregation for the Doctrine of the Faith

John Paul II Address on Nutrition and Hydration for the Comatose

Of Human Life [Humanae Vitae], Pope Paul VI

On the Christian Meaning of Human Suffering [Salvifici Doloris], Pope John Paul II

The Ethical and Religious Directives for Catholic Health Services, U.S. Conference of Catholic Bishops

The Gospel of Life [Evangelium Vitae], Pope John Paul II

CCC #2270-2279

CCC #2290-2291

CCC #2292-2295

Possible Essay Topics:

• In what ways was Pope Paul VI's *Humanae Vitae* prophetic?

• In what ways does devaluing the sanctity of life alter the focus of health care?

• How are abortion and breast cancer linked? [one possible informational source— www.lifeissues.net]

• Read *CCC* #2275 & 2292-2295. How might the medical use of adult stem cells prove superior to fetal stem cells, from both medical and ethical standpoints? List at least two ethical considerations and two medical considerations [one possible informational source— www.lifeissues.net]. Quote from the *Catechism* in your essay.

• Research and write about Catholic contributions to leprosy treatment and care, past and current. Include historical attitudes and references to leprosy from the Old and New Testaments.

• Read *CCC* #2290-2291. 'The virtue of temperance disposes us to avoid every kind of excess: the abuse of food, alcohol, tobacco...' Research the health effects of each of these abuses; include illegal drug use in your research. E.g., marijuana abuse is linked to an alarming rise in the incidence of schizophrenia [a permanent, debilitating mental illness]. Write an essay about healthful temperance, including your findings and referring to the *Catechism*.

• Report on obesity-related illnesses, including Type II Diabetes, heart disease, and joint deterioration. [one resource: www.msuextension.org/nutrition/]

• Given the opportunity, what dreams do you have for a future in health-related fields? List your dreams, plans, and goals. Arrange them in order of 'attack.' Outline steps toward their achievement. Write about your dream.

Research:

You may, in conjunction with your text and field work, wish to investigate the following topics in greater depth. Credit may be obtained through reading and hands-on, experiential learning including field trips, volunteering, and apprenticeships. Learning is demonstrated through the production of projects, experiments, essays or reports. Reports may be based on note-taking and observation and might include graphs, charts, illustrations and diagrams.

To aid in research, ask and answer, "Who, what, where, when and why?" [For example: *Where* is the pituitary gland found? *What* caused the spread of the disease? *Who* discovered.....? *When* do congenital defects occur? *Why* does blood...?]

- allergies
- disorders of the blood
    hemophilia
    leukemia
- first aid
- cancer
    abortion-breast cancer link
- communicable diseases and prevention
    bacterial and viral illnesses
    vaccinations
- disorders of the heart
    congenital valve defects
    aneurysms
    arteriosclerosis
    heart attack
- disorders of the respiratory system
    asthma
    bronchitis
    pneumonia
    lung cancer
- glandular disorders
    diabetes, thyroid
- neurological disorders
    cerebral palsy

    stroke
- disorders of the skeletal and muscular
    system
    scoliosis
    arthritis
    muscular dystrophy
- dental health
- nutrition
    vitamins and minerals
    dietary deficiency diseases
    balanced diet

See also Biology: Fetology

Famous Names Related to Health Sciences: Read and Report

In what ways did the Catholic Church aid in advancements in the field of health?

How did the person's faith [or lack thereof] influence his/her work?

What might have motivated the person to become involved in the field of health?

In what ways did his/her discoveries/ inventions change the accepted approach to health or medical practice?

In what ways did his/her discoveries/ inventions ultimately change society?

Rose Hawthorne [Hawthorne Dominicans]

Edward Jenner

Alexander Fleming

Mary Walker [homeschooled]

Robert Koch

Joseph Lister

Helen Brooke Taussig

Linus Pauling [homeschooled]

Catherine McCauley, Sisters of Mercy

Walter Reed

Clara Barton [homeschooled]

Louis Pasteur

St. Damien of Molokai

Hippocrates

Florence Nightingale [homeschooled]

Dorothea Day

Jonas Salk

Experiential Learning/Career and Vocational Bridge:

[See Table of Contents for *Process Project Outline* and *Following in Their Footsteps* projects.]

Health Projects:

• Find out about combining legumes and grains to make a complete protein. Plan balanced, meatless Friday meals for a week. Include dishes that create complete proteins using grains and legumes, or by adding milk, eggs, or cheese to the menu. Don't forget that thrifty favorite of ground legumes smeared generously over milled and baked whole-wheat grains! [That's a peanut butter sandwich.]

• Practice the Corporal Works of Mercy. Find out about illnesses and conditions common to the elderly and how those conditions are treated. Volunteer with adult day care/geriatrics.

• Find out about the role of food groups in a healthful diet. Draw, or create on the computer, a chart, graph, wheel or other illustration that displays each food group. Portray in the illustration/chart the percentages of each group needed to equal a balanced diet.

• Find out about volunteer opportunities at a local hospital.

• Take a Certified Nursing Assistant course.

• How did British sailors earn the nickname 'limeys'? In previous centuries, why were sailors sometimes derogatorily referred to as 'scurvy knaves'? Websearch scurvy [which is still found in impoverished countries and in college-age men who are shopping and cooking for themselves for the first time] and the history of its treatment. How is it caused? What are its effects? How is it cured? Prepare a scurvy-fighting snack or beverage and serve it to your family; tell them that you're saving them from a future lived as 'scurvy knaves.'

• Sign up for CPR instruction.

• Take First Aid classes.

• For those who are not currently engaged in a regular program of physical exercise: if you have no physical illness that would make heavy exertion unwise, do 100 jumping jacks without stopping to rest. Immediately take your pulse for one minute. Record the pulse rate and also the date. Start a physical exercise program. After choosing one of the following activities, exercise for at least half an hour, five days per week, for four weeks. After four weeks, again do 100 jumping jacks without stopping to rest. Immediately take your pulse for one minute. After four weeks of exercise, how has your heart rate changed? [A lower pulse rate is indicative of a strengthened heart.]

   —swim

   —jog

   —exercise to a video

   —take a *brisk* walk

   —jump rope

• Draw, or illustrate in some other fashion, a series of humorous posters that would appeal to and teach young children about simple personal health care, e.g., brushing teeth, washing hands, proper diet, proper sleep habits. Be sure to include attendance at Holy Mass for spiritual health! Using the posters, give a presentation to children.

• Ronald McDonald Houses provide temporary 'homes away from home' for families of critically ill children who are undergoing medical treatment. Find a Ronald McDonald House near you [www.rmhc.com]. Call and ask about volunteer opportunities. [Rules vary from house to house; many welcome high school-age volunteers; others require that volunteers be age 18 or older.] To increase your understanding, research the illnesses for which family members are being treated.

• Volunteer as an aide in an elementary classroom for disabled children. Learn about their various disabilities and therapies used in their treatment. Find Matt. 25:40 in your Bible. Cut a 3x5 index card in half, discard one half, and write the verse on the other. Laminate and carry it in your pocket.

[see also *Midwifery, Biology* projects]

HISTORY, CANADIAN

S=*The Penguin History of Canada*, Robert Bothwell

S, T/AK=*Canadian History, Patterns and Transformation*—Irwin Publishing, www.nelson.com [Gr. 12]

NCC, AK=*Canadian History & Government*, 12 Lifepacs from ADS—Heritage Resources

S, T/AK=*Canada, Our Century, Our Story [1890-1999]*—www.nelson.com [Gr. 9-11]

C=*Catholic in English Canada: A Popular History*, Murray Nicolson

C=*Under Mary's Mantle: Our Lady's Love for Canada*

Supplemental Reading:

C, B=*Madeleine Takes Command*, Ethel Brill

C=*Kateri Tekakwitha*, Evelyn Brown—Ignatius

C=*Saint Among Savages: The Life of St. Isaac Jogues*, Francis Talbot

C=*The Popes and Slavery*, Leonard Kennedy

C, B=*With Pipe, Paddle and Song*, Elizabeth Yates

Links:

www.canadahistory.com/Index.htm—Canadian history site

C=www.catholiceducation.org—orthodox Catholic writers; excellent resource for history articles

www.collectionscanada.gc.ca/index-e.html—Library and Archives of Canada www.owensound.ca/live/underground-rail-road—Underground Railroad, Canada

http://www.ipl.org/div/subject/—Internet Public Library

Church Teaching:

C=www.newadvent.org/cathen—Catholic encyclopedia

C=www.catholic-pages.com/—Catholic documents and teaching, current events, more

C=www.zenit.org/en—Vatican news; recent and archived Papal/Church statements

Slavery, Catholic Encyclopedia

On the Abolition of Slavery, In Plurimus—Pope Leo XIII

CCC #2414

Possible Report/Essay Topics:

• Research the history of slavery and abolition in Canada. Include reference in your report to at least one document from Church Teaching [see also Anti-Slavery Society of Canada].
• What role did the Church play in the exploration and development of Canada? What group was largely responsible for the settlement of Montreal? Include in your report mention of Fr. Jacques Marquette and Fr. Isaac Jogues and companions. How might the development of Canada have been different if not for the presence of the Church?

• Research the history of your community. When was it first settled, and by whom? What were the circumstances that brought the first non-native settlers to the community? When was the first parish established? Was there a second or third 'wave' of immigration and, if so, from what country/countries? What problems/hardships did they encounter in their settlement, including basic human needs, discrimination, and survival in general? What was the economic or industrial base of the community two hundred years ago? One hundred years ago? In what ways has the economic base changed? Are there ethnic parishes in your community? Find the history of their founders. Do their descendents still live in the community? If possible, interview some of the descendents, particularly the elderly. How has the community changed since they were young? In what ways were their lives different when they were your age? Include their stories in your report.

Experiential Learning:

[See Table of Contents for *Experiential Historical and Cultural Sites, U.S. and Canada,* listing hands-on opportunities including ancient Native Peoples' sites, battlefields, fortresses, historical homes, Canadian stations on the Underground Railroad, and much more.]

[See Table of Contents for *Process Project Outline* projects.]

Canadian History Projects:
• Volunteer at historical sites, museums.
• Visit historical sites and history museums in your province. What makes the history of your province unique? Using your talents, create a tribute to that unique history, e.g., sew a quilt with representations of significant historical events, compose a musical piece, build a small replica of the first fortress or settlement, or execute an artistic rendering that captures the spirit of the event. Be prepared to explain the history that your creation depicts.
• How has the Canadian diet changed in the last two centuries? Locate old cookbooks or their reprints, e.g., *Fannie Farmer Cookbook.* Find out what might have been served in a rural area at a typical 18th or 19th century meal. Prepare and serve a typical meal.

HISTORY, ROMAN EMPIRE

S, V/DVD, Audio=*The History of Ancient Rome*—The Great Courses

S=*The Complete Idiot's Guide to the Roman Empire,* Eric Nelson

S=*The Roman Republic*—Michael Crawford

S, AK=*World History the Easy Way, Vol. 1*—Charles Frazee, Barron's [early civilizations, Greece and Rome]

Supplemental Reading:

C=*Son of Charlemagne,* Barbara Willard—Ignatius

NCC/C=*The Ides of April,* Mary Ray

S=The Roman Empire in the First Century [PBS video]

C=*The Tiber Ran Red,* Frank Korn

Links:

C=www.steveraysstore.com—Catholic videos, history of Church

www.fordham.edu/halsall/ancient/asbook01.asp—Internet Ancient History Sourcebook

www.pbs.org/empires/romans/— PBS: lesson plans and materials, more

http://www.ipl.org/div/subject/ —Internet Public Library

Possible Report/Essay Topics:

• Research and report on Roman engineering feats, some of which are still in use today, e.g, roads, aqueducts, sewer systems, and bridges. [The Roman Empire boasted more than 51,000 miles of paved thoroughfares.]

• Read *The Tiber Ran Red*, an account of Christian martyrdom, by Frank Korn. Report.

• Research and report on the ancient Roman cities of Pompeii and Herculaneum.

• Almost 1,000 years passed between the founding of the Roman Republic and the fall of the Roman Empire. In what ways were the years of the Republic different from those of the Empire? List at least three ways in which these two Roman eras differed. In what way did governance change under Augustus Caesar in 27 B.C.?

• Read and report on the martyrdom of St. Polycarp.

• Write about at least three monumental changes to the Empire brought about by Constantine I.

• If you could travel back in time to ancient Rome, what would you most like to see? Is there an event in which you might like to participate? Would you in any way try to influence the course of Roman history? If so, in what way?

• Read and report on *The Bones of St. Peter* [archaeological discoveries beneath the Vatican], by John Walsh.

Famous Names in Roman History: Read and Report

What might have motivated the historical figure to his/her actions?

How might his faith [or lack thereof] have influenced his actions?

How did his/her actions impact the government and/or society of his time?

How did his/her actions impact governments and/or societies of later eras?

How might the person's country have been different in later eras without the influence of this person?

How might the world have been different in later eras without the influence of this person?

Flavius Josephus

Caesar Nero

Herod Agrippa

St. Paul

Pliny the Elder

Pliny the Younger

Caesar Caligula

Emperor Hadrian

Experiential Learning:

[See Table of Contents for *Process Project Outline* projects.]

Roman History Projects:

• View the Catholic videos 'Peter, Keeper of the Keys' and 'Apostolic Fathers: Handing on the Faith.' Perhaps your parish would be interested in their purchase. [www.steveraysstore.com]

• Map the military conquests—and eventual losses—of the Empire. Create maps showing the boundaries of the Empire for each century from the establishment of the Roman Republic in 509 B.C., to the Visigoths' Sack of Rome in 410 A.D.

• Study mosaics from Pompeii. Create a Christian-themed mosaic.

• Find a vocabulary book about Latin roots in the English language. Create a series of colorful teaching posters for children, depicting Latin roots and the modern English words from which they grew. [One possibility: depict a tree with exposed roots; label the roots with a single Latin word. In the branches, write several words sharing the Latin root.] Using your posters, give a presentation.

HISTORY, U.S.

NCC, CP, Teacher's Guide=*A Basic History of the United States,* Clarence B. Carson—American Textbook Committee in 6 small, paperback volumes:

1. The Colonial Experience
2. The Beginning of the Republic
3. The Sections and the Civil War
4. The Growth of America
5. The Welfare State
6. America in Gridlock and Teacher's Guide

S, V/DVD=*American Civil War*—The Great Courses

S, B=American Heritage: Merit Badge Series

S, AK=*E-Z American History,* William Kellogg—Barron's

C, B=*Christ and the Americas* with workbook [CHC]

S, V/DVD=*Early American History: Native Americans through the Forty-Niners*—The Great Courses

S, T/AK=*U.S. History for Dummies*—www.dummies.com

S, T/AK=*Let's Review: U.S. History and Government*— Barron's

Supplemental Reading:

S, V/DVD=*Abraham Lincoln: In His Own Words*—The Great Courses

C=*The History of Black Catholics in the United States,* Fr. Cyprian Davis

S=*American History Magazine*—www.historynet.com/american-history [also Civil War, Wild West, other history magazines]

S, V/DVD=*Americas in the Revolutionary Era*—The Great Courses

C=*Cathedrals in the Wilderness*, J. Herman Schauinger [settlement of Kentucky Territory, Bishop Flaget]

C, B=*Chaplain in Gray: Abram Ryan*, H.J. Heagney [Catholic Fr. Ryan, Confederate Chaplain]

C=*Charles Carroll of Carrollton, Faithful Revolutionary*, Scott McDermott

S, T/AK=*Civil War for Dummies*, www.dummies.com

NCC=*Columbus and Cortez: Conquerors for Christ*, John Eidsmoe

S=*Conversations with Bullwhackers, Muleskinners...*, Fred Lockley [true stories of the settlement of the Northwest]

S=*Conversations with Pioneer Women*, Fred Lockley [true stories of the settlement of the Northwest]

S=*Day of Infamy*, Walter Lord [World War II]

S=*Ethnic America: A History*, Thomas Sowell

C=*Faith in the Wilderness*, Margaret and Stephen Bunson [Catholic Indian missions]

C=*Fr. Marquette and the Great River*, August Derleth—Ignatius

S, T/AK=*AP United States History*—Barron's

S, T/AK=*AP U.S. Government and Politics*—Barron's

C, B=*Madeleine Takes Command*, Ethel Brill

C=*Memoir of Pierre Toussaint, Born a Slave*, Hannah Lee

C=*Saint Among Savages—The Life of St. Isaac Jogues*, Francis Talbot

C=*St. Katherine Drexel, Friend of the Oppressed*—Ignatius

S, V/DVD=*The Civil War*, Ken Burns

S=*The Coming Fury*, Bruce Catton [Civil War]

C=*The Grunt Padre: Service and Sacrifice of Fr. Vincent Robert Capodanno*, Fr. Daniel Mode [Vietnam]

C=*The Life of Fr. DeSmet: Apostle of the Rocky Mountains*, Fr. Laveille, S.J.

C=*The Man Who Founded California*, Couve de Murville—Ignatius [Bl. Junipero Serra]

C, B=*The Marylanders*, Anne Heagney [story of the Puritan revolt in Catholic Maryland]

C=*The Popes and Slavery*, Joel Panzer

C=*The Reb and the Redcoats*, Constance Savery—Ignatius

S,V/DVD=*United States and the Middle East: 1914-9/11*—The Great Courses

S=*Up from Slavery*, Booker T. Washington

C=*When Hell Was in Session*, Jeremiah Denton [Viet Nam War, POW]

Links:

C="Slavery," Fr. William Most—www.ewtn.com/library/answers/slavery.htm

C=www.catholiceducation.org—orthodox Catholic writers; excellent resource for history articles

www.nps.gov/—National Parks Service historic landmarks, military history, more

www.nps.gov/learn/

www.cr.nps.gov

www.cr.nps.gov/nr/travel/underground—history and location of Underground Railroad 'stations'

www.enchantedlearning.com/Home.html—printables: maps, geology, anatomy, astronomy, botany, more

www.freedomcenter.org—National Underground Railroad Freedom Center, magazine available

http://eawc.evansville.edu/index.htm

www.tcr.org/tcr/index.htm—The Concord Review History Essay

www.fordham.edu/halsall/mod/modsbook26.html

www.history.com/topics/space-race

http://history.hanover.edu/project.php

http://historymatters.gmu.edu/—designed for high school and college teachers and students; contains a wealth of web links and other materials for the study of U.S. history

www.historyplace.com/unitedstates/revolution/decindep.htm

www.law.ou.edu/hist/—historical documents

www.nationalarchives.gov.uk/museum/

C=www.newadvent.org/cathen—Catholic encyclopedia

www.nps.gov/subjects/ugrr/education/lesson_plans.htm

www.discoveryeducation.com/teachers/—free lessons and lesson plans for history

www.historynet.com—history magazines

http://avalon.law.yale.edu/default.asp—historical documents

www.spartacus.schoolnet.co.uk/

http://www.ipl.org/div/subject/—Internet Public Library

Church Teaching:

C=www.newadvent.org/cathen—Catholic encyclopedia

C=www.catholic-pages.com/—Catholic documents and teaching, current events, more

C=www.zenit.org/en—Vatican news; recent and archived Papal/Church statements

Slavery, Catholic Encyclopedia

On the Abolition of Slavery [*In Plurimus*]—Pope Leo XIII

The Church and Racism: Towards a More Fraternal Society, Pontifical Commission on Justice and Peace [curial document]

CCC #2414

Possible Report/Essay Topics:

• Research the life of Bishop James Augustine Healy, born into slavery. [Two of his brothers were also ordained priests; three sisters entered the religious life.] Include reference in your report to at least one of the above-listed Church documents on slavery.

• Research the history of your community. When was it first settled, and by whom? What were the circumstances that brought the first non-native settlers to the community? When was the first parish established? Was there a second or third 'wave' of immigration and, if so, from what country/countries? What problems/hardships did they encounter in their settlement, including basic human needs, discrimination, and survival in general? What was the economic or industrial base of the community two hundred years ago? One hundred years ago? In what ways has the economic base changed? Are there ethnic parishes in your community? Find the history of their founders. Do their descendents still live in the community? If possible, interview some of the descendents, particularly the elderly. How has the community changed since they were young? In what ways were their lives different when they were your age? Include their stories in your report.

• The Civil War is often thought of simplistically as 'the war to end slavery.' Read about states' rights and their link to the Civil War. How did the Theory of Nullification and the Tenth Amendment guide the belief of secessionists? From a Constitutional standpoint, did the Southern states have a right to secede from the Union? Choose a side and defend your position.

• What was Manzanar? Find out. In retrospect, write two reasons supporting it, and two against. Read the Bill of Rights. Was the use of Manzanar constitutional?

• Who or what were the Code Talkers of WWII? Report.

• How effective was the League of Nations in its quest to mediate conflict and bring an end to war? Did Japan, Italy, and Germany follow its guidelines? How effective has been the United Nations in its quest to mediate conflict and bring an end to war? Report, listing in your paper the occurrence and location of armed conflicts worldwide since the United Nations' founding.

• Find out about the U.S. Army's 100th/442nd 'Go For Broke' Regimental Combat Team, the most decorated unit for its size and length of service in WWII, comprised entirely of Japanese-American soldiers.

• Compare Supreme Court rulings *Plessy v. Ferguson* with *Brown v. Board of Education.*

Research:

You may, in conjunction with your text and field work, wish to investigate the following topics in greater depth. Credit may be obtained through reading and hands-on, experiential learning including field trips, volunteering, and apprenticeships. Learning is demonstrated through the production of projects, experiments, essays or reports. Reports may be based on note-taking and observation and might include graphs, charts, illustrations and diagrams.

To aid in research, ask and answer, "Who, what, where, when and why?"

• Native American cultures prior to European settlement
    Algonquian
    Pueblo
    Salish
    Seminole
• European settlements: the Spanish were here first!
    St. Augustine
    Santa Fe, New Mexico
• English settlements
    Jamestown
    Plymouth
• Dutch and French settlements
• Maryland Colony
• French and Indian War
• The Revolution
• The Constitution
• The Louisiana Purchase
• The War of 1812
• Missouri Compromise
• The Mexican War
• Immigration in the mid-19th century
    German
    Irish
• Civil War
• Spanish-American War
• World War I
    Treaty of Versailles
    League of Nations
• The Depression
• World War II

United Nations
- The Korean War
- Civil Rights Movement
- Viet Nam War
- The Supreme Court: not strictly Constitutional
  Roe v. Wade

Famous Names in U.S. History: Read and Report

What might have motivated the historical figure to his/her actions?

How might his faith [or lack thereof] have influenced his actions?

How did his/her actions impact the government and/or society of his time?

How did his/her actions impact governments and/or societies of later eras?

How might the person's country have been different in later eras without the influence of this person?

How might the world have been different in later eras without the influence of this person?

Bl. Junipero Serra

Lord Baltimore

Thomas Jefferson

Merriwether Lewis and William Clark

Nathaniel Hawthorne

Tecumseh

Dred Scott

Frederick Douglass

Robert E. Lee

Ulysses S. Grant

Chief Joseph

Sequoyah

Fr. Pierre De Smet

Fr. Joseph Machebeuf

Jefferson Davis

St. Katherine Drexel

Theodore Roosevelt

Franklin Delano Roosevelt

Ven. Archbishop Fulton J. Sheen

Fr. Vincent Capodanno

Martin Luther King

Commander Lloyd Bucher

Ronald Reagan

Experiential Learning:

[See Table of Contents for Experiential Historical and Cultural Sites, U.S. and Canada]
[See Table of Contents for Process Project Outline projects.]

U.S. History Projects:
- Visit historical sites and history museums in your county and state. What makes the history of your state unique? Using your talents, create a tribute to that unique history, e.g., sew a quilt with representations of significant historical events, compose a musical piece, build a small replica of the first fortress or settlement. Be prepared to explain the history that your creation depicts.
- Volunteer at historical sites, museums.

  http://portal.hud.gov/hudportal/
  HUD?src=/topics/volunteering

- Watch 'Horatio's Drive.' [PBS video about the first cross-country trip by auto, traveled in 1903—prior to the creation of the national highway system.] Draw or purchase a large map and retrace Horatio's route with a highlighting pen; mark breakdowns in red.

How long did his trip take? Find out when construction on the national highway system began. Using a road atlas or internet route mapping, find out how long the auto trip would take today.

• Interview a Viet Nam veteran. In which branch of the Armed Services did he or she serve? Prior to military service, did he/she believe that helping the free South to fight off Communist attack was a worthy cause? How did he/she view American involvement in Indo-China before being sent to Viet Nam? Did his/her view of the war change during or after service? If so, in what way? If he/she had been in command of military forces, how might he/she have directed operations differently?

• How has the American diet changed in the last two centuries? Locate old cookbooks or their reprints, e.g., *Fannie Farmer Cookbook*. Find out what might have been served at a typical 18th or 19th century meal. Prepare and serve a typical meal.

• Find out about early photography and photographers, particularly Matthew Brady and cohorts, who photographed the Civil War. How have cameras and photography changed since that time?

• Research the art of Frederic Remington, N.C. Wyeth, Winslow Homer, Howard Pyle, and Gilbert Stuart, who in their paintings and sculpture chronicled the history of our nation. Obtain postcard-size samples of their work; make an album. Write a paragraph's explanation of the historical event portrayed by each composition; paste it alongside the work.

NOTE: Some may plan to include first-hand exposure to historical sites in their governmental and U.S. History studies. Those who wish to tour the White House, Capitol, Supreme Court, and House and Senate Galleries in Washington, D.C., may contact their senators/representatives, well in advance of a visit, to obtain tickets/passes for these tours. See Table of Contents for Experiential Historical And Cultural Sites, U.S. and Canada *for hands-on study including ancient Native American sites, battlefields, fortresses, historical homes, stations on the Underground Railroad, and much more.*

> *...part of the motivation for Catholic homeschooling is to expose the student to the profound wisdom and moral clarity of our Holy Faith, that he will see the world through the eyes of Jesus and His Church. What might be Our Lord's "worldview" of euthanasia? Of abortion? Of legislation that flies in the face of holy wisdom?*

S, B=Archaeology: Merit Badge Series

C=*Christ the King, Lord of History*, Anne W. Carroll with workbook [CHC]

S, T/AK=*World History: Connections to Today*, Elisabeth Gaynor Ellis—Pearson Prentice Hall

C, CP=*How the Catholic Church Built Western Civilization*, Thomas Woods, Jr.

S, AK=*World History the Easy Way*, [Vols. 1 & 2] Charles Frazee—Barron's

C, CP=*The History of Christendom*—series in six volumes—Warren H Carroll

C=*Seven Lies about Catholic History*, Diane Moczar—debunks biased arguments in regard to the 'Dark Ages,' Inquisition, and more

Supplemental Reading:

B=*Beowulf the Warrior*, Ian Serraillier—Ignatius

C=*Between the Forest and the Hills*, Ann Lawrence—Ignatius [ancient Britain during Roman occupation]

C=*Beyond the Desert Gate*, Mary Ray [1st century Palestine]—Ignatius

C=*Blood-Drenched Altars*, Francis Kelley—History of Mexico

C=*Characters of the Inquisition*, William Walsh

C=*Characters of the Reformation*, Hilaire Belloc

C=*Citadel of God*, de Wohl [St. Benedict; 6th century Europe]—Ignatius

✓ C=*Come Rack! Come Rope!*, Msgr. Robert Benson [persecution of Catholics in England]

C=*Defenders of the Faith in Word and Deed*, Fr. Charles Connor

C, B=*Edmund Campion*, Fr. Harold Gardiner, S.J.—Ignatius

B=*Enemy Brothers*, Constance Savery [WWII]—Ignatius

C=*Europe and the Faith*, Belloc

S, V/DVD=*Greek Tragedy*—The Great Courses

C=*A History of the Protestant Reformation in England and Ireland*, William Cobbett—TAN

S, V/DVD=*History of Hitler's Empire*—The Great Courses

C=*How the Reformation Happened*, Belloc

S, T/AK=*AP European History*—Barron's

S, T/AK=*AP World History*—Barron's

C=*If All the Swords in England*, Barbara Willard [St. Thomas Becket]—Ignatius

C=*Isabella of Spain: The Last Crusader*, William Thomas Walsh

C=*Isabel of Spain: The Catholic Queen*, Warren H. Carroll

C, T/TM=*Lepanto*, G.K. Chesterton

C=*Mary's House*, Donald Carroll—archaeology/discovery of St. John's and Our Lady's home in Ephesus

S=*Persia and the Bible*, Edwin Yamauchi

C=*Pius XII and the Second World War: According to the Archives of the Vatican*, Fr. Pierre Blet

C, B=*Saint Thomas More*, Elizabeth Ince

C=*Science of Today and the Problems of Genesis*, Fr. Patrick O'Connell [archaeological/origin of man]

C=*Son of Charlemagne,* Barbara Willard—Ignatius

C=*Song at the Scaffold,* Gertrud on LeFort

C=*The Bones of St. Peter,* John Walsh [archaelogical discovery beneath the Vatican]

S=*The Campaigns of World War II Day-by-Day,* Chris Bishop

C=*The Crusades,* Hilaire Belloc

C=*The Crusaders,* Regine Pernoud—Ignatius

The Dead Sea Scrolls

C=*The Defamation of Pius XII,* Ralph McInerny—Ignatius

C=*The Guillotine and the Cross,* Warren H. Carroll

NCC=*The Hiding Place,* Corrie ten Boom [WWII Holocaust]

C=*The Ides of April,* Mary Ray [1st century Rome]—Ignatius

C=*The King's Good Servant But God's First,* James Monti [St. Thomas More]—Ignatius

C=*The Pope and the Holocaust,* Fr. John S. Rader and Kateryna Fedoryka

C=*The Quiet Light,* de Wohl [St. Thomas Aquinas]—Ignatius

C =*The Red Horse,* Eugenio Corti [WWII]—Ignatius

C=*The Restless Flame,* de Wohl [St. Augustine]—Ignatius

✓ C, B=*The Winged Watchman,* Hilda van Stockum [WWII]—Ignatius

C=*Those Terrible Middle Ages,* Regine Pernoud—Ignatius

C=*To Quell the Terror,* William Bush [French Revolution]

C=*What Were the Crusades?,* Jonathan Riley-Smith—Ignatius

C=*William the Conqueror,* Hilaire Belloc—TAN

C=*With God in Russia,* Fr. Walter Cizek, S.J. —Ignatius

S, V/DVD=*United States and the Middle East: 1914-9/11*—The Great Courses

S, V/DVD=*World War II: A Military and Social History*—The Great Courses

S, T/AK=*World War II for Dummies*—www.dummies.com

Links:

"A Righteous Gentile: Pope Pius XII and the Jews," Rabbi David Dalin—http://catholiceducation.org/articles/facts/fm0020.html

C=www.catholiceducation.org—orthodox Catholic writers; excellent resource for history articles

www.enchantedlearning.com/Home.html—printables: maps, geology, anatomy, astronomy, botany, more

C=www.steveraysstore.com—10+ video series, Steve Ray—Holy Land, apostles, Mary, figures in early Church

www.fordham.edu/halsall/ancient/asbook01.asp—Internet Ancient History Sourcebook

www.tcr.org/tcr/index.htm—The Concord Review History Essay

www.gwpda.org/photos/greatwar.htm

http://history.hanover.edu/project.php

http://historywired.si.edu/index.html

http://history.howstuffworks.com/

www.nationalarchives.gov.uk/museum/

www.pbs.org/empires/thegreeks/
htmlver/—PBS: lesson plans and
materials, more

http://users.binary.net/polycarp/piusxii.
html

www.catholicleague.org/category/
pope-pius-xii-and-the-hoocaust/

www.spartacus.schoolnet.co.uk/

www.historynet.com—history
magazines, including WWII and Viet
Nam

http://isurvived.org/Lustig_
AuschwitzAlbum.html

http://www.ipl.org/div/subject/
—Internet Public Library

Possible Essay Topics:

• Do you suppose it's coincidental that Pharaoh Akehenaten [or Akhenaton] who ruled during the Hebrew captivity in Egypt, was the one Pharaoh to reject polytheism and embrace monotheism? Read Genesis chapters 46-50 and Exodus chapters 1-12. Research Akehenaten and his religious beliefs. Write about your conclusions.

• Read *The Tiber Ran Red*, an account of Christian martyrdom in the Roman Empire, by Frank Korn. Report.

• Research and report on the ancient Roman cities of Pompeii and Herculaneum.

• Read and report on *The Bones of St. Peter* [archaeological discoveries beneath the Vatican], by John Walsh.

• If you could travel back in time to ancient Rome, what would you most like to see? Is there an event in which you might like to participate? Would you in any way try to influence the course of Roman history? If so, in what way?

• How would you gently correct and inform those who have been mislead about the nature of the Inquisition? Read *Characters of the Inquisition*, by William Walsh and prepare a point-by-point defense based in historical fact.

• Who were the Martyrs of Nagasaki? How were they evangelized and by whom?

• Read and report on *Mary's House* [archaeo-logical discovery, Our Lady's home at Ephesus], by Donald Carroll.

• How would you answer those who are of the erroneous opinion that Pope Pius XII did little to help the Jewish people escape the Nazi Holocaust of WWII? Why did the Chief Rabbi of Rome, Israel [Eugenio] Zolli become a Catholic after WWII? Using listed books and websites, research the evidence that demonstrates the heroic and fruitful efforts of the Holy Father.

• Did you know that more Christians were martyred in the 20th century than in the early years of the Church? Select one of the following 20th century persecutions and report:

—Catholics in Mexico, 1920's [see Bl. Miguel Pro]

—Catholics in Europe under Nazi rule, 1940's [see St. Maximilian Kolbe and St. Teresa Benedicta of the Cross]

—Catholics in China, 1950's [*God's Under-ground in Asia*, by Gretta Palmer]

—Catholics in the Soviet Union, 1920's-1980's [see books by Fr. Walter Cizek, or *God's Underground in Asia*, by Gretta Palmer]

—Catholics in Viet Nam, 1970's [see *The Miracle of Hope*, by Andre Nguyen and Van Chau]

—Catholics in East Timor, 1980's to 1990's

—Catholics in the Sudan, 1990's to present

Research:

You may, in conjunction with your text and field work, wish to investigate the following topics in greater depth. Credit may be earned through reading, book reports, essays or student-developed projects inspired by the topic.

- Roman Empire, Christian persecution [*The Tiber Ran Red*, Frank Korn]
- Middle Eastern history [*Persia and the Bible*, Edwin Yamauchi]
- Roman Empire, occupation of Britain [*Between the Forest and the Hills*, Ann Lawrence]
- Roman Empire, occupation of Palestine [*Beyond the Desert Gate*, Mary Ray]
- Fall of the Roman Empire through Medieval Civilization, feudalism, and beyond [*Europe and the Faith*, Hilaire Belloc—excellent]
- France in the 'Dark Ages' [*Son of Charlemagne*, Barbara Williard]
- Europe, the 'Dark Ages' [*Citadel of God*, Louis de Wohl or *Those Terrible Middle Ages*, Regine Pernoud]
- The Crusades [*The Crusades*, Hilaire Belloc]
- Muslim Moors driven from Spain in 1492 [*Isabella of Spain*, William Walsh or *Characters of the Inquisition*, William Walsh]
- 'Reformation' in 16th century Europe [*Characters of the Reformation*, Hilaire Belloc]
- Explosive growth of the Faith in, and conquest of, 16th century Mexico [*Our Lady of Guadalupe*, Warren Carroll and *Columbus and Cortez, Conquerors for Christ*]
- 16th century Muslim attack on Italy [*Lepanto*, G.K. Chesterton, edited by Dale Ahlquist]
- 16th century Asia and evangelization by St. Francis Xavier [*Set All Afire*, Louis de Wohl]
- Elizabeth I, English persecution of Catholics [*Come Rack! Come Rope!*, Msgr. Robert Benson, and *Edmund Campion*, Fr. Harold Gardiner]

- 18th century French Revolution [*The Song at the Scaffold*, Gertrud von LeFort, or *To Quell the Terror*, William Bush, or *The Guillotine and the Cross*, Warren Carroll]
- 1917 Revolution in Mexico [*1917: Red Banners, White Mantle*, Warren Carroll or *Mexican Martyrdom*, Wilfrid Parsons]
- 1930's Spanish persecution of the Church and Civil War in Spain [*The Last Crusade*, Warren Carroll]
- 1940's, World War II and Holocaust [*Pius XII and the Second World War: According to the Archives of the Vatican*, Fr. Pierre Blet, or *The Hiding Place*, Corrie ten Boom, or *A Righteous Gentile: Pope Pius XII and the Jews*, Rabbi David Dalin]
- Nazi occupation, to Soviet domination, to his part in the fall of Communism: through the remarkable, holy life of Pope John Paul II [*Witness to Hope: the Biography of Pope John Paul II*, George Weigel]
- Soviet Union and Communism [*With God in Russia*, Fr. Walter Cizek, S.J.]
- China and Communism [*The Pagoda and the Cross: The Life of Bishop Ford of Marynoll*, John Donovan, and *Four Years in a Red Hell: The Story of Fr. Rigney*, Fr. Harold Rigney]
- Africa's Christian history and heritage [*2,000 Years of Christianity in Africa*, Fr. John Baur]

Experiential Learning/Career and Vocational Bridge/Volunteer:

[See Table of Contents for *Process Project Outline* projects.]

World History Projects:

• For what were the Iconoclasts famous? Read, then design and create an icon.

• At Fatima, Our Lady foretold the expansion of Communism. From which countries did the founders of Communist thought—Lenin, Marx, Engels—originate? Create a world map; mark the location of Our Lady's appearance at Fatima, Portugal, and the birthplaces of Lenin, Marx, and Engels. Outline in yellow all countries that are now, or at one time were, under Communist attack or domination. [For example, Communists took an active role in the Spanish Civil War, but Spain successfully resisted Communist control.] Outline in red those countries that are currently under Communist domination. [Some countries will have both yellow and red outlines.] Did all or parts of the countries of Lenin, Marx, and Engels become Communist? Did the country of Our Lady's appearance become Communist? Did the number of Communist-dominated countries increase or decrease during the pontificate of Pope John Paul II?

• Create a 'History of Transportation Portfolio.' Draw or in some way illustrate and label methods of transportation used in the ancient Middle East, ancient Rome, ancient Japan, medieval Europe, Scandinavia's Viking Era, and 17th, 18th, 19th, and 20th century North America.

• Create a 'History of Style Portfolio.' Draw or in some way illustrate and label clothing styles worn in the ancient Middle East, ancient Rome, ancient Japan, the Aztec culture, medieval Europe, the court of Louis XVI of France, 19th century Russia or Poland, 20th century Nigeria and Egypt, and 17th, 18th, 19th, and 20th century North America. Include information about popular fabrics and why they might have been popular in their respective cultures.

• Research the development of written language. Create a portfolio including representations of hieroglyphics [including North American discoveries], Phoenician, Greek, Roman, Cyrillic alphabets, Arabic, Hebrew, Hangul, and Japanese Kanji characters. Include a sample of Sequoyah's alphabet and explain its origins. Who invented the Cyrillic alphabet and for what purpose? Where and how did Japanese Kanji originate? What can be learned about interactions between cultures by observing the development of writing forms?

Home Economics

C=*A Continual Feast,* Evelyn Birge Vitz [cookbook]

C=*Cooking with the Saints,* Ernst Schuegraf

S, B=Cooking: Merit Badge Series

S, T/AK=*Guide to Good Food* [The Goodheart-Wilcox Home Economics series], Velda Langen

S=*Miserly Moms: Living on One Income in a Two-Income Economy,* Jonni McCoy

S=*Stories and Recipes of the Great Depression,* Rita Van Amber

S=*Where's Mom Now That I Need Her?: Surviving Away from Home,* Betty Rae Frandsen [recipes, laundry, nutrition, and shopping tips]

[See also *Family Management* for titles]

Links:

www.4-h-canada.ca/core/—4-H Canada

www.4-h.org—4-H

http://crochet.about.com—free crochet patterns and instructions

www.crochetpatterncentral.com/free_crochet_patterns.php

www.khake.com/page77.html—free lessons and lesson plans: health, nutrition, child care, meals

www.kingarthurflour.com/recipes—baking tips and recipes

http://knitting.about.com—free knitting patterns and instructions

www.knitting-crochet.com—free knitting and crochet patterns

http://ohioline.osu.edu—Ohio State University Extension—food, agricultural, and environmental information

www.recipegoldmine.com—recipes unlimited

www.stretcher.com/index.cfm—money-saving tips for the home: food, electrical usage, clothing, more

www.psnh.com/downloads/Home%20Appliance%20Usage%20Costs.pdf?id=4294968770&dl=t

www.psnh.com/CustomerSupport/Home/Tips-for-Reducing-Your-Bill.aspx

http://www.ipl.org/div/subject/—Internet Public Library

Experiential Learning/Career and Vocational Bridge:

[See Table of Contents for *Process Project Outline* and *Following in Their Footsteps* projects.]

Home Economics Projects:

• Create a 'Home Economics Notebook.' Decorate the cover appropriately, then include as many of the following projects as you might find helpful for credit and future use in your own home.

• Compile a cookbook of favorite family recipes from parents, aunts, uncles, and grandparents. Interview grandparents to learn how cooking and meal preparation has changed in their lifetimes.

• Using weekly grocery ads, plan dinner menus for your family for one month, including sale items wherever possible. No mixes of any sort are allowed; fresh and canned fruits and vegetables are acceptable. [Do not purchase or prepare the foods, just plan the menus.] Each week, visit the grocery store and record prices for all menu ingredients and items. Save all menus. At the end of the month, using the same menus, visit the grocery store and record non-sale prices of all items when the sales have ended. Total menu costs for the month at sale and non-sale prices. How much money was saved by centering menus around sale items?

• Ask permission to advertise a 'doll collection' in your parish bulletin. Sew doll clothes to fit collected dolls, then donate all to Children's Services for foster children's use, particularly as they transition from one home to another.

• Plan a month's worth of dinner menus for your family based on foods that they enjoy. [Do not purchase or prepare the foods, just plan the menus.] Include prepared frozen dishes and prepared boxed meals. Visit the grocery store and record the prices of all ingredients and items listed on the menus. How did the month's grocery bill differ from the menus based on sale prices?

• Knit or crochet a variety of soft pastel baby booties to donate to your local Crisis Pregnancy Center.

• Find out about the effect of cooking on vitamins.

http://ohioline.osu.edu/lines/food.html

• What is the dietary need for:
calcium
Vitamin A
Vitamin E
Vitamin C
iron
folic acid/folates

http://ohioline.osu.edu/lines/food.html

• Select a favorite salad dressing, noting price, total calories per serving and total fat calories per serving. Using reduced-fat mayonnaise, and your own unique blend of spices, create a lower calorie dressing. Calculate the price, total calories per serving, and total fat calories per serving of your salad-crowning creation.

• Can housecleaning be made simpler/cheaper? Add housecleaning tips and money-saving home-made cleaning solutions to your 'Home Economics Notebook.'

www.stretcher.com/index.cfm

• Using weekly grocery ads, plan dinner menus for your family for two weeks, including sale items wherever possible. No mixes of any sort are allowed; fresh and canned fruits and vegetables are acceptable. Prepare the meals for your family.

• Find out about the role of food groups in a healthful diet. Draw, or create on the computer, a chart, graph, wheel or other illustration that displays each food group. Portray in the illustration/chart the percentages of each group needed to equal a balanced diet.

• Do you have favorite saints from Africa or Asia? Prepare an international meal on their feast days.

• How and where can money be shaved from the family electrical bill? Which appliances consume the most electricity? Create or add to your Home Economics Notebook. [Resources: www.psnh.com/downloads/ Home%20Appliance%20Usage%20Costs. pdf?id=4294968770&dl=t and www.psnh. com/CustomerSupport/Home/Tips-for-Reducing-Your-Bill.aspx and www.stretcher. com/index.cfm]

See also: Family Management

Journalism

S, T=*Basic Media Writing,* Melvin Mencher

S, B=Journalism: Merit Badge Series

S, T=*Journalism Today,* Donald Ferguson

S=*Newspaper Workshop,* Howard Decker

S=*Writing and Reporting News: A Coaching Method,* Carole Rich

Links:

www.aim.org—Accuracy in Media

www.doleta.gov—apprenticeships by state, county, and occupation

C=www.catholiceducation.org—orthodox Catholic writers; excellent resource for articles on the media

C=www.catholicpress.org—Catholic Press Association of U.S. and Canada

www.khake.com/page43.html—broadcast media/journalism career guide, requirements

www.khake.com/page58.html—apprenticeship info, training resources, U.S. and Canada

www.mrc.org—Media Research Center for bias in journalism

www.spj.org—Society of Professional Journalists—conduct essay contests

http://townhall.com—journalism, current topics

www.catholicpress. org/?page=CatholicJournalist

http://catholicmediajournal.com/ category/cj/

http://catholicacademy.org

http://www.ipl.org/div/subject/ —Internet Public Library

Church Teaching:

C=www.newadvent.org/cathen—Catholic encyclopedia

C=www.catholicnews.com/—Catholic News Service

C=www.cctn.org/—Catholic Community Television Network

C=www.catholic-pages.com/—Catholic documents and teaching, current events, more

C=www.vatican.va/news_services/—Vatican News Services

C=www.zenit.org/en—Vatican news; recent and archived Papal/Church statements

Dawn of a New Era [Aetatis Novae], Pontifical Council for Social Communications

Decree on the Media and Social Communication [Inter Mirifica], Second Vatican Council

Ethics in Advertising, Pontifical Council for Social Communications

Ethics in Communication, Pontifical Council for Social Communications

Pastoral Instruction on the Means of Social Communication [Communio et Progressio], ibid

CCC #2494-2497

Possible Essay Topics:

• Research and write about anti-Catholic/ Christian bias in the media.

www.catholiceducation.org

• What does the Church teach about the responsibilities of those working in the field of journalism? In what ways might Catholic journalists provide a positive influence on society through their work? For example, how might the world's response to governmental persecution—indeed, slaughter— of Catholics in East Timor or in the Sudan have been altered if reports by Catholic journalists had been widely published?

• List, compare, and contrast the differences between Catholic homeschooling and public education. Include in your essay the comparative cost of parochial school vs. homeschooling. Submit your article to the diocesan newspaper.

• Read *CCC* #2494-2497 in full. In part, the teaching admonishes that "...information provided by the media is at the service of the common good. Society has a right to information based on truth..." [#2494] and "...journalists have an obligation to serve the truth and not offend against charity in disseminating information." [#2497] Think of examples in which the media has not followed this guidance. In what ways were individuals or the public harmed by reporting based on half-truths? How might media adherence to the quoted catechetical counsel have changed the outcome of the story's printing/broadcast? [E.g., false reporting on a purported 'need' for partial birth abortion, or printing allegations against an individual to 'scoop' the story before thoroughly checking the veracity of the allegation's source.]

• Not infrequently, misconceptions and inaccuracies about the Catholic Faith find their way into local newspapers. Carefully monitor your paper for articles on religion [often published on Saturdays and Sundays], and also for religious-themed letters to the editor. ['Always be prepared to make a defense to any one who calls you to account for the hope that is in you, yet do it with gentleness and reverence...' 1 Pet. 3:15] Write charitable rebuttals and explanations and submit them to the editor.

• Read and summarize *Decree on the Media and Social Communication [Inter Mirifica]* or another Church document. Compose a news report about the document. Write as if for a secular newspaper, writing as to inform a non-Catholic audience.

• Given the opportunity, what dreams do you have for a future in journalism? List your dreams, plans, and goals. Arrange them in order of 'attack.' Outline steps toward their achievement. Write about your dream.

Experiential Learning/Career and Vocational Bridge:

[See Table of Contents for *Process Project Outline* and *Following in Their Footsteps* projects]

Journalism Projects:

• Write and produce a yearbook for a local homeschool group.

[The project might also gain Photography, Computer, and Business Cluster credit for taking orders and selling.]

• Write and produce a Catholic homeschool newsletter/magazine. The newsletter may include announcements of upcoming events, report on current activities, feature ideas for celebrating the liturgical season, and interviews of homeschooling families. Additionally, the newsletter might invite written contributions from other student authors.

• Interview elderly residents of a nursing home for local history, or retired religious for local history of their order. Submit articles based on your interviews to the local or diocesan newspaper, or create a 'news bulletin' with their stories and send to the home.

• Interview two or three couples from your parish who have been married fifty years or more. Ask how their Faith has strengthened their marriage. What other marriage advice do they have? Think of at least ten questions for your interview. Write and submit your article to the local and diocesan newspapers.

• Write articles on topics of interest to Catholics and submit to the diocesan newspaper.

• Write news stories about three fairy tales. The story should inform the reader primarily of the simple facts: who, what, when, where, and why. For example:

> *On June 13, 1912, the home of Mr. Second Pig, located at 23 Sheepskin Rd., was reportedly destroyed by unusually heavy wind gusts of undetermined origin. The stick-built home was uninsured; Mr. Second Pig has moved temporarily to the home of his brother, and was unavailable for comment.*
>
> *While yet to be confirmed, eyewitness accounts indicate the presence of a 'scruffy-looking canine-type' who hastily departed the scene immediately following the disaster.*

• Volunteer to help with parish bulletin and announcement flyers.

• Volunteer at the diocesan newspaper.

LANGUAGES

S=Audio-Forum, catalog with 285 courses in 103 languages—www. audioforum.com

S=Rosetta Stone—[French, German, Italian, Latin, Spanish], CD-ROM interactive, text

S=*Learnables,* Harris Winitz, Ph.D.—[Spanish, French, German], CD-ROM, readers, and workbooks [CHC]

S, T/AK=*Easy American Sign Language*— Barron's

NCC, V/DVD, T=*Sign Language for Everyone,* Cathy Rice [CHC]

S, T/AK=*French*—Cliff's

S, T/AK=*AP French Language and Culture*—Barron's

S=*Wheelock's Latin 7th Edition,* Richard LaFleur

S=*Thirty-Eight Latin Stories Designed to Accompany Wheelock's Latin,* Anne Groton

C, CP, AKA=*Henle's Latin and Study Guide* [4 volumes, 4 levels]

C=*Latin Grammar,* Charles and Cora Scanlon—Church Latin, 1st year

C=*Second Latin,* Charles and Cora Scanlon—Church Latin for reading philosophy, theology, canon law

S, T/AK=*AP Spanish*—Barron's

S, T/AK=*Spanish*—Cliff's

Supplemental Reading:

C, TM, CD=*Lingua Angelica,* Latin hymns with translations—Memoria Press

Links:

www.nle.org—National Latin Exam

www.internet4classrooms.com/flang.htm—interactive foreign language study

www.spartacus.schoolnet.co.uk/REVlanguages.htm—scroll down for interactive foreign language activities

http://www.ipl.org/div/subject/—Internet Public Library

Church Teaching:

Musicam Sacram, Documents of Vatican II, Vol. 2

Possible Essay Topics:

• "According to the Constitution on the Liturgy, 'the use of the Latin language, with due respect to particular law, is to be preserved in the Latin rites...Pastors of souls should take care that besides the vernacular, 'the faithful may also be able to say or sing together in Latin those parts of the Ordinary of the Mass which pertain to them.' " [*Musicam Sacram*]. Write a short essay about the usefulness of Latin for international Church communication and liturgy in 'churches...in large cities...where many come together with faithful of different languages.'

• Given the opportunity, what dreams do you have for a future in foreign languages? List your dreams, plans, and goals. Arrange them in order of 'attack.' Outline steps toward their achievement. Write about your dream.

Experiential Learning/Career and Vocational Bridge:

[See Table of Contents for *Process Project Outline* and *Following in Their Footsteps* projects.]

Foreign Language Projects:
• Volunteer with diocesan outreach to immigrants/ethnic vicariates/minority groups whose second language is English.
• Volunteer with the Deaf Apostolate.
• Translate a nursery rhyme or fairy tale into the language of your choice.
• Teach a class of homeschool youngsters the basics of the language of your choice, e.g., colors, counting, songs.
• Find a translator—school, court, medical—and 'shadow.'

Elective choices are limited only by one's imagination.

LOGIC

NCC, T, V/DVD=*Traditional Logic I and II,* Martin Cothran—Memoria Press

S, V/DVD=*Argumentation: The Study of Effective Reasoning*—The Great Courses

Links:

http://www.ipl.org/div/subject/
—Internet Public Library

Church Teaching:

The Splendor of Truth [Veritatis Splendor]—Pope John Paul II, encyclical letter

Faith and Reason [Fides et Ratio]—Pope John Paul II, encyclical letter

CCC #158

Possible Essay Topics:

• 'I believe, in order to understand; and I understand, the better to believe.' [St. Augustine] How should the proper study of Logic enhance our Faith? Read *CCC #158* and respond in a short essay.

MATHEMATICS

S=*All the Math You'll Ever Need: A Self-Teaching Guide* [Wiley Self-Teaching Guides], Steve Slavin [1999]

S, T/AKA, B=*Basic Mathematics for Occupational and Vocational Students*—Pearson Prentice Hall

S, V/DVD=The Great Courses [with workbook]: *Basic Math, Algebra I, Algebra II, Geometry*

S, AKA, B=*Budgeting and Spending Skills 1 and 2*—Fearon

S=*E-Z Business Math*—Barron's

S=*Consumer Math,* Kathleen Harmeyer [CHC]

S, AKA, B=*Consumer Math*—Steck-Vaughn—money management, car and home purchases, taxes

S, T/AK, B=Barron's: *Essential Math* [math for the job, bank, shopping, sales tax], *Math the Easy Way* [general math], *AP Calculus*

S=*Everyday Math for Dummies,* Charles Seiter—www.dummies.com

S=*Everyday Math for Everyday Life: A Handbook for When It Just Doesn't Add Up,* Mark Ryan

S=*Math to Build On: A Book for Those Who Build,* Johnny Hamilton

S=*Mathematics for Carpentry and the Construction Trades,* Alfred Webster

S=*Mathematics for Technical and Vocational Students,* Richard Spangler

S=*Math Basics for the Healthcare Professional,* Michele Benjamin-Lesmeister

S=*Math the E-Z Way*—Barron's

S, AK=*The Only Math Book You'll Ever Need,* Stanely Kogelman—checkbook, taxes, measurement, comparison shopping, recipe conversion, etc.

S, AKA, B=*Pacemaker Practical Arithmetic Series: Buying with Sense, Working Makes Sense, Using Dollars and Sense, Money Makes Sense*—Fearon

S=*Practical Math Success in 20 Minutes a Day*—LearningExpress Editors

S=*Practical Problems in Mathematics: For Automotive Technicians* [Applied Mathematics], Todd Sformo

S=*Practical Problems in Mathematics for Carpenters*, Mark Huth

S=*Practical Problems in Math for Health Occupations*, Louise M. Simmer

S, B=*AGS Pre-Algebra* [for Secondary students with learning difficulties]

S, CP, T/AK=Saxon: *Algebra 1/2, Algebra I, Algebra II, Advanced Math, Calculus, Geometry* [Saxon teaching videos also available—DIVE]

S, V/DVD=Standard Deviants: The Pumped-Up World of Pre-Algebra, Adventurous World of Algebra, Many-Sided World of Geometry, The Twisted World of Trigonometry, Dangerous World of Pre-Calculus, Calculus

S, CP, T/AK=*Algebra I,* www.teachingtextbooks.com [also titles for Algebra II, Geometry, and Pre-Calculus]

S, CP, T/AK=*Geometry: Seeing, Doing, Understanding,* Harold Jacobs—W.H. Freeman

S, CP, T/AKA=*Precalculus: Graphical, Numerical, Algebraic*—Pearson

Links:

http://agutie.homestead.com/—geometry

www.khanacademy.org—math tutorials

http://library.thinkquest.org/2647/index.html—interactive math

http://nlvm.usu.edu/—interactive virtual mathematics—algebra, geometry, etc.

http://www.ipl.org/div/subject/—Internet Public Library

Experiential Learning/Career and Vocational Bridge:

• Tutor young math students in an after-school or summer program.

Famous Names in Mathematics:

In what ways did the Catholic Church aid in discoveries/inventions/advancement?

How did the person's faith [or lack thereof] influence his/her work?

What might have motivated the person to become involved in the field?

In what ways did his/her discoveries/inventions/advancement change the field of study?

In what ways did his/her discoveries/inventions/advancement ultimately change society?

Archimedes

Euclid

Pythagoras

Blaise Pascal

Johannes Kepler

Research:

You may, in conjunction with your text and field work, wish to investigate the following topics in greater depth. Credit may be obtained through reading and hands-on, experiential learning including field trips, volunteering, and apprenticeships. Learning is demonstrated through the production of projects, experiments, essays or reports. Reports may be based on note-taking and observation and might include graphs, charts, illustrations and diagrams. Find out about the following careers that require extensive studies in mathematics.

- accountant
- architect
- architectural engineer
- astronomer
- bookkeeper
- business manager
- chemist
- cryptologist
- economist
- electrician
- engineer, chemical
- engineer, construction
- engineer, electrical
- nurse
- physician
- scientist, computer
- scientist, research
- scientist, space
- statistician
- surveyor

MECHANICAL SCIENCE, AUTOMOTIVE

Science Labs:

Labs essentially provide students an opportunity to test theories against reality, i.e., allow students to apply what they have learned from their texts in hands-on settings.

Most colleges don't require documented science labs as part of a high school science course. In fact, there is no national standard or definition of what exactly constitutes a high school science lab. However, since some colleges do require documented science lab work, it is best to include at least 20 hours of lab work in each science course that your student takes.

Keeping in mind that 'lab' means hands-on learning that applies book-learning to reality, credit for a Geology lab might be earned by visiting a fossil bed and searching for fossils. Students might photograph the rock formations where the fossils were found, identify the type of rock in which the fossils were found, and identify the types of fossils therein. Brief descriptions or notations about why and how fossils were found in this type of geological structure might be included. All of this information would then be assembled into a lab report.

An Environmental Science lab might include similar notations about discoveries made in a pond ecosystem, including a description and photographs of the pond, plant and animal aquatic life, and conclusions as to how and why those particular plants and animals live in that environment.

In essence, no matter which science courses are chosen, students will devote at least 20 hours of class time to lab work—that is, hands-on projects, exploration, and conclusions about what the student learned—which will be documented in a hard-copy notebook or portfolio.

Parents might also double-check with colleges to which students might apply to determine whether or not there are lab requirements.

Please also note that students who enroll in science classes at local colleges gain those lab credits while simultaneously earning both high school and college credit.

Book List:

S=*Auto Fundamentals,* Martin W. Stockel, Heritage Resources

S, B=Auto Mechanics: Boy Scout Merit Badge Handbook

S=*Auto Repair for Dummies,* www.dummies.com

S=*Repairing Your Outdoor Power Equipment,* Jay Webster

www.delmarlearning.com/—curricula: automotive studies

http://store.im.tamu.edu/Transportation-Distribution-Logistics-C51.aspx#

Links:

http://auto.howstuffworks.com

www.doleta.gov—apprenticeships by state, county, and occupation

http://www.magazines.com/popular-mechanics/7066-MA,default,pd.html

http://www.magazines.com/magazines/auto-cycles-magazines,default,sc.html

www.carparts.com/classroom

www.khake.com/page12.html —automotive career descriptions, requirements

www.khake.com/page20.html—engine technology career guide, requirements

www.khake.com/page58.html— apprenticeship info, training resources, U.S. and Canada

www.magazines.com/popular-mechanics/7066-MA,default,pd.html

www.motor.com/—automotive magazine and manuals

www.popularmechanics.com—Popular Mechanics magazine: automotive, aviation, computers, home improvement, robotics, woodworking, more

http://technicaljobsearch.com/job-banks/apprenticeships.htm— apprenticeships U.S. and Canada

http://www.ipl.org/div/subject/ —Internet Public Library

Possible Essay Topics:

• 'The human person is called to be a worker; work is one of the characteristics which distinguish human beings from the rest of creatures. From this it is evident that it is not enough to posses a vocational identity, an identity which involves the whole person, if it is not lived.' [*Les laics Catholiques, Documents of Vatican II, Vol. 2*]

In what ways might a person live his 'vocational identity,' using his mechanical gifts in God's service?

• In what ways are diesel powered vehicles different from gasoline powered? List differences and compare advantages and disadvantages. If you could choose between a diesel powered vehicle and a gasoline powered vehicle, which would you choose and why?

• Given the opportunity, what dreams do you have for a future in automotive mechanics? List your dreams, plans, and goals. Arrange them in order of 'attack.' Outline steps toward their achievement. Write about your dream.

Experiential Learning/Career and Vocational Bridge:

[See Table of Contents for *Process Project Outline* and *Following in Their Footsteps* projects]

Automotive Mechanics Projects:

Note: If you are doing major body work on a vehicle, replacing an engine, or any repairs that would be evident in a photograph, be sure to take step-by-step photographs to document your work.

• Make a list of safety rules to observe before and during any work on a vehicle. [For example, always work on the vehicle in an open, well ventilated area.] Post one copy of the rules on your bedroom wall and one copy on the wall above your automotive tools.

• Journal, journal, journal. As soon as the day's mechanical labors are concluded, wash your hands, pick up your pen, and write. What unexpected difficulties did you encounter? How were problems solved? What would you do differently next time? How do you feel about your work? You may wish to write in a 3-ring binder; clear plastic pages containing photographs of your automotive project may be inserted between written sheets.

• Watch 'Horatio's Drive.' [PBS video about the first cross-country trip by auto, traveled in 1903— prior to the creation of the national highway system.] Take notes during the video. Of the automobile manufacturers mentioned in the video, how many are still manufacturing today? How many times did his vehicle break down? How were repairs made on the vehicle? Would it be possible to repair a modern vehicle in the same way? Why or why not? Had you accompanied Horatio, what automotive advice might you have given him before or during the trip? If you could design a vehicle to make the same trip, covering unpaved ground, what type of vehicle would you design and build?

• Find out: How frequently should a vehicle's coolant be changed? How frequently should the oil be changed? And filters for fuel, oil, and air? How often should fluid levels, including brake fluid, automatic transmission fluid, windshield washing fluid, and fluid for power steering, be checked? Why are these maintenance procedures necessary? What happens if they are neglected? Perform these operations; create a notebook and make note of dates that maintenance was done. Take photos!

METEOROLOGY

Science Labs:

Labs essentially provide students an opportunity to test theories against reality, i.e., allow students to apply what they have learned from their texts in hands-on settings.

Most colleges don't require documented science labs as part of a high school science course. In fact, there is no national standard or definition of what exactly constitutes a high school science lab. However, since some colleges do require documented science lab work, it is best to include at least 20 hours of lab work in each science course that your student takes.

Keeping in mind that 'lab' means hands-on learning that applies book-learning to reality, credit for a Geology lab might be earned by visiting a fossil bed and searching for fossils. Students might photograph the rock formations where the fossils were found, identify the type of rock in which the fossils were found, and identify the types of fossils therein. Brief descriptions or notations about why and how fossils were found in this type of geological structure might be included. All of this information would then be assembled into a lab report.

An Environmental Science lab might include similar notations about discoveries made in a pond ecosystem, including a description and photographs of the pond, plant and animal aquatic life, and conclusions as to how and why those particular plants and animals live in that environment.

In essence, no matter which science courses are chosen, students will devote at least 20 hours of class time to lab work—that is, hands-on projects, exploration, and conclusions about what the student learned—which will be documented in a hard-copy notebook or portfolio.

Parents might also double-check with colleges to which students might apply to determine whether or not there are lab requirements.

Please also note that students who enroll in science classes at local colleges gain those lab credits while simultaneously earning both high school and college credit.

Book List:

S=*A Field Guide to the Atmosphere*—Peterson's

S=*Meteorology Today*, C. Donald Aherns

S=*The Atmosphere: An Introduction to Meteorology*, Frederick Lutgens

S=*The Handy Weather Answer Book*, Walter Lyons

S=*The Weather Book: An Easy-to-Understand Guide to the USA's Weather*, Jack Williams

S=*Tying Down the Wind*, Eric Pinder

S, B=*Weather: Merit Badge Series*

Links:

1,200 page, free science supplies catalog!—www.wardsci.com—Ward's Natural Science—1-800-962-2660

www.ametsoc.org/—American Meteorological Society

www.afn.org/~afn09444/weather/skywarn.html

www.ec.gc.ca—Environment Canada—meteorology and environmental information

www.noaa.gov—weather, oceans, satellite information

www.ncdc.noaa.gov/cdo-web/

www.nssl.noaa.gov—National Severe Storm Laboratory

www.nssl.noaa.gov/people/jobs/careers.php—career info meteorology

www.oar.noaa.gov/—atmospheric research

www.ncdc.noaa.gov/cdo-web/

http://meso-a.gsfc.nasa.gov/goes/—Geostationary Operational Environmental Satellite

www.discoveryeducation.com/teachers/—free lessons and lesson plans for weather

www.skywarn.org

www.stormchaser.com—stormchasers, meteorology links

www.weather.unisys.com

www.weather.gov

http://som.ou.edu—career info, meteorology

www.wunderground.com/satellite/vis/1k/US.html—U.S. and international satellite images, updated every 20 min.

http://www.ipl.org/div/subject/—Internet Public Library

Possible Essay Topics:

• Compare and contrast: what are the differences in systems, collection of information, and benefits/disadvantages between the U.S. NEXRAD weather radar system and NESDIS satellite imaging?
• Compare and contrast the differences in purpose between GOES [Geostationary Operational Environmental Satellites] and POES [Polar Orbiting Environmental Satellites].
• Given the opportunity, what dreams do you have for a future in meteorology? List your dreams, plans, and goals. Arrange them in order of 'attack.' Outline steps toward their achievement. Write about your dream.

Research:

• What type of education is needed to become a meteorologist? Which classes should be studied in high school? At the college level?
• Find out about the following careers in meteorology:

operational meteorologist
synoptic meteorologist
environmental meteorologist
climatologist
physical meteorologist
hydrometeorologist
broadcast meteorologist
- Find out about:
  VORTEX
  Doppler Radar
  Defense Meteorological Satellite Program
  Space Environment Center & space
     weather alerts and warnings
  mesocyclones
  supercell thunderstorms
  convective windstorms
  downbursts
  microbursts

Experiential Learning/Career and Vocational Bridge:

[See Table of Contents for *Process Project Outline* and *Following in Their Footsteps* projects]

Meteorology Projects:
- Set up a weather station at home. Record wind speed, precipitation, and temperatures at set times throughout the day. Keep careful notes. How did your findings differ from broadcast forecasts?

  www.wardsci.com—Ward's Natural Science—1-800-962-2660—home weather stations

- Volunteer as a weather spotter with a television station.
- Do an internet track of El Nino over the past decade. Find out how drought and flooding cycles were affected by El Nino in those same years.
- Research and compile a list of safety measures to be taken during a lightning storm.

If possible, illustrate. Create a poster that would be suitable for distribution.
- Check into becoming part of SKYWARN.
- Research and compile a list of weather conditions and signs, including unusual cloud formations, that could signal a developing tornado. If possible, illustrate. Create a booklet that would be suitable for distribution.

Books, videos, and websites listed as references for the courses in this volume are not 'recommended' or 'preferred,' but rather widely used options from which to choose, depending on the intended field of study, educational goals, and the mental and spiritual maturity of the student.

METEOROLOGY

MIDWIFERY

Science Labs:

Labs essentially provide students an opportunity to test theories against reality, i.e., allow students to apply what they have learned from their texts in hands-on settings.

Most colleges don't require documented science labs as part of a high school science course. In fact, there is no national standard or definition of what exactly constitutes a high school science lab. However, since some colleges do require documented science lab work, it is best to include at least 20 hours of lab work in each science course that your student takes.

Keeping in mind that 'lab' means hands-on learning that applies book-learning to reality, credit for a Geology lab might be earned by visiting a fossil bed and searching for fossils. Students might photograph the rock formations where the fossils were found, identify the type of rock in which the fossils were found, and identify the types of fossils therein. Brief descriptions or notations about why and how fossils were found in this type of geological structure might be included. All of this information would then be assembled into a lab report.

An Environmental Science lab might include similar notations about discoveries made in a pond ecosystem, including a description and photographs of the pond, plant and animal aquatic life, and conclusions as to how and why those particular plants and animals live in that environment.

In essence, no matter which science courses are chosen, students will devote at least 20 hours of class time to lab work—that is, hands-on projects, exploration, and conclusions about what the student learned—which will be documented in a hard-copy notebook or portfolio.

Parents might also double-check with colleges to which students might apply to determine whether or not there are lab requirements.

Please also note that students who enroll in science classes at local colleges gain those lab credits while simultaneously earning both high school and college credit.

S=*Paths to Becoming a Midwife: Getting an Education*—www. midwiferytoday.com

NCC=*The Christian Childbirth Handbook,* Jennifer Vanderlaan

S=*Texas Midwifery Basic Information and Instructor's Manual* [see **Links**]

Supplemental Reading:

C=*Catholic Bioethics and the Gift of Human Life,* William May

C=*Communicating the Catholic Vision of Life,* Russell Smith [available through NCBC]

C=*Pro-Life: Defending the Culture of Life against the Culture of Death,* Fr. John Pasquini

NCC=*Ethics for Doctors, Nurses and Patients,* H.P. Dunn

S=*Midwifery Today* magazine—www. midwiferytoday.com

C=*Redeemer in the Womb: Jesus Living in Mary,* John Saward

Links:

www.midwife.org—American College of Nurse-Midwives

C=www.all.org—American Life League, topical index, end of life care, euthanasia, eugenics, fetal development, stem cell research

http://12.aamishop.com—[apprentice program] Ancient Art Midwifery Institute [Christian]

http://avivacollege.org—online midwifery and health education

www.birthcenters.org—midwifery, birth centers by state

C=www.cathmed.org—Catholic Medical Association

www.birthingnaturally.net/christian/directory/organizations.html

www.christianchildbirth.org/Links.html

www.christianmidwives.org/wp/

http://fetus.ucsfmedicalcenter.org

www.gentlebirth.org—information on ultrasound, risks

C=www.lifeissues.net—site in association with OMI

www.midwiferycollege.org—National College of Midwifery

www.midwiferytoday.com—books, midwifery magazine

C=www.marquette.edu/nursing/index.shtml—College of Nursing, Marquette University

C=www.ncbcenter.org—National Catholic Bioethics Center

www.nrlc.org—National Right to Life

www.nursesforlife.org—National Association of Prolife Nurses

C=http://onemoresoul.com—One More Soul

www.sfuhl.org—Science for Unborn Human Life—learning in the womb

www.texasmidwives.com—Association of Texas Midwives

C=www.wf-f.org/MedicalMoral.html—Women for Faith and Family

http://www.ipl.org/div/subject/—Internet Public Library

Church Teaching:

C=www.newadvent.org/cathen—Catholic encyclopedia

C=www.catholic-pages.com/—Catholic documents and teaching, current events, more

C=www.zenit.org/en—Vatican news; recent and archived Papal/Church statements

Instructions on the Respect for Human Life in its Origin and on the Dignity of Procreation [Donum Vitae], Congregation for the Doctrine of the Faith

Of Human Life [Humanae Vitae], Pope Paul VI

CCC #2270-2279

Possible Essay Topics:

• In what ways was Pope Paul VI's *Humanae Vitae* prophetic? Read, list the ways, and cite the encyclical.

• In what ways does devaluing the sanctity of life alter the focus of maternity and neonatal care?

[See also *Biology, Fetology* for essay topics]

• "Prenatal diagnosis is morally licit, 'if it respects the life and integrity of the embryo and the human fetus and is directed toward its safeguarding or healing as an individual...It is gravely opposed to the moral law when this is done with the thought of possibly inducing an abortion, depending upon the results: *a diagnosis must not be the equivalent of a death sentence.'* " [CCC #2274] Compare and contrast the positive and negative effects of amniocentesis, CVS, and ultrasound testing. Include information about maternal and fetal risks and benefits, and false positive readings for nonexistent birth defects. What should be the Catholic response if 'birth defects' are found?

• Given the opportunity, what dreams do you have for a future in midwifery? List your dreams, plans, and goals. Arrange them in order of 'attack.' Outline steps toward their achievement. Write about your dream.

Research

You may, in conjunction with your text and field work, wish to investigate the following topics in greater depth. Credit may be obtained through reading and hands-on, experiential learning including field trips, volunteering, and apprenticeships. Learning is demonstrated through the production of projects, experiments, essays or reports. Reports may be based on note-taking and observation and might include graphs, charts, illustrations and diagrams.

To aid in research, ask and answer, "Who, what, where, when and why?" [See also *Biology: Fetology*]

- Pregnancy complications
   ectopic pregnancy
   placenta previa
   premature birth
   breech birth
   premature separation of the placenta
   multiple births
   maternal diabetes, gestational and
      pre-existing

Experiential Learning/Career and Vocational Bridge:

[See Table of Contents for *Process Project Outline* and *Following in Their Footsteps* projects]

Midwifery Projects:
- Sign up for First Aid classes.
- Volunteer with Right to Life:
   Study stages of fetal development. Borrow fetal models and give a presentation to a youth group.
- Volunteer at a hospital nursery.
- Investigate classes toward a CNA license.
- Volunteer at a Crisis Pregnancy Center.
- Check into Church-connected bio-ethics or pro-life outreaches.
- Contact One More Soul and find out about their purpose.
- Sign up for CPR Classes.

Music

[See public library for video
and audio resources]

S=*Music in Theory and Practice*, Bruce
Benward

S=*The Complete Idiot's Guide to Music
Theory*, Michael Miller

S, V/DVD, Audio=*The Symphony*—The
Great Courses

S=*Understanding Music*, Jeremy
Yudkin [look for copy with CD]

Links:

C=http://musicasacra.com—Catholic
Music Association of America

C=www.adoremus.org—Adoremus
Hymnal, Church documents on music

C=http://comp.uark.edu/~rlee/
otherchant.html—Gregorian chant and
polyphony resources, recordings, choir
contacts

C=http://easterncatholichymns.
homestead.com/spasihospodi.html—
Eastern Rite Catholic hymns

C=www.fisheaters.com/hymns.html—
traditional Catholic hymns

www.khake.com/page48.html—
performing arts career guide,
requirements

C=http://midihymns.homestead.com/
midiindex.html—traditional Catholic
hymns

http://www.ipl.org/div/subject/
—Internet Public Library

Church Teaching:

C=www.adoremus.org—Church
documents

C=www.newadvent.org/cathen—
Catholic encyclopedia

C=www.catholic-pages.com/—Catholic
documents and teaching, current
events, more

C=www.zenit.org/en—Vatican news;
recent and archived Papal/Church
statements

*Musicam Sacram, Documents of
Vatican II, Vol. 1*

*Sacrosanctum Concilium, Documents
of Vatican II, Vol. 1*

CCC #1156-1158, 2513

Possible Essay Topics:

• In the *General Instruction of the Roman
Missal*, #41, [pub.2002], the Church teaches
that '...Gregorian chant holds pride of place
because it is proper to the Roman Liturgy.'
This instruction is also found in *Sacrosanctum
Concilium* and *Musicam Sacram*. In what
ways is it wise that liturgical music should
differ from 'popular' music? Discuss some of
the reasons why the Church may have issued
this directive.

• 'The treasury of sacred music is to be
preserved and cultivated with great care.'
[*Sacrosanctum Concilium,*#114] How has
the treasury of sacred music been preserved
in your parish? As a musician, how might you
help to 'cultivate with great care' the use of
sacred music in your parish? Brainstorm ideas
and write. You may wish, when your essay is
complete, to present it to your pastor and/or
music director.

• Write about a work that has influenced your
approach to music. In what ways did the
composer or his work change your perspective?

• Given the opportunity, what dreams do you
have for a future in music? List your dreams,
plans, and goals. Arrange them in order of

'attack.' Outline steps toward their achievement. Write about your dream.

Famous Names Related to Music: Read and Report

In what ways did the Catholic Church aid in the composer's work?

How did the person's faith influence his/her work?

What might have motivated the person to compose as he did?

Wolfgang Amadeus Mozart

Giuseppe Verdi

Anton Bruckner

Giovanni Palestrina

Experiential Learning/Career and Vocational Bridge:

See Table of Contents for *Process Project Outline* and *Following in Their Footsteps* projects]

Music Projects:
• Participate in church choir.
• Participate in a community orchestra or band.
• According to *CCC #1158*, '...texts intended to be sung must always *be in conformity with Catholic doctrine. Indeed they should be drawn chiefly from the Sacred Scripture and from liturgical sources.*' Compose a musical piece, drawn from Sacred Scripture or liturgical sources, that teaches a doctrine of our Holy Faith. You may wish to present your piece at a Catholic homeschool meeting, perhaps engaging other Catholic homeschoolers in your project and presentation.
• Provide private music lessons to young students, particularly to the disadvantaged or in an after-school program.

• Prepare and present a musical selection at a local nursing home, perhaps on a regular basis.
• With other Catholic homeschoolers, organize a 'Mom's Day Out.' Set a time and location, then provide an afternoon of activities for children from ages 3-8. [This might be done in conjunction with a parish mission or retreat to provide babysitting; students seeking Family Management or Psychology credit could provide care while observing the under-3 age group.] Create art or craft projects, music/songs, physical activities and games, cooking, or hobby demonstrations that can be used to teach the Faith to young children.
• Contact and 'shadow' the director of a community orchestra.

...during the high school years when parents are available for guidance, and for the student to be fully prepared for college courses, it is not necessarily imprudent to study secular materials alongside those that present Catholic teaching.

PHYSICAL EDUCATION

For those who are following academic guidelines of a particular state, some states allow Health to be substituted for 1/2 year of P.E.

C=*A Catholic Perspective: Physical Exercise and Sports,* Robert Feeney

S=*Homeschool Family Fitness,* Dr. Bruce Whitney [CHC]

S, B=Athletics: Merit Badge Series

S, B=Canoeing: Merit Badge Series

S, B=Cycling: Merit Badge Series

S, B=Golf: Merit Badge Series

S=*Physical Best Activity Guide: High School Level,* NASPE

S, B=Skating: Merit Badge Series

S, B=Snow Sports: Boy Scout Merit Badge Handbook

S, B=Sports: Merit Badge Series

S, B=Swimming: Merit Badge Series

S, B=Waterskiing: Merit Badge Series

Links:

www.fitness.gov/about-pcfsn/—President's Council on Physical Fitness and Sports

www.fitness.gov/resource-center/research-and-reports/—free publications for physical education

www.pecentral.org/lessonideas/middlehigh/highschoolideas.asp—ideas and lessons plans for P.E.

Church Teaching:

C=www.newadvent.org/cathen—Catholic encyclopedia

C=www.catholic-pages.com/—Catholic documents and teaching, current events, more

C=www.zenit.org/en—Vatican news; recent ard archived Papal/Church statements

CCC #2288, 2289

Possible Essay Topics:

Yes, P.E. credit may be awarded for writing about physical education topics!

• Compare and contrast the physical growth and rewards gained by participating in organized sports with the spiritual growth and rewards gained by participating in the Holy Sacrifice of the Mass. Discuss the temporal and eternal effects of each activity. How might the value of these two goods be weighed when sports events conflict with Holy Mass?
• Research the connection between physical exercise and mental health, e.g., alleviation of depression and delay in onset of Alzheimer's. Report.
• 'Life and physical health are precious gifts entrusted to us by God. We must take reasonable care of them, taking into account the needs of others...' [*CCC #2288*] 'If morality requires respect for the life of the body, it does not make it an absolute value. It rejects a neo-pagan notion that tends to promote the cult of the body, to sacrifice everything for its sake, to idolize physical perfection and success at sports. By its selective preference of the strong over the weak, such a conception can lead to the perversion of human relationships.' [*CCC #2289*] Think of and write about examples of the 'cult of the body' and the idolization of 'sports heroes' as described in these quotes from the *Catechism*. In what ways has the abuse of steroid drugs by athletes been part of this 'cult'? Quoting *CCC #2288* in your response, contrast the Christian

attitude to physical health as opposed to the 'cult of the body.'

Experiential Learning/Career and Vocational Bridge:

[See Table of Contents for *Process Project Outline* projects.]

Physical Education Projects:

• With other Catholic homeschoolers, organize a 'Mom's Day Out.' Set a time and location, then provide an afternoon of activities for children from ages 3-8. [This might be done in conjunction with a parish mission or retreat to provide babysitting; students seeking Family Management or Psychology credit could provide care while observing the under-3 age group.] Create art or craft projects, music/songs, physical activities and games, cooking, or hobby demonstrations that can be used to teach the Faith to young children.

• If you live in northern climes, create a temporary ice-skating or hockey rink in your back yard.

• Physical activities for one or two:
  bike
  jog
  walk
  swim
  ice or roller blade
  badminton
  tennis
  jump rope
  trampoline
  horseshoes
  Tae Kwon Do
  tetherball
  croquet
  archery

• Physical activities for a group:
  square dance
  baseball
  tag football
  basketball
  soccer
  croquet
  tennis
  badminton
  swim
  gymnastics
  roller skate
  ice skate
  jump rope
  Tae Kwon Do
  tug-of-war
  volleyball

• Organize a homeschool field day or track meet with:
  foot races
  softball throw
  sack race
  three-legged race
  relay race with a raw egg as the relay 'baton' [first team to make it to the finish line with a whole egg wins]
  running long jump
  standing long jump

• Select a sport and write. What were its origins? Rules? In what ways has the sport changed since its beginning?

• Study Olympic events and their origins. Create an artistic rendition of one of the events and write a brief history of the activity pictured.

Physics

Science Labs:

Labs essentially provide students an opportunity to test theories against reality, i.e., allow students to apply what they have learned from their texts in hands-on settings.

Most colleges don't require documented science labs as part of a high school science course. In fact, there is no national standard or definition of what exactly constitutes a high school science lab. However, since some colleges do require documented science lab work, it is best to include at least 20 hours of lab work in each science course that your student takes.

Keeping in mind that 'lab' means hands-on learning that applies book-learning to reality, credit for a Geology lab might be earned by visiting a fossil bed and searching for fossils. Students might photograph the rock formations where the fossils were found, identify the type of rock in which the fossils were found, and identify the types of fossils therein. Brief descriptions or notations about why and how fossils were found in this type of geological structure might be included. All of this information would then be assembled into a lab report.

An Environmental Science lab might include similar notations about discoveries made in a pond ecosystem, including a description and photographs of the pond, plant and animal aquatic life, and conclusions as to how and why those particular plants and animals live in that environment.

In essence, no matter which science courses are chosen, students will devote at least 20 hours of class time to lab work—that is, hands-on projects, exploration, and conclusions about what the student learned—which will be documented in a hard-copy notebook or portfolio.

Parents might also double-check with colleges to which students might apply to determine whether or not there are lab requirements.

Please also note that students who enroll in science classes at local colleges gain those lab credits while simultaneously earning both high school and college credit.

Book List:

S, B=Atomic Energy: Merit Badge Series

S=Basic Physics: A Self-Teaching Guide [Wiley Self-Teaching Guides], Karl Kuhn

S, TM, OI, V/DVD=Conceptual Physics, Paul Hewitt—Pearson Prentice Hall

S=CRC Handbook of Chemistry and Physics, David Lide

C=Experiences in Physics, Mark Julicher—Homeschool Science Press [physics lab for homeschool]

S, TM, S, CP, T/AK=SAXON Physics [CHC]

S, T/AK=Physics—Cliff's

S, T/AK=E-Z Physics—Barron's

Supplemental Reading:

C, V/DVD=The Reason: What Science Says about God, Fr. Robert Spitzer, S.J., Ph.D [CHC]

S, V/DVD=Einstein's Relativity and the Quantum Revolution: Modern Physics for Non-Scientists=The Great Courses

S=Hands-On Physics Activities with Real-Life Applications: Easy-to-Use Labs and Demonstrations for Grades 8-12, James Cunningham

S, AK=AP Physics—Barron's

C=The Reason Series: What Science Says about God, Fr. Robert Spitzer, S.J., Ph.D

Madame Curie: A Biography, Eve Curie

S, V/DVD=Physics—Standard Deviants

C=Scientist and Catholic: An Essay on Pierre Duhem, Fr. Stanley Jaki, O.S.B.

S=Six Easy Pieces: Essentials of Physics Explained by Its Most Brilliant Teacher, Richard Feynman

S=*The Flying Circus of Physics*, Jearl Walker

C=*The Science Before Science*, Art Rizzi

S=*Turning the World Inside Out and 174 Other Simple Physics Demonstrations*, Robert Erlich

Links:

www.spsnational.org—Society of Physics Students

http://vaticanobservatory.org—Vatican Observatory, Tucson

www.conceptualphysics.com

www.cpepweb.org/—Contemporary Physics Education Project

http://csee.lbl.gov/—Center for Science and Engineering Education

www.aavso.org/education/vsa—Hands-On Astrophysics

www.lbl.gov/abc/—ABC's of nuclear science

www.nrao.edu/—National Radio Astronomy Observatory

www.physics.uoguelph.ca/tutorials/ohm/index.html—electricity

http://scienceworld.wolfram.com/physics—World of Physics

www.physicsclassroom.com

http://www.ipl.org/div/subject/—Internet Public Library

Church Teaching:

C=www.newadvent.org/cathen—Catholic encyclopedia

C=www.catholic-pages.com/—Catholic documents and teaching, current events, more

C=www.zenit.org/en—Vatican news; recent and archived Papal/Church statements

Compendium of the Social Doctrine of the Church, Pontifical Council for Justice and Peace

Possible Essay Topics:

• Read #457 of the *Compendium of the Social Doctrine of the Church.* As scientific knowledge advances, so too, does man's responsibility to use that knowledge 'according to the design and will of God, to humanity's true good.' In what ways do you see that the study of Physics might fit God's design for the good of humanity?

Research:

You may, in conjunction with your text and field work, wish to investigate the following physics-related careers in greater depth. Credit may be obtained through reading and hands-on, experiential learning including field trips to labs and science museums, and volunteering. Learning is demonstrated through the production of projects, experiments, essays or reports. Reports may be based on note-taking and observation and might include graphs, charts, illustrations and diagrams. Find out more about these professions:

• atmospheric scientist
• bio-engineer
• chemical engineer
• computer scientist
• electrical engineer
• forensic scientist
• geophysicist
• mechanical engineer
• nuclear physicist
• nuclear reactor operator

Famous Names Related to the Science of Physics: Read and Report

In what ways did the Catholic Church aid in discoveries/inventions/advancement?

How did the person's faith [or lack thereof] influence his/her work?

What might have motivated the person to become involved in the field?

In what ways did his/her discoveries/inventions/advancement change the field of study?

In what ways did his/her discoveries/inventions/advancement ultimately change society?

Andre-Marie Ampere [devout Catholic]

Archimedes

Pierre and Marie Curie [both homeschooled]

Albert Einstein [homeschooled]

Michael Faraday

Enrico Fermi

Steven Hawking

Fr. Stanley Jaki, O.S.B.

Theodore Maiman

Isaac Newton

Wilhelm Roentgen

Carlo Rubbia

William Shockley

Samuel Ting

Experiential Learning/Career and Vocational Bridge:

[See Table of Contents for *Experiential Learning: Discovery Centers*]

[See Table of Contents for *Process Project Outline* projects.]

PSYCHOLOGY

S, T/AK=*Developmental Psychology*, George Zquorides—Cliff's [194 pages]

S, T/AK=*E-Z Psychology*, Nancy Melucci—Barron's

S=*What's Going on in There?: How the Brain and Mind Develop in the First Five Years of Life*, Lise Eliot [child psychology]

Supplemental Reading:

C=*Arise from Darkness: When Life Doesn't Make Sense*, Fr. Benedict Groeschel, C.F.R.

C=*Discipline That Lasts a Lifetime*, Dr. Ray Guarendi [child development]

NCC=*Day Care Deception: What the Child Care Establishment Isn't Telling Us*, Brian Robertson

S=*King Solomon's Ring: New Light on Animal Ways*, Konrad Lorenz

C=*Feeling and Healing Your Emotions*, Dr. Conrad Baars

S=*Psychopathology of Everyday Life*, Sigmund Freud

C=*Stumbling Blocks or Stepping Stones: Spiritual Answers to Psychological Questions*, Fr. Benedict Groeschel, C.F.R.

C=*The Cross and the Beatitudes: Lessons on Love and Forgiveness*, Archbishop Fulton J. Sheen

Links:

C=www.catholiceducation.org—orthodox Catholic writers; excellent resource for psychology articles [see 'Culture and Civilization']

C=www.guidetopsychology.com/catholic.htm—Catholic psychology

C=www.cathmed.org—Catholic Medical Association, some articles on psychological issues

C=www.guidetopsychology.com/be_psy.htm—information on becoming a psychologist

C=http://ipsciences.edu—Institute for Psychological Science

www.muskingum.edu/~psych/psycweb/history.htm—History of Psychology—bios of famous names and pioneers in the field of psychology; some theory

http://brainconnection.positscience.com

http://www.ipl.org/div/subject/—Internet Public Library

Church Teaching:

C=www.newadvent.org/cathen—Catholic encyclopedia

C=www.catholic-pages.com/—Catholic documents and teaching, current events, more

C=www.zenit.org/en—Vatican news; recent and archived Papal/Church statements

The Christian Family in the Modern World [*Familiaris consortio*], Documents of Vatican II, Vol. 2

On the Christian Meaning of Human Suffering [*Salvifici Doloris*], Pope John Paul II, apostolic letter

CCC #1500-1505; 2221

Possible Essay Topics:

• 'The role of parents in education is of such importance that it is almost impossible to provide an adequate substitute. The right and the duty of parents to educate their children are primordial and inalienable.' [*CCC* #2221]

Research and write about the effects of day care on children vs. children whose 'primary caregivers' are their own parents. [One possible search aid: www.highbeam.com—e.g., search 'negative effects of childcare' or www.cato.org/research/early-childhood]

• Read *On the Christian Meaning of Human Suffering*, particularly Section VII. "Everyone who stops beside the suffering of another person, whatever form it may take, is a Good Samaritan. The stopping does not mean curiosity but availability. It is like the opening of a certain interior disposition of the heart...'Good Samaritan' fits every individual who is sensitive to the sufferings of others..." In what ways might Christian compassion be actively expressed through psychology?

• '...a man is called upon to ensure the harmonious and united development of all the members of the family: he will perform this task by exercising generous responsibility for the life conceived under the heart of the mother...and by means of the witness he gives of an adult Christian life which effectively introduces the children into the living experience of Christ and the Church.' [*The Christian Family in the Modern World*, #25] Research the psychological impact on children raised in homes with fathers and without. In your essay, quote from the document cited, above. [You may wish to read the entire document.]

• 'Illness can lead to anguish, self-absorption, sometimes even despair...It can also make a person more mature, helping him discern in his life what is not essential so that he can turn toward that which is.' [*CCC* #1501] Contrast these two reactions to illness and discuss the role that a Catholic psychologist might play in helping the patient move from the first state of mind to the second.

• Given the opportunity, what dreams do you have for a future in psychology? List your dreams, plans, and goals. Arrange them in order of 'attack.' Outline steps toward their achievement. Write about your dream.

Research:

You may, in conjunction with your text and field work, wish to investigate the following topics in greater depth. Credit may be obtained through reading and hands-on, experiential learning; as you research and learn about conditioning, you may think of experiments to conduct with pets or siblings. Be sure to present your ideas to your parents before conducting experiments! Observe, take notes, and report.

- classical conditioning
    - conditioned response
    - conditioned stimulus
    - unconditioned response
    - unconditioned stimulus
- operant conditioning
    - positive reinforcer
    - negative reinforcer
    - avoidance behavior
    - primary reinforcer
    - timing of reinforcement
        - continuous reinforcement
        - intermittent reinforcement

Research illness and treatments:
    aversion therapy
    desensitization therapy

    bipolar
    depression
    obsessive-compulsive disorder
    phobias
    schizophrenia

Famous Names Related to Psychology: Read and Report

    Konrad Lorenz

    Ivan Pavlov

    B.F. Skinner

    Edward Thorndike

Experiential Learning/Career and Vocational Bridge:

[See Table of Contents for *Process Project Outline* and *Following in Their Footsteps* projects.]

Psychology Projects:
- With other Catholic homeschoolers, organize a 'Mom's Day Out.' Set a time and location, then provide an afternoon of activities for children from ages 3-8. [This might be done in conjunction with a parish mission or retreat to provide babysitting; students seeking Family Management or Psychology credit could provide care while observing the under-3 age group.] Create art or craft projects, music/songs, physical activities and games, cooking, or hobby demonstrations that can be used to teach the Faith to young children.
- Find out about early childhood development. Websearch 'developmental milestones children' or log on to:

    www.ldonline.org/article/6313

    www.health.state.ny.us/publications/0527

    www.firstsigns.org/healthydev/milestones.htm

    www.mhmrabv.org/early-childhood-intervention

At what age should a child be able to:
    —speak in three to five word sentences
    —walk alone
    —drink from a cup
    —recognize pictures of objects and respond appropriately, e.g., 'moo' at a picture of a cow
    —recite simple rhymes and say the blessing before meals
    —wave good-bye
    —put two blocks in a 'stack'
    —reach for and grasp objects

—point to eyes, nose, ears, mouth, and hair on command
—identify circles, squares, and triangles
—identify at least one color
—tell his first and last name
—sit alone
—count to five
—say three or four individual words
—respond to her name
—follow simple commands like 'Please bring me the spoon.'
—lift his head and chest when lying on his stomach
—speak in two-word sentences like 'want down' or 'more milk.'
—understand simple prepositions like 'under,' 'over,' 'behind,' 'on'
—babble
—pull himself up to a standing position on furniture

• If you gather information on early childhood development, you may wish to arrange your findings in chronological order and/or chart, then compose age-appropriate tests based on your findings. Contact parents with children in those age groups and ask permission to test and observe. Find out how many hours of television children in your test group are allowed to watch each day. Find out how frequently children are read to, and for what length of time. Remember that not all children reach every milestone at the same time!

• Find out, based on early childhood research, methods to provide a stimulating learning environment.

SCIENCE, GENERAL

Science Labs:

Labs essentially provide students an opportunity to test theories against reality, i.e., allow students to apply what they have learned from their texts in hands-on settings.

Most colleges don't require documented science labs as part of a high school science course. In fact, there is no national standard or definition of what exactly constitutes a high school science lab. However, since some colleges do require documented science lab work, it is best to include at least 20 hours of lab work in each science course that your student takes.

Keeping in mind that 'lab' means hands-on learning that applies book-learning to reality, credit for a Geology lab might be earned by visiting a fossil bed and searching for fossils. Students might photograph the rock formations where the fossils were found, identify the type of rock in which the fossils were found, and identify the types of fossils therein. Brief descriptions or notations about why and how fossils were found in this type of geological structure might be included. All of this information would then be assembled into a lab report.

An Environmental Science lab might include similar notations about discoveries made in a pond ecosystem, including a description and photographs of the pond, plant and animal aquatic life, and conclusions as to how and why those particular plants and animals live in that environment.

In essence, no matter which science courses are chosen, students will devote at least 20 hours of class time to lab work—that is, hands-on projects, exploration, and conclusions about what the student learned—which will be documented in a hard-copy notebook or portfolio.

Parents might also double-check with colleges to which students might apply to determine whether or not there are lab requirements.

Please also note that students who enroll in science classes at local colleges gain those lab credits while simultaneously earning both high school and college credit.

Book List:

Also see Astronomy, Biology, Botany, Chemistry, Earth Science, Environmental Science, Health, Meteorology, Midwifery, Physics

S, T/AK= *Conceptual Physical Science,* Paul Hewitt [CHC]

S, AK=*E-Z Earth Science*—Barron's

S, CP, T/AKA=*Essentials of Oceanography*—Prentice Hall

S, T/AK, B=*Pacemaker General Science*—Globe Fearon

S, T/AK=*Passage to General Science*—Globe Fearon

S, B=*Physical Science*—Student Text, AGS Secondary

Supplemental Reading:

C=*Adventures in Nature,* Edwin Way Teale

C=*Origin of the Human Species,* Dennis Bonnette

C=*Copernicus, Galileo, and the Catholic Sponsorship of Science,* Mary Daly [CHC]

C=*Creator and Creation,* Mary Daly [CHC]

C=*Darwin's Black Box,* Michael Behe

S=Discover Magazine—http://discovermagazine.com

S, B=Energy: Merit Badge Series

S=*Everyday Science Sourcebook,* Lawrence Lowery—homeschool-friendly science experiments

C=*Faith, Science, and Reason: Theology on the Cutting Edge,* Christopher Baglow [CHC]

C, V/DVD=*The Reason: What Science Says about God,* Fr. Robert Spitzer, S.J., Ph.D [CHC]

C=*God and the Atom,* Ronald Knox

S=*King Solomon's Ring,* Konrad Lorenz

S, B=Nature: Merit Badge Series

S, B=Oceanography: Merit Badge Series

S=*Peterson's Field Guides* [insects, animals, minerals]

S, B=Plant Science: Merit Badge Series

S=*Popular Mechanics Magazine*

C=*Science and Evidence for Design in the Universe,* Michael Behe

C=*Science of Today and the Problems of Genesis,* Fr. Patrick O'Connell

S=*Scientific American Magazine*—www.scientificamerican.com

S=*The Anatomy Coloring Book,* Wynn Kapit

The Dancing Bees, Karl Von Frisch

NCC=*The Flood: In the Light of the Bible, Geology, and Archaeology,* Alfred Rehwinkel

C=*The Life of the Fly,* John Henri Fabre

C=*The Limits of a Limitless Science,* Fr. Stanley Jaki, O.S.B.

C=*The Science Before Science,* Art Rizzi

S, V/DVD=*Understanding the Universe: An Introduction to Astronomy*—The Great Courses

Links:

1,200 page, free science supplies catalog!—www.wardsci.com—Ward's Natural Science—1-800-962-2660

C=www.catholiceducation.org—orthodox Catholic writers; excellent resource for science articles

http://education.jlab.org/indexpages/index.html—all about elements and atoms, games and puzzles http://education.usgs.gov/common/secondary.htm—geologic maps, fossils, minerals; excellent

www.enchantedlearning.com/Home.html—printables: maps, geology, anatomy, astronomy, botany, more

www.eyeofscience.de—scientific photography; microscopic world: botany, zoology, etc.

http://junkscience.com—scientific evidence challenging global warming, etc.

http://scienceandpublicpolicy.org

www.worldclimatereport.com

www.khanacademy.org—science tutorials

www.nsf.gov—National Science Foundation

www.soinc.org—Science Olympiad

www.rocketcontest.org—Team America Rocketry Contest

www.exploravision.org—Toshiba Exploravision

www.bestinc.org—robotics

http://bridgecontest.usma.edu/index.htm—West Point Bridge Design Contest

www.discoveryeducation.com/teachers/—free lessons and lesson plans for astronomy, space, earth science, life science, animals, ecology, human body, microscopic world, plants, physical science, technology, weather

www.wunderground.com/satellite/vis/1k/US.html—U.S. and international satellite images, updated every 20 min.

http://ww2010.atmos.uiuc.edu/(Gh)/guides/mtr/home.rxml

http://www.ipl.org/div/subject/—Internet Public Library

Church Teaching:

C=www.newadvent.org/cathen—Catholic encyclopedia

C=www.catholic-pages.com—Catholic documents and teaching, current events, more

C=www.zenit.org/en—Vatican news; recent and archived Papal/Church statements

Humani Generis, Pope Pius XII

Statement on Evolution, Pope John Paul II, Address to Pontifical Academy of Sciences, 1997

Possible Essay Topics:

• Scientific and technological advancements have led some to the conclusion that science has the answer to every question and human need. Some would go so far as to say that anything that can't be proven scientifically to exist, must not have existence. Is scientific reasoning the only form of reasoning, or scientific measurement the only valid measurement? Does not even science require a faith in the unseen, the unknown, the unmeasurable? How does one measure anguish, love, self sacrifice, or holiness? Read the encyclical letter of Pope John Paul II, *Fides et Ratio*. Discuss the complementary balance of science and reason in light of the statement, 'Faith and reason are like two wings on which the human spirit rises to the contemplation of truth.' [It is suggested that the student purchase *Fides et Ratio*, available from the Daughters of St. Paul and elsewhere, rather than attempting to read it online.]

• Read *Humani Generis* and/or *Statement on Evolution*. Just what does the Church teach about evolution and the origins of man? Summarize the document/s and report.

• 'Science and its technical applications offer new and immense possibilities...Still, as a consequence of political choices that decide the direction of research and its applications, science is often used against its original purpose, which is *the advancement of the human person.*' [*The Christian Family in the Modern World*] Brainstorm three specific ways that scientific developments could advance humanity, and three ways that scientific development has harmed or could harm humanity. Compare and contrast.

Research:

You may, in conjunction with your text and field work, wish to investigate select science topics in greater depth. See: Astronomy, Biology, Botany, Earth Science, Health, Meteorology, Midwifery, Physics, and their subtopics. First, decide which of these branches of science, in addition to General Science, you are likely to study for your three or four high school science credits. From each of the remaining categories of science, select *at least* three topics to investigate. [E.g., Astronomy: solar flares, Milky Way, natural satellites; Biology: Anatomy: nervous system, heart & circulation, digestive system.] Be sure to check related websites listed with the courses you choose.

Credit may be obtained through reading and hands-on, experiential learning including field trips, volunteering, and apprenticeships. Learning is demonstrated through the production of projects, experiments, essays or reports. Reports may be based on note-taking and observation and might include graphs, charts, illustrations and diagrams.

Famous Names Related to Science: Read and Report

In what ways did the Catholic Church aid in discoveries/inventions/ advancement?

How did the person's faith [or lack thereof] influence his/her work?

What might have motivated the person to become involved in the field?

In what ways did his/her discoveries/ inventions/advancement change the field of study?

In what ways did his/her discoveries/ inventions/advancement ultimately change society?

Andre-Marie Ampere—physics [devout Catholic]
Archimedes—physics, mathematics
St. Albert the Great—astronomy, biology, chemistry, zoology
Benjamin Banneker—astronomy
Antoine Henri Becquerel—radioactivity
Alexander Graham Bell—electronics [homeschooled]
Robert Boyle—chemistry
George Washington Carver—botany [homeschooled]
Nicolaus Copernicus—astronomy
Pierre and Marie Curie—radioactivity
Baron Cuvier—anatomy
Thomas Edison—electronics [homeschooled]
Albert Einstein—atomic theory
Michael Faraday—chemistry, physics
Enrico Fermi—physics
Alexander Fleming—bacteriology
Luigi Galvani—anatomy, medical research [devout Catholic]
Edmond Halley—astronomy
Stanley Jaki, O.S.B.—physics
Edward Jenner—medicine
Robert Koch—bacteriology
Shibasaburo Kitasato—bacteriology
Antoine Lavoisier—chemistry [devout Catholic]
Anton van Leeuwenhoek—microbiology
Carolus Linnaeus—botany, biology
Joseph Lister—medicine

Guglielemo Marconi—electricity
[homeschooled]
Fr. Gregor Mendel—botany
Maria Mitchell—astronomy
Isaac Newton—physics
Marshall Nirenberg—genetics, biochemistry
Louis Pasteur—chemistry and microbiology
Wilhelm Roentgen—physics
Helen Brooke Taussig—medicine
Mary Walker—Civil War physician
[homeschooled]
Andreas Vesalius—anatomy

Experiential Learning/Career and Vocational Bridge:

[See Table of Contents for *Process Project Outline* and *Following in Their Footsteps* projects.]

General Science Projects:

• Grow a plant or raise an animal to show in the county fair.

• Map or chart tsunami damage in the historical record. Include dates, location, and magnitude. In which oceans do most tsunamis occur?

www.tsunami.noaa.gov

• Build a solar system model and give a presentation to a homeschooling group.

www.noao.edu/education/peppercorn/pcmain.html

www.exploratorium.edu/ronh/solar_system

• Find out about Newton's Third Law of Motion. Build and launch a model rocket. Compose a brief written explanation of the ways that the rocket demonstrates Newton's Third Law.

• Visit a Marine Science Center or Sanctuary. Find out which marine animals are studied or protected there and why. If the animals are considered to be endangered, are they found in any other areas outside this particular sanctuary?

• Start an herb garden, planting herbs beneficial to health. Press and dry samples of each herb in a notebook. Label herbs by scientific name, common name, and list health benefits of each.

• Track volcanic activity for three months. Note whether the activity is from a shield, composite, or cinder cone volcano. How does volcanic action differ amongst the different types of volcanoes? [http://volcano.oregonstate.edu]; chart or graph activity.

• Practice the Corporal Works of Mercy. Find out about illnesses and conditions common to the elderly and how those conditions are treated. Volunteer with adult day care/geriatrics.

• Track earthquake activity for three months. Select three specific countries/regions to track; chart or graph activity.

http://earthquake.usgs.gov/earthquakes/map/

www.iris.edu/seismon

• Find out about the role of food groups in a healthful diet. Draw, or create on the computer, a chart, graph, wheel or other illustration that displays each food group. Portray in the illustration/chart the percentages of each group needed to equal a balanced diet.

• Research and compile a list of weather conditions and signs, including unusual cloud formations, that could signal a developing tornado. If possible, illustrate. Create a booklet that would be suitable for distribution.

SOCIAL PROBLEMS TODAY

NCC=*Answering Islam: The Crescent in Light of the Cross,* Norman Geisler

S=*Barbarians Inside the Gates and Other Controversial Essays,* Thomas Sowell

S=*Black Rednecks and White Liberals,* Thomas Sowell

C=*Collected Works of Chesterton Vol. IV: What's Wrong With the World, Superstition of Divorce, Eugenics and Other Evils*—Ignatius

S=*Population and Development in Poor Countries,* Julian Simon

C=*Population Control,* Eamonn Keane [myths of overpopulation]

S=*Race and Culture: A World View,* Thomas Sowell

S=*The Economic Consequences of Immigration,* Julian Simon

C=*The Human Person: Dignity Beyond Compare,* Sr. Terese Auer, O.P. [CHC]

C=*Called to Happiness: Guiding Ethical Principles,* Sr. Terese Auer, O.P. [CHC]

S=*The True State of the Planet,* Ronald Bailey

S=*The Ultimate Resource,* Julian Simon [pollution, population and continuing availability of resources]

C=*The War Against Population: The Economics and Ideology of World Population Control,* Dr. Jacqueline Kasun—Ignatius

C=*Ungodly Rage,* Donna Steichen [feminism]—Ignatius

C=*What's Wrong With the World,* G.K. Chesterton—Ignatius

Links:

www.acton.org/public-policy—poverty, environment, economics

C=www.all.org—American Life League, topical index, end of life care, euthanasia, eugenics, fetal development, stem cell research

C=www.catholiceducation.org— orthodox Catholic writers; excellent resource for articles on current topics including population growth, feminism, animal rights, modern-day persecution of Christians, abortion, euthanasia, and more

C=www.catholic-pages.com—articles on the myth of overpopulation, life issues, social concerns, feminism

C=www.catholic-pages.com/dir/culture_ wars.asp—articles about anti-Christian bias in today's culture

www.cato.org/research—numerous current topics: immigration, environment, health care, civil rights, welfare

C=www.catholicnews.com—Catholic News Service

www.cloninginformation.org

www.eppc.org—Ethics and Public Policy Center, established in 1976 to clarify and reinforce the bond between the Judeo-Christian moral tradition and the public debate over domestic and foreign policy issues

www.hrw.org—Human Rights Watch, violations of human rights worldwide

C=www.lifeissues.net—excellent resource for life issues in the news; site in association with OMI

C=www.lifesitenews.com—daily news, current events; Canada, U.S., world

www.naiaonline.org—'animal rights'

C=www.ncbcenter.org—National Catholic Bioethics Center, articles on medical ethics, some papal addresses

www.notdeadyet.org—disabled and disability advocates against euthanasia and anti-life legislation

www.pop.org—Population Research Institute—articles on the myth of overpopulation

C=www.priestsforlife.org—life issues, abortion, euthanasia, etc.

C=www.vatican.va—Church documents

C=www.vatican.va/news_services—Vatican News Services

C=www.wf-f.org/MedicalMoral.html—Women for Faith and Family—search for feminism, other current topics

http://www.ipl.org/div/subject/ —Internet Public Library

Church Teaching:

C=www.newadvent.org/cathen—Catholic encyclopedia

C=www.catholic-pages.com—Catholic documents and teaching, current events, more

C=www.zenit.org/en—Vatican news; recent and archived Papal/Church statements

Atheistic Communism [Divini Redemptoris], Pope Pius XI

Declaration on Euthanasia [Iura et Bona], Congregation for the Doctrine of the Faith

Letter to the Bishops of the Catholic Church on the Collaboration of Men and Women in the Church and in the

World Of Human Life, Congregation for the Doctrine of the Faith

Humanae Vitae, Pope Paul VI

Instruction: "The Love of Christ Towards Migrants," Pontifical Council for the Pastoral Care of Migrants & Itinerant People, May, 2004 [see zenit. org/english]

On the Condition of the Working Classes [Rerum Novarum], Pope Leo XIII

On the Development of Peoples [Populorum Progressio], Pope Paul VI

On Human Work [Laborem Exercens], Pope John Paul II

On the Hundredth Anniversary of Rerum Novarum [Centesimus Annus], Pope John Paul II

On Social Reconstruction [Quadragesimo Anno], Pope Piux XI

The Church and Racism, Pontifical Council for Justice and Peace

We Remember: A Reflection on the Shoah, Pontifical Commission for Religious Relations with the Jews

CCC #2241, 2270-2279, 2295

Possible Essay Topics/Research:

• Research the myth of overpopulation. In what ways has Malthus been proved wrong? Document incidents demonstrating that war, deliberate governmental starvation of ethnic populations, and misguided governmental policies are the primary causes of 'global hunger.' See Genesis 1:28. Could an omniscient God have miscalculated the ability of His earth to feed His children?

• Research and evaluate the opinion that the world's resources are limited. [See **Links**]

• 'Experimentation on human beings is not morally legitimate if it exposes the subject's life or physical and psychological integrity to disproportionate or avoidable risks. Experimentation on human beings does not conform to the dignity of the person if it takes place without the informed consent of the subject or those who legitimately speak for him.' [CCC #2295] Would it be legitimate to conduct medical experiments, that would result in the death of the individual, on newborn infants? On premature infants? From biological and spiritual standpoints, it is understood that human life begins at conception, so there is therefore no moral difference in regard to the age of the human being who is the object of experimentation. What then should be the attitude of the Catholic toward cloning and embryonic stem cell research, in light of CCC #2295?

• Research and write about 21st century persecution of Christians in Sudan, China, East Timor, and Saudi Arabia. To get you started, see www.catholiceducation.org and enter 'persecution of Christians' in the search box. Also see www.zenit.org/article-4369?l=english.

• Read The Church and Racism, a curial document from the Pontifical Council for Justice and Peace. [See www.catholic-pages.com] Research the contributions of 16th century priest and bishop, Bartolome de Las Casas, O.P., in defense of native peoples. Discuss and enumerate the consistent teaching of the Church, reflecting Gal. 3:28.

• Research and write about 'politically correct speech' and 'hate crimes' legislation being used to curb the free speech and actions of Christians in Canada and the United States.

• '...prosperous nations are obliged...to welcome the foreigner in search of the security and the means of livelihood which he cannot find in his country of origin.' [CCC #2241] Most North American citizens are descendents of immigrants. Immigrants tend to be young, motivated, and contribute to strengthening the societies to which they immigrate. Research the history and impact of immigration and write about what you have learned. [E.g., see—www.acton.org/public-policy and www.cato.org/research]

• Is it possible for mankind to have dominion over the earth and subdue it, without destroying the environment? What is the 'Cornwall Declaration'? Read the Declaration and summarize. Does the Declaration's approach address environmental concerns in a balanced manner? Discuss. [E.g., see—www.acton.org/public-policy]

• Assisted suicide was legalized in Oregon in 1997; similar legislation has been proposed in other states and Canadian provinces. Discuss compassionate care alternatives that would provide the terminally ill with a dignified and peaceful end to life and joyous entrance into eternity. [E.g., see—www.all.org and www.pccef.org—Physicians for Compassionate Care Educational Foundation]

• Research the Church's teaching on vitro fertilization and the medical and moral complications involved with the procedure. What might be some other options for childless couples who desire the blessing of children? [Read The Christian Family in the Modern World, Documents of Vatican II, Vol. 2, #14; also see— www.all.org]

• Compendium of the Social Doctrine of the Church [#208] addresses the question of poverty: 'It is undoubtedly an act of love, the work of mercy by which one responds here and now to a real and impelling need of one's neighbor, but it is an equally indispensable act of love to strive to organize and structure society so that one's neighbor will not find himself in poverty...' How might changing societal conditions that lead to poverty ultimately be a greater good than simply addressing immediate needs of food and clothing? List some moral or other conditions that lead to poverty, e.g, single parenthood, drug abuse, lack of education or job skills, and discuss means to eliminate these conditions. What role might Catholics take in instituting these changes?

Experiential Learning/Career and Vocational Bridge:

See Table of Contents for *Process Project Outline* and *Following in Their Footsteps* projects.]

Social Problems Projects:

• *Compendium of the Social Doctrine of the Church* [#208] addresses the social problem of poverty. Find out about, and volunteer with, outreaches to the poor in your area. Contact your parish or diocesan offices for diocesan service agencies and apostolates, or contact orders that work with the disadvantaged by logging on to websites, below.

www.motherteresa.org/07_family/ Volunteering/v_cal.html—Missionaries of Charity

http://societyofourlady.net/laity. html—Society of Our Lady of the Most Holy Trinity

www.franciscanfriars.com—Franciscan Friars of the Renewal

• What programs does your parish/diocese offer for migrant assistance? Contact your diocesan office of migrant concerns and find out about volunteer opportunities.
• Volunteer at a parish or diocesan food pantry.
• Lack of education is one cause of poverty. Volunteer with an after-school or summer tutoring program.
• A society is only as safe as its weakest member; if any one citizen is judged 'disposable' or 'unworthy' of life, no citizen is safe. [What greater social problem can there be than society's murder of its own members?] In what ways can you support Christ in the disguise of the 'disabled'? Inquire about parishioners who are caring for family members with Alzheimer's, or severely disabled children. Offer your services: help with shopping, meal preparation, or in-home care. 'As you did it to one of the least of these my brethren, you did it to me.'
• Volunteer in, or make visits to, Veteran's Hospitals that serve disabled veterans.

Books, videos, and websites listed as references for the courses in this volume are not 'recommended' or 'preferred,' but rather widely used options from which to choose, depending on the intended field of study, educational goals, and the mental and spiritual maturity of the student.

SPEECH

S, T/AKA=*Going Public: A Practical Guide to Public Talk,* Virginia Richmond

S, T/DVD=*Introduction to Policy Debate,* Christy Shipe [CHC]

S, B=Public Speaking: Merit Badge Series

S, V/DVD=Public Speaking—Standard Deviants

S=*The Complete Book of Speech Communication: A Workbook of Ideas and Activities for Students of Speech and Theatre,* Carol Marrs and Lafe Locke

Links:

www.ncfca.org—National Christian Forensics and Communications Association

www.ja.org/—Junior Achievement—hands-on business and economics

www.toastmasters.org/—Toastmasters International—public speaking for leadership, business

http://www.ipl.org/div/subject/ —Internet Public Library

Possible Speech Topics:

Use **Essay Topics** from *Social Problems Today* and other courses in this volume to develop speaking topics.

Experiential Learning/Career and Vocational Bridge:

Speech Projects:
• Memorize poetry, a dramatic selection, or a musical piece for presentation at a retirement or nursing home.
• Volunteer with a local political party.
• Join Toastmasters International for public speaking and leadership opportunities.
• Research speech contests with local, state, and national Right to Life Committees, American Legion, civic groups.
• Study stages of fetal development and create a five-minute teaching presentation. Borrow fetal models and speak to a youth group. Include references to Ps. 139:13-16 and other Church teaching.
• Assist in teaching an elementary level CCD class.
• Volunteer as a teacher's aide in a public or private school classroom.
• Organize a group of homeschooled students and jointly select a topic for debate. You may wish to draw straws and assign half of the participants to take the opposing side of the topic. Set time limitations for presenting speeches; allow time for a rebuttal. [Suggested times: four or five minutes to present; two minutes for challenge from the opponent; two minutes for the original speaker to rebut the challenge.] If desired, judges might be appointed and a contest made of the debate.
• Demonstrate a hobby, craft, or school project, e.g., quilting, model aircraft, fossil and mineral collection, to a homeschool group, nursing or retirement home, day care, nursery or elementary school.

THEOLOGY

C=*A Map of Life*, F.J. Sheed—Ignatius

C, TM, T/AK=*Didache High School Religion Series* [CHC]

> Introduction to Catholicism [9th gr.]
>
> Understanding the Scriptures [10th gr.]
>
> The History of the Church [11th gr.]
>
> Our Moral Life in Christ [12th gr.]

C=*YOUCAT: Youth Catechism of the Catholic Church* [CHC]

C=*Introduction to the Bible, High School Religion Series*, Fr. John Laux—TAN

C, T, V/DVD=*LifeWork: Finding Your Purpose in Life*, Rick Sarkisian, Ph.D. [CHC]

C=*The Adoremus Bulletin*—current issues in the Church—www.adoremus.org

C=*The Faith Explained*, Fr. Leo J. Trese [CHC]

C=*The Human Person: Dignity Beyond Compare*, Sr. Terese Auer, O.P. [CHC]

C=*Called to Happiness: Guiding Ethical Principles*, Sr. Terese Auer, O.P. [CHC]

C=*Theology for Beginners*, F.J. Sheed

C=*Theology of the Body for Beginners*, Christopher West

C=*Voices*—magazine published by Women for Faith and Family—www.wf-f.org

C, V/DVD=*Catholicism Youth Pilgrimage*, Fr. Robert Barron [CHC]

Links:

http://www.newmanconnection.com/institute/courses/exploring-youcat—Exploring YOUCAT

C=www.newmanconnection.com/institute/courses/rich-gift-of-love—Theology of the Body course

C=www.catholic.com—the Catholic Faith

C=www.catholicfirst.com/index.cfm—Catholic Information Center—Search the Catechism, Early Church Fathers

C=www.catechismclass.com

C=www.vatican.va—Church documents

C=www.clairval.com/sample.en.php—saint biographies

Church Teaching:

C=www.adoremus.org —Church documents

C=www.newadvent.org/cathen —Catholic encyclopedia

C=www.catholic-pages.com —Catholic documents and teaching, current events, more

C=www.zenit.org/en—Vatican news; recent and archived Papal/Church statements

Reconciliation and Penance In the Mission of the Church Today [Reconciliatio et Paenitentia], Pope John Paul II

Letter to the Bishops of the Catholic Church on the Collaboration of Men and Women in the Church and in the World of Human Life, Congregation for the Doctrine of the Faith

CCC #841-848, 1691-1698

Possible Essay Topics:

• How different our lives would be had Adam and Eve not fallen. Why, had there been no Fall, there might have been no need for high school at all! Brainstorm the effects of original sin and discuss.

• What is meant by the Church's statement, 'Outside the Church there is no salvation'? Read *CCC* # 841-848, paying special attention to #846. According to this document, do the faithful still have an obligation to bring those outside the Church to the fullness of the Truth? Outline the main points of these paragraphs from the *CCC* and expound on Church teaching. Write as if to explain the teaching to a non-Catholic.

• What are the fruits of the Holy Spirit? Discuss the great graces from, and necessity for, the Sacrament of Confirmation.

• Aren't there many paths to God? If so, does it really matter to which church we belong? Find out about the sin of indifferentism and answer these questions.

• Explain the two great privileges that Our Lord granted His beloved Mother: her Immaculate Conception and Assumption.

• What is the difference between a vice and actual sin? Discuss and explain the seven capital sins, or vices.

Experiential Learning/Career and Vocational Bridge:

[See Table of Contents for *Experiential Learning: Shrines*]
[See Table of Contents for *Process Project Outline* and *Following in Their Footsteps* projects.]

Theology Projects:

• Volunteer your services as an aide with your parish catechetical program.
• Visit a shrine in your area. If distance permits, volunteer there.

TYPING

S=*Mastering Computer Typing: A Painless Course for Beginners and Professionals*, Sheryl Roberts

S=www.bbc.co.uk/schools/typing—free online typing program

Experiential Learning/Career and Vocational Bridge:

• Volunteer as a parish office aide.
• Volunteer as an aide in your parochial school office.

Do you begin to tremble at the specter of teaching Chemistry or Biology, particularly to the college-bound student? There are options!

VOCATIONS

C=*A Map of Life,* F.J. Sheed—Ignatius

C=*An Introduction to the Devout Life,* St. Francis de Sales

C=*'...And You Are Christ's': The Charism of Virginity and the Celibate Life,* Fr. Thomas Dubay—Ignatius

C=*A Right to Be Merry,* Mother Mary Francis, P.C.C.

C=Completely Christ's—DVD about consecrated life by those living it [http://lifeworkpress.stores.yahoo.net]

C=*Dark Night of the Soul,* St. John of the Cross

C=*Forth and Abroad,* Mother Mary Francis, P.C.C.—Ignatius

C, T, V/DVD=*LifeWork: Finding Your Purpose in Life,* Rick Sarkisian, Ph.D. [CHC]

C, T/TM, AK=*Our Moral Life in Christ: The Didache Series* [CHC]

C=*Religious Life Magazine*—published by Institute on Religious Life [http://religiouslife.com]

C=*Self-Abandonment to Divine Providence,* Jean-Pierre de Caussade

C=*The Faith Explained,* Fr. Leo Trese [CHC]

C=*The Meaning of Vocation in the Words of Pope John Paul II*—Scepter Publishers

C=*The Three Ages of the Interior Life,* Fr. Garrigou-Lagrange, O.P.

C=*The Training of the Will,* Fr. Johann Lindworsky, S.J.

Links:

http://laymc.bizland.com—Lay Missionaries of Charity

www.religiouslife.com—Institute on Religious Life, communities and orders faithful to the Holy Father and Magisterium

Church Teaching:

C=www.adoremus.org—Church documents

C=www.newadvent.org/cathen—Catholic encyclopedia

C=www.catholic-pages.com/—Catholic documents and teaching, current events, more

C=www.zenit.org/en—Vatican news; recent and archived Papal/Church statements

Consecrated Life [Vita Consecrata], Pope John Paul II

Instruction on the Contemplative Life and on the Enclosure of Nuns [Verbi Sponsa], Congregation for Institutes of Consecrated Life and for Societies of Apostolic Life

On Reserving Priestly Ordination to Men Alone [Ordinatio Sacerdotalis], Pope John Paul II

CCC #851, 1536-2012

Possible Essay Topics:

• Read *Ordinatio Sacerdotalis.* Why does the Church ordain men alone? Isn't this discrimination on the basis of gender? Isn't the Church a democracy? List reasons for the Church's—and Christ's—stance and expound. Quote from *Ordinatio Sacerdotalis* in your essay.

- Define and explain the difference among cloistered, contemplative, and active communities. Which life most appeals to you, and why?
- How do the lives of diocesan and ordered priests differ? Compare and contrast. If possible, interview both an ordered and diocesan priest.
- In what ways does the priesthood differ from Protestant ministerial service? Include in your essay discussion of sacramental differences, and the indelible spiritual character, conferred at priestly ordination, that is lacking in Protestant ordination. Read *CCC* #1536-2012 and reference in your paper.
- What is a secular institute? Write a short paper of explanation.

Experiential Learning/Career and Vocational Bridge:

[See Table of Contents for *Experiential Learning: Shrines*]
[See Table of Contents for *Process Project Outline* and *Following in Their Footsteps* projects.]

Vocations Projects:
- Find out about the Institute of Religious Life and its links to orthodox religious communities [www.religiouslife.com].
- Pray for direction; contact a religious community and arrange for a visit. Keep a journal of your holy adventure.
- Interview a priest, brother, or religious sister. When did he/she first realize that he/she had a vocation to the priesthood or religious life? In what way did his/her family contribute to their vocation? What method of discernment or preparation do they recommend?
- Write to a religious community and request more information about their charism or apostolate. When was this order founded, and by whom? Find out about the founder/foundress.

Men's Communities: [for a more extensive listing of orthodox communities, see www.religiouslife.com]

Fathers of Mercy—
   http://fathersofmercy.com
Franciscan Friars of the Renewal—www.franciscanfriars.com
Norbertines—www.stmichaelsabbey.com
Oblates of the Virgin Mary—www.omvusa.org
Oratorians—www.oratory-toronto.org
Society of Our Lady of the Most Holy Trinity—http://societyofourlady.net

Women's Communities: [for a more extensive listing of orthodox communities, see www.religiouslife.com]

Carmelite Sisters of the Divine Heart of Jesus—www.carmelitedcj.org
Carmelite Sisters of the Most Sacred Heart of Los Angeles—www.carmelitesistersocd.com
Dominican Sisters of Hawthorne—www.hawthorne-dominicans.org
Dominican Sisters of Mary, Mother of the Eucharist—www.sistersofmary.org
Fr. Kolbe Missionaries of the Immaculata—www.kolbemission.org
Little Sisters of the Poor—www.littlesistersofthepoor.org
Marian Sisters of Lincoln Diocese, NE—www.mariansisters.org
Parish Visitors of Mary Immaculate, Marycrest—www.parishvisitorsisters.org
Poor Clare Nuns, Our Lady of Guadalupe Monastery—www.poor-clares.org
Sisters of Life—www.sistersoflife.org

WILDLIFE SCIENCE

Science Labs:

Labs essentially provide students an opportunity to test theories against reality, i.e., allow students to apply what they have learned from their texts in hands-on settings.

Most colleges don't require documented science labs as part of a high school science course. In fact, there is no national standard or definition of what exactly constitutes a high school science lab. However, since some colleges do require documented science lab work, it is best to include at least 20 hours of lab work in each science course that your student takes.

Keeping in mind that 'lab' means hands-on learning that applies book-learning to reality, credit for a Geology lab might be earned by visiting a fossil bed and searching for fossils. Students might photograph the rock formations where the fossils were found, identify the type of rock in which the fossils were found, and identify the types of fossils therein. Brief descriptions or notations about why and how fossils were found in this type of geological structure might be included. All of this information would then be assembled into a lab report.

An Environmental Science lab might include similar notations about discoveries made in a pond ecosystem, including a description and photographs of the pond, plant and animal aquatic life, and conclusions as to how and why those particular plants and animals live in that environment.

In essence, no matter which science courses are chosen, students will devote at least 20 hours of class time to lab work—that is, hands-on projects, exploration, and conclusions about what the student learned—which will be documented in a hard-copy notebook or portfolio.

Parents might also double-check with colleges to which students might apply to determine whether or not there are lab requirements.

Please also note that students who enroll in science classes at local colleges gain those lab credits while simultaneously earning both high school and college credit.

Book List:

S=*Ecology and Field Biology,* Robert Smith

S=*Wildlife and Natural Resource Management,* Kevin Deal

S=*Wildlife Ecology and Management,* Eric Bolen

S=*Managing the White Tailed Deer*— http://store.im.tamu.edu/B-6227-Managing-the-White-Tailed-Deer-A-Wildlife-Management-Curriculum-for-High-School-P2763.aspx

Supplemental Reading:

S=*Peterson Field Guide to Animal Tracks,* Olaus Murie

S=*A Practical Guide for the Amateur Naturalist,* Gerald Durrell

S, B=Bird Study: Merit Badge Series

S= *Peterson Field Guide to Edible Wild Plants,* Lee Peterson

S, B=Fish and Wildlife Management: Merit Badge Series

S=*Fur Trapping in North America,* Steven M. Geary

S=*Journal of Wildlife Management,* published by The Wildlife Society, www.wildlife.org

S, B=Wilderness Survival: Merit Badge Series

www.deeranddeerhunting.com—magazine

www.trapperpredatorcaller.com—magazine

Links:

www.doleta.gov—apprenticeships by state, county, and occupation

C=www.catholiceducation.org—orthodox Catholic writers; excellent articles on environmental issues

www.ec.gc.ca—nature and wildlife, regulations, Canada

www.tcu.gov.on.ca/eng/employmentontario/training/

www.fws.gov—U.S. Fish and Wildlife Service

www.huntingpa.com—wildlife articles

www.invasivespeciesinfo.gov—invasive animals, plants, and control

http://icwdm.org/—research, damage, animal diseases, management

www.khake.com/page46.html—environmental, biology career guide, requirements

www.khake.com/page58.html—apprenticeship info, training resources, U.S. and Canada

www.naiaonline.org—National Animal Interest Alliance

www.nationaltrappers.com—National Trappers Association and *American Trapper Magazine*

www.raptorsinthecity.org

http://rurallivingcanada.4t.com—Rural Living in Canada

www.taxidermy101.com/—taxidermy home school courses, videos

www.taxidermy.net/—taxidermy information, magazines

http://technicaljobsearch.com/job_banks/apprenticeships.htm

www.usgs.gov/science.html—U.S. Geological Survey—wildlife links

http://www.ipl.org/div/subject/—Internet Public Library

Church Teaching:

C=www.newadvent.org/cathen—Catholic encyclopedia

C=www.catholic-pages.com/—Catholic documents and teaching, current events, more

C=www.zenit.org/en—Vatican news; recent and archived Papal/Church statements

Compendium of the Social Doctrine of the Church

CCC #340, 353, 2417

Possible Essay Topics:

• Select for study an animal or fowl that is common to your area. What is the history of the animal in your state? Does it have an 'unbroken' presence, or has the population been re-introduced after a period of decline? If the animal was re-introduced, how long ago? How has its population grown since that time? In what ways does habitat affect its feeding patterns? Does the animal feed primarily in undeveloped areas, on farmland or developed areas, or both? Has the animals' presence had an impact on human activity?

• 'God wills the interdependence of creatures... Creatures exist only in dependence on each other, to complete each other, in the service of each other.' Read *CCC #340*. Select for study two animals/birds that are predator and prey. Find out about their respective feeding habits. What role does camouflage play in their survival? What might be the effect if either predator or prey were eliminated? Discuss in your paper the interdependence of animals, the way they complete each other, and their different roles.

• Numerous states are struggling with the problem of deer over-population. What have been the causes of the overpopulation? How has this overpopulation affected agricultural production? In what ways has it affected the health of the deer themselves? What methods are states employing to reduce deer populations, and how effective have those measures been? Chart or graph populations, indicating the year that control measures were introduced.

[E.g., see http://www.naiaonline.org/articles/article/bambi-has-outgrown-the-forest-and-alternatives-for-control-are-elusive-inef]

• Which local animals may be listed as endangered? How are local/state regulations safeguarding the animal?

• Given the opportunity, what dreams do you have for a future in wildlife sciences? List your dreams, plans, and goals. Arrange them in order of 'attack.' Outline steps toward their achievement. Write about your dream.

Experiential Learning/Career and Vocational Bridge:

[See Table of Contents for *Process Project Outline* and *Following in Their Footsteps* projects.]

Wildlife Science Projects:

• Visit a taxidermist. What type of training did he/she access to learn the trade?

• Which animals are trapped in your state, and why? Are some of the animals nuisance animals, or disease carriers? Create a calendar that highlights trapping seasons; use a different color for each animal. Indicate briefly why each animal is trapped, e.g., to control disease or prevent overpopulation.

• Does your state or province's Division of Wildlife have programs for improving endangered species habitat? Find out and participate.

• Visit and volunteer at a fish hatchery.

• Peregrine falcons, once considered endangered in some locations, are now thriving in metropolitan areas. Falcon families nest on ledges of downtown office buildings from Toronto to Cleveland to Seattle, hunting and feasting on pigeons snatched from streets below. Find out about the rebounding populations of Peregrine falcons and measures that have successfully increased the numbers of this bird in North America. Document your findings and participate in local programs.

> www.njfishandwildlife.com/peregrinecam/
>
> www.dnr.state.oh.us/wildlife/dow/falcons/columbus.aspx *or do a websearch for 'peregrine falcon webcam'*
>
> www.peregrine-foundation.ca— Canadian Peregrine Foundation
>
> www.peregrinefund.org—Peregrine Fund

• Visit and volunteer at a wildlife rehabilitation center. Find an agency in your province or state by doing an internet search for 'wildlife rehabilitation,' followed by the name of your state or province.

> www.wildlifeinternational.org/EN/public/agencies/agencysearch.html— Wildlife International

• Zebra Mussels, inadvertently introduced into the Great Lakes in 1988, have now spread not only throughout the Lakes but also throughout the entire Mississippi River system, seriously threatening native mussels populations. Find out about nuisance species such as kudzu, brown tree snakes, and purple loosestrife that compete for food and habitat with native populations of fish, plants, and animals. What means are used for control? Document your findings and find out if you can participate in control programs.

> www.invadingspecies.com—Canada, invasive species
>
> www.invasivespeciesinfo.gov—U.S., invasive species

WOODWORKING/ METAL SHOP

S, T, AKA=*Arc Welding,* John Walker

S=*The Complete Book of Woodworking,* Tom Carpenter— Landauer Corporation Publishing

S, T, TM, AKA=*Exploring Woodworking,* Fred Zimmerman [workbook available]

S, B=Metalwork: Merit Badge Series

S=*Practical Shielded Metal ARC Welding,* Mike Gellerman

S, T, AKA=*Small Gas Engines,* Alfred Roth [workbook available]

S, B=Woodwork: Merit Badge Series

http://store.im.tamu.edu/Search.aspx?c=49—metal technology, welding, metal trades

http://new.4-hcurriculum.org/catalog.aspx?cid=210&c=Woodworking

Links:

www.doleta.gov—apprenticeships by state, county, and occupation

www.tcu.gov.on.ca/eng/employmentontario/training/index.html

www.habitat.org—Habitat for Humanity International

www.khake.com/page58.html —apprenticeship info, training resources, U.S. and Canada

www.khake.com/page14.html —carpentry and construction career guide, requirements

www.khake.com/page29.html —metalworking and welding career guide, requirements

www.khake.com/page82.html —free lessons and lesson plans: construction, carpentry, metalwork

www.popularmechanics.com —Popular Mechanics magazine: automotive, aviation, computers, home improvement, robotics, woodworking, more

Possible Essay Topics:

• 'Work honors the Creator's gifts and the talents received from him. It can also be redemptive. By enduring the hardship of work in union with Jesus, the carpenter of Nazareth... man collaborates in a certain fashion with the Son of God in his redemptive work.' Read *CCC #2427.* In what ways might you use your talents in a redemptive way? Brainstorm and write about possibilities, including the creation of sacred art or furniture for your parish and repairs or construction for those who might lack the means to otherwise afford them.

• Keep a daily journal of your welding or woodworking activities. Note skills learned, including names of equipment on which you have trained. Note errors, how they were corrected, and why. Photograph your work! If you are assisting or working with a professional, record names and contact information of those for and with whom you worked. All of this information may be used in job resumes for future employment.

• Given the opportunity, what dreams do you have for a future in wood or metal working? List your dreams, plans, and goals. Arrange them in order of 'attack.' Outline steps toward their achievement. Write about your dream.

Experiential Learning/Career and Vocational Bridge:

[See Table of Contents for *Process Project Outline* and *Following in Their Footsteps* projects.]

Woodworking/Metal Shop Projects:
• Volunteer with *Habitat for Humanity*, that constructs housing for the poor in the U.S., Canada, more.
• Build folding kneelers for a Perpetual Adoration chapel or for your home.
• Design and weld a shrine with votive holders for your home or for a chapel.
• Locate and interview cabinet makers in your area. [see *Following in Their Footsteps*]

EXPERIENTIAL LEARNING

EXPERIENTIAL LEARNING: VOLUNTEER/PAID/CAREER BRIDGE POSITIONS

Students may gain volunteer experience, class credit, and potential employment by searching and participating in volunteer opportunities at www.volunteer.gov, www.volunteermatch.org, or by participating in programs that follow.

after-school program, parish or other [child care or tutoring]
credit for: Family Management, Home Ec., Psychology; Education

American Cancer Society
credit for: Biology, Health
www.cancer.org/involved/volunteer/index

American Red Cross
credit for: Midwifery, Biology, Health
www.redcross.org/support/volunteer

aquarium
credit for: Biology, Oceanography

Catholic Summer Camps
credit for: Social Problems, Family Management, Psychology, Theology, Vocations
www.mysummercamps.com/camps/ Religious_Camps/Catholic/index. html—volunteer opportunities at Catholic summer camps

Catholic Social Services [see diocesan directory]
credit for: Social Problems, Theology, Foreign Language, Typing, Business Cluster
www.catholicvolunteering.org

Civil Air Patrol
credit for: Aeronautics

http://gocivilairpatrol.com—Civil Air Patrol

community service, general
Key Club—www.keyclub.org/home.aspx
Rotarians—www.rotary.org/en/studentsandyouth/Pages/ridefault.aspx
Ruritans—www.ruritan.org

concrete contractors
credit for: Building Cluster

crisis pregnancy center
credit for: Theology, Social Studies, Psychology, Home Ec., Typing, Business Cluster
www.heartbeatinternational.org/ worldwide-directory-of-pregnancy- help/—international directory of crisis pregnancy centers

day care, parish or other
credit for: Family Management, Home Economics, Psychology, Education, Pediatric Nursing

fire department

food pantry
credit for: Social Problems Today
Missionary of Charities and many others within your diocese

www.motherteresa.org/07_family/ Volunteering/v_cal.html—Missionaries of Charity; volunteer sites

Service dogs puppy training program
credit for: Agricultural Science

www.guidedogs.com/site/ PageServer?pagename=programs_dog_ puppy

www.guidedogs.org [Southeast USA]

www.thepuppyplace.org/international. html [international]

http://tdi-dog.org

www.assistancedogsinternational.org/
standards/training-programs/

Habitat for Humanity
  *credit for: Building Construction,
  Electronics, Woodworking*
  Habitat for Humanity: Volunteer opportunities in construction of housing for
  the poor in U.S., Canada, more. www.
  habitat.org

hospital
  *credit for: Midwifery, Biology, Family
  Management, Health*

Kiwanis, Key Club
  credit for: community volunteering
  www.keyclub.org/home.aspx

landscaping/groundskeeping for parish,
      nursing home
  credit for: Agricultural Science, Botany

library
  *credit for: English, Typing, Business
  Cluster, Computer*

maintenance, parish or nursing home
  *credit for: Electronics, Building
  Construction, Woodworking*

nursing home aide
  credit for: Biology, Health

nursing home for retired religious
  credit for: Biology, Health
parish office [computer and office skills]
  *credit for: Business Cluster, Typing,
  Computer*

police cadet
  credit for: Criminal Justice

political involvement

*credit for: Political Science, Government,
  Social Studies, pro-life credit*
[Not limited to election years. Contact
  local party headquarters, elected
  officials for townships, counties,
  states, provinces and political action
  committees such as National Right to
  Life Committee for volunteer opportu-
  nities]
www.nrlc.org/—National Right to Life
  Committee—life issues and political
  action contacts

preschool aide
  *credit for: Family Management,
  Psychology*

Ronald McDonald Houses
  credit for: Health
  Ronald McDonald Houses provide a
  temporary 'home away from home'
  for families of critically ill children
  who are undergoing treatment. Find
  a Ronald McDonald House near you
  [www.rmhc.com]. Call and ask about
  volunteer opportunities. [Rules vary
  from house to house; many welcome
  high school-age volunteers; others
  require that volunteers be age 18 or
  older.]

Rotary International
  credit for: community volunteering
  http://rotary.org/en/StudentsAndYouth/
  Pages/ridefault.aspx

St. Vincent de Paul stores
Home Ec., Health, Business
[serving in food kitchen, office, store]
www.svdpusa.org/AssistanceServices.
aspx—Society of St. Vincent de Paul,
directory of centers

science museum
credit for: Sciences

soup kitchen
credit for: Social Problems Today
Missionary of Charities and other within
your diocese
www.motherteresa.org/07_family/
Volunteering/v_cal.html—Missionaries
of Charity; volunteer sites
http://societyofourlady.net/laity.html—
Society of Our Lady of the Most Holy
Trinity
http://franciscanfriars.com—Franciscan
Friars of the Renewal

teacher's aide, religious education
credit for: Family Management,
Theology, Vocations, Apologetics,
Psychology, Speech

teacher's aide, parish or public school
credit for: Family Management,
Theology, Vocations, Apologetics,
Psychology, Speech
[for more ideas, student might inquire
at parish offices, or look through
diocesan directory]
Assisting with or mentoring a Little
Flowers Girls' Club

tutoring positions
credit for: Math, English
Boys & Girls Clubs, literacy programs,
Salesian Boys & Girls Clubs

EXPERIENTIAL LEARNING: SHRINES, MUSEUMS, AND SCIENCE DISCOVERY CENTERS

The following listings offer a brief sampling of countless opportunities for experiential learning. More detailed information about listed sites may be found at the websites noted below, or through a Google or MapQuest search.

However, students should be aware that internet or directory searches can offer nearly limitless possibilities for hands-on learning, not listed here for lack of space. Searches by budding aviators and mechanics will be rewarded with aviation and automobile museums; history buffs will discover sites that played significant roles in the Revolutionary or Civil Wars, and reconstructed medieval and Native American dwellings. And then there are the tours of law enforcement laboratories, agricultural research stations, and nuclear submarines!

After browsing through the educational sites listed in the next thirty pages of this manual, students are encouraged to search the websites provided below, refer to telephone directories, or contact travel services to locate the multitude of educational and Faith-related sites *not* included in the next thirty pages!

www.cs.cmu.edu/~mwm/sci.html

http://en.wikipedia.org/wiki/List_of_
museums_in_the_United_States

www.umich.edu/~motherha/museums.
html

www.museumstuff.com

www.museevirtuel-virtualmuseum.ca/
index-eng.jsp [Canada]

CATHOLIC SHRINES/HISTORIC SITES, U.S. AND CANADA

United States

Alabama

Ave Maria Grotto, St. Bernard Abbey, Cullman, www.avemariagrotto.com

Cathedral of the Immaculate Conception, Mobile, www.mobilecathedral.org

EWTN, Irondale, www.ewtn.com

Shrine of the Most Blessed Sacrament, Hanceville, http://olamshrine.com

Arizona

Mission San Xavier del Bac, Tucson, www.sanxaviermission.org

Shrine of St. Joseph of the Mountains, Yarnell, www.stjoseph-shrine.org

Arkansas

Our Lady of the Ozarks Shrine, Hwy. 71, Winslow

St. Mary's Catholic Church, Altus, http://stmarysaltus.org

California

[Most missions have on-site museums.]
http://www.missionscalifornia.com

Cathedral of the Blessed Sacrament, Sacramento, www.cathedralsacramento.org

La Purisima Mission State Historic Park, Lompoc, www.lapurisimamission.org

Mission Basilica San Diego de Alcala, San Diego, www.missionsandiego.com

Mission San Antonio de Padua, King City, http://missionsanantonio.net

Mission San Carlos Borromeo del Rio Carmelo, Carmel, www.carmelmission.org/museum

Mission San Fernando Rey de Espana, Mission Hills, www.missionscalifornia.com/keyfacts/san-fernando-rey.html

Mission San Francisco de Asis, San Francisco, www.missiondolores.org/old-mission/visitor.html

Mission San Jose Chapel, Fremont, www.missionsanjose.org

Mission San Juan Bautista, San Juan Bautista, www.oldmissionsjb.org

Mission San Juan Capistrano, San Juan Capistrano, www.missionsjc.com

Mission San Luis Obispo de Tolosa, San Luis Obispo, www.missionsanluisobispo.org

Mission San Luis Rey de Francia, Oceanside, www.sanluisrey.org

Mission San Miguel Arcangel, San Miguel, www.missionsanmiguel.org

Mission San Rafael Arcangel, San Rafael, www.saintraphael.com

Mission Santa Barbara, Santa Barbara, www.santabarbaramission.org

Mission Santa Clara de Asis, Santa Clara

San Buenaventura Mission, Ventura, www.sanbuenaventuramission.org

Colorado

Mother Cabrini Shrine, Golden, www.mothercabrinishrine.org

Shrine of the Stations of the Cross, San Luis, www.sdcparish.org/the-stations-shrine.html

Connecticut

Knights of Columbus Museum, New Haven, www.kofcmuseum.org

Lourdes in Litchfield, Litchfield, www.shrinect.org

District of Columbia

The Basilica of the National Shrine of the Immaculate Conception, www.nationalshrine.com

Franciscan Monastery, www.myfranciscan.org

Florida

Cathedral of St. Augustine [oldest Catholic parish in U.S.], St. Augustine, http://thefirstparish.org

*Mission of Nombre de Dios and Shrine of
Our Lady of La Leche,*
San Marco Ave., St. Augustine

Georgia

Cathedral of St. John the Baptist,
Savannah, ww.savannahcathedral.org

Hawaii

Cathedral of Our Lady of Peace
[1843], Honolulu, Oahu,
www.cathedralofourladyofpeace.com

St. Benedict's Church ['Painted
Church,' 1899], Honaunau,
www.thepaintedchurch.org

St. Raphael Catholic Church [1841],
Koloa, Kauai,
http://st-raphael-kauai.org

Idaho

Coeur D'Alene's Old Mission State Park
[Sacred Heart Mission], Cataldo

Illinois

Church of the Holy Family, Cahokia,
www.holyfamily1699.org

*Franciscan Shrines of St. Francis and St.
Anthony, St. Peter's Church,* Chicago,
www.stpetersloop.org

Mother Cabrini Shrine [Columbus
Hospital], Chicago,
http://cabrinishrinechicago.com

*National Shrine of Our Lady of the
Snows,* Belleville, www.snows.org

Shrine of St. Anne, St. Anne

Shrine of St. Maximilian Kolbe, Marytown,
Libertyville, www.marytown.com

Indiana

Carmelite Shrines, Munster,
www.carmelitefathers.com

Our Lady of Monte Cassino Shrine, St.
Meinrad, www.saintmeinrad.edu/
the-monastery/monte-cassino-shrine

St. Francis Xavier Church,
205 Church St., Vincennes

University of Notre Dame Campus, South
Bend, http://tour.nd.edu *[Basilica
of the Sacred Heart, Grotto of Our
Lady of Lourdes, Log Chapel]*

Iowa

*St. Donatus Church and Way
of the Cross,* St. Donatus,
www.stjosephbellevue.org/st-donatus

Kansas

St. Fidelis Catholic Church, Victoria,
www.stfidelischurch.com

Shrine of St. Philippine Duchesne,
Mound City

Kentucky

Basilica of St. Joseph Proto-Cathedral,
Bardstown,
www.bardstown.com/~stjoe

Cathedral of the Assumption, Covington,
www.covcathedral.com

Cathedral of the Assumption, Louisville,
www.cathedraloftheassumption.org

*Lourdes Rosary Shrine, St. Louis
Bertrand Church,* 1104 S. 6th St.,
Louisville

Mother of God Church, Covington,
http://mother-of-god.org

*Shrine of the Little Flower, St. Therese
Church,* Alexandria Pike, Southgate

Shrine of St. Ann, 1274 Parkway Ave,
Covington

Louisiana

Immaculate Conception Catholic Church,
Natchitoches, www.minorbasilica.org

St. Louis Cathedral, New Orleans,
http://stlouiscathedral.org

St. Martin de Tours Catholic Church,
133 S. Main St., St. Martinville

Maine

St. Anthony Monastery and Shrines,
Kennebunkport

St. Patrick's Church [1808], Newcastle,
www.allsaintsmaine.com/churches/
st-patrick

Maryland

*Basilica of the National Shrine of the
Assumption of the Blessed Virgin
Mary,* [first cathedral in the U.S.],
Baltimore, www.baltimorebasilica.org

National Shrine Grotto of Lourdes,
Emmitsburg, www.msmary.edu/grotto
Shrine of St. Elizabeth Ann Seton,
Emmitsburg, www.setonheritage.org

Massachusetts
LaSalette Shrine, Attleboro,
www.lasalette-shrine.org
St. Anne's Church and Shrine, Fall River,
www.stanneshrine.com

Michigan
Assumption Grotto Church, Detroit,
www.assumptiongrotto.com
The Solanus Center [Ven. Solanus Casey],
Detroit, www.solanuscenter.org
St. Mary's of Mount Carmel Shrine,
Manistee, http://
catholiccommunityofmanistee.com
Cross In The Woods National Shrine
[St. Kateri Tekakwitha], Indian River,
www.crossinthewoods.com

Minnesota
Assumption Chapel, Cold Spring,
www.stboniface.com/parish/
assumption-chapel.htm
Schoenstatt Shrine, Sleepy Eye,
www.schoenstattmn.com

Mississippi
St. Augustine Seminary,
199 Seminary Dr., Bay St. Louis

Missouri
Black Madonna Shrine and Grottos,
Eureka, www.franciscancaring.org/
blackmadonnashri.html
*St. Martin's, Shrine of Our Lady
of Sorrows,* Starkenburg,
www.historicshrine.com
*St. Mary of the Barrens Church, Shrine
of Our Lady of the Miraculous Medal,*
Perryville, www.amm.org/MarysShrine/
Visit%20the%20Shrine.aspx
St. Philippine Duchesne Shrine,
St. Charles, http://duchesneshrine.org

Montana
Cathedral of St. Helena, Helena,
www.sthelenas.org

St. Francis Xavier Church, Missoula,
http://sfxmissoula.com
St. Ignatius Mission, St. Ignatius,
www.rockymtnmission.org/index.
php?page=st-ignatius-mt
St. Mary's Mission, Stevensville,
www.saintmarysmission.org

Nebraska
Christ the King Eucharistic Shrine
['Pink Sisters'], Lincoln,
www.holyspiritadorationsisters.org
St. Cecilia's Cathedral, Omaha,
www.stceciliacathedral.org

New Hampshire
La Salette Shrine and Center, Enfield,
www.lasaletteofenfield.org

New Jersey
Holy Face Monastery, Clifton,
www.holyfacemonasterygiftshop.
blogspot.com
*Rosary Shrine, Monastery of Our Lady of
the Rosary,* Summit,
http://nunsopsummit.org
St Cecilia's Church [Little Flower Shrine],
Englewood. www.stceciliachurch.com
St. Lucy's/National Shrine of St. Gerard,
Newark, www.saintlucy.net
*Shrine of the Immaculate Heart of
Mary* [Blue Army], Washington,
www.wafusa.org

New Mexico
Cathedral of St. Francis of Assisi,
Santa Fe, www.cbsfa.org
Cristo Rey Church, Santa Fe, www.
cristoreysantefe.parishesonline.com
Loretto Chapel, Santa Fe,
www.lorettochapel.com
San Esteban del Rey, Acoma,
http://acoma.sks.com
San Francisco de Asis Church,
Hwy. 68, Taos
San Miguel Mission Church,
401 Old Santa Fe Tr., Santa Fe
San Miguel Mission, Socorro,
www.sdc.org/~smiguel

Santa Nino de Atocha, Hurley,
www.santoninodeatochashrine.com

New York

Cathedral of the Immaculate Conception,
Albany, www.cathedralic.com

Marian Shrine, Stony Point,
www.marianshrine.org

*National Shrine of North American
Martyrs* [St. Isaac Jogues et al],
Auriesville, www.martyrshrine.org

St. Patrick's Cathedral, New York,
www.saintpatrickscathedral.org

Shrine of Our Lady of the Island, Manor-
ville, www.ourladyoftheisland.org

*The National Shrine of St. Kateri Tekak-
witha and Native American Exhibit,*
Fonda, www.katerishrine.com

Ohio

*Basilica and National Shrine of
Our Lady of Consolation,* Carey,
www.olcshrine.com

National Shrine of Our Lady of Lourdes,
Euclid, www.srstrinity.com/2136

National Shrine of St. Dymphna, Massillon,
www.natlshrinestdymphna.org

Portiuncula, Franciscan University of
Steubenville, Steubenville,
www.franciscan.edu/
ChapelMinistries/Portiuncula

Saint Peter in Chains Cathedral,
Cincinnati,
www.stpeterinchainscathedral.org

Shrine of Our Sorrowful Mother, Bellevue,
http://sorrowfulmothershrine.org

Shrine of the Holy Relics, Maria Stein,
www.mariasteinshrine.org

Oklahoma

*Our Lady of Mt. Carmel and St. Therese
the Little Flower Church,*
1125 S. Walker St., Oklahoma City

*St. Wenceslaus Church, Shrine of the
Infant Jesus of Prague,* Prague,
www.shrineofinfantjesus.com

Oregon

Mt. Angel Abbey, St. Benedict,
www.mountangelabbey.org

*The Grotto [Sanctuary of Our Sorrowful
Mother],* Portland, www.thegrotto.org

Pennsylvania

Basilica of the Sacred Heart of Jesus,
Hanover, www.sacredheartbasilica.com

National Shrine of St. John Neumann,
Philadelphia, www.stjohnneumann.org

Old St. Joseph's Church
[pre-Revolutionary War], Philadelphia,
http://oldstjoseph.org

Old St. Mary's Church [late 18th century],
Philadelphia, www.oldstmary.com

St. Katharine Drexel Shrine, Bensalem,
www.katharinedrexel.org

South Carolina

St. Mary's Church, Charleston,
www.catholic-doc.org/saintmarys

South Dakota

*Fatima Family Shrine, St. Mary
of Mercy Church,* Alexandria,
www.stmaryofmercyalexandria.
parishesonline.com

*St. Joseph's Indian School, Our Lady
of the Sioux Chapel,* Chamberlain,
http://www.stjo.org/site/
PageServer?pagename=chapel

Shrine of the Nativity, Bethlehem

Texas

La Lomita Chapel, Mission

La Purisima de Socorro Mission, El Paso,
www.elpasodiocese.org/
la-purisima-socorro-mission

*Mission Nuestra Senora de La
Concepcion de Acuna,* San Antonio,
http://loscompadres.org/
the-missions/mission-concepcion

*Mission San Jose y San Miguel
de Aguayo,* San Antonio,
http://loscompadres.org/
the-missions/mission-san-jose

Mission San Juan Capistrano, San
Antonio, http://loscompadres.org/
the-missions/mission-san-juan
San Fernando Cathedral, San Antonio,
www.sfcathedral.org

Utah

Cathedral of the Madeleine,
Salt Lake City, www.utcotm.org

Washington

St. Francis Xavier Mission [1838], Toledo,
www.toledotel.com/~stfrancis
St. Mary's Mission, Omak,
www.rockymtnmission.org/index.
php?page=omak-wa
St. Paul's Mission [log church, 1845],
12 miles north of Colville on US 395

Wisconsin

Basilica of St. Josaphat, Milwaukee,
http://thebasilica.org
Grotto Gardens and Wonder Cave,
Rudolph, www.rudolphgrotto.org
Holy Hill, Hubertus, https://holyhill.com
St. Joan of Arc Chapel, Milwaukee,
www.marquette.edu/chapel

Canada

Alberta

Basilian Fathers Museum, Mundare,
www.basilianmuseum.ca
Father Lacombe Chapel, St. Albert,
www.history.alberta.ca/
fatherlacombe/default.aspx

British Columbia

St. Joseph's Church,
Chilcotin St., Kamloops
Westminster Abbey [1861, mission
to Native Peoples], Mission,
www.westminsterabbey.ca

Manitoba

*Immaculate Conception Church and
Grotto of Our Lady of Lourdes,*
Ukrainian Catholic, 3km north on
Hwy. 212, Cooks Creek

New Brunswick

*Historic Church of St. Henri
de Barachois,* Barachois,
www.eglisehistoriquebarachois.org
Popes' Museum [Musee des Papes],
Grand-Anse, http://rmne.ca/en/
content/pope-museum
*St. Michael's Basilica, Museum and
Genealogy Centre,* Miramichi,
www.saintmichaelsmuseum.com

Newfoundland

Basilica Cathedral of St. John the Baptist,
St. John's, www.thebasilica.ca

Nova Scotia

Chapel of Our Lady of Sorrows, Halifax,
http://holycrosshalifax.ca
St. Mary's Museum, Church Point, www.
museeeglisesaintemariemuseum.ca
St. Patrick's Museum, Sydney,
www.oldsydney.com

Ontario

*St. Ann's Roman Catholic
Church,* Penetanguishene,
www.1812bicentennial.com/
st-anns-church.html
The Cathedral Basilica of Notre-Dame,
Ottawa, www.notredameottawa.com
The Martyrs' Shrine, Midland,
www.martyrs-shrine.com
Saint-Ignace II [mission site of Canadian
Martyrs], Midland
Sainte-Marie Among the Hurons,
Midland, www.hhp.on.ca

Prince Edward Island

*Our Lady of Mont-Carmel Acadian
Church,* Hwy. 11, Mont-Carmel
St. Dunstan's Basilica, Charlottetown,
www.stdunstans.pe.ca

Quebec

Basilica of Notre Dame, Montreal,
www.basiliquenddm.org/en
Basilica of Ste-Anne-de-Beaupre,
Ste-Anne-de-Beaupre,
www.shrinesaintanne.org

Beauvoir Shrine, Sherbrooke,
www.sanctuairedebeauvoir.qc.ca

Cathedral of Marie-Reine-du-Monde,
Montreal, www.
cathedralecatholiquedemontreal.org

*Chapel of Notre Dame and Marguerite
Bourgeoys Museum,* Montreal, www.
marguerite-bourgeoys.com

Grey Nuns Museum, [St. Marguerite],
Montreal, www.concordia.ca/
about/major-projects/grey-nuns

Montmartre Canadien [grotto], Sillery,
www.lemontmartre.net

Shrine of Notre-Dame-du-Cap, Cap-de-
la-Madeleine, http://sanctuaire-ndc.ca

*St. Francis Xavier Mission and Shrine
of Kateri Tekakwitha,* Kahnawake,
http://kateritekakwitha.net

St. Joseph's Oratory, Montreal [St. Andre
Bessette], www.saint-joseph.org/en

The Old Chapel [site of oldest Indian
mission in Canada], rue Bord de l'Eau,
Tadoussac

The Ursulines Museum, Quebec,
www.museedesursulines.com/en

Trois Rivieres Cathedral, Trois-Rivieres,
www.tourismetroisrivieres.com/
en/attractions-and-activities/
trois-rivieres-cathedral-of-the-
assumption/115

Ursuline Monastery and Museum, Trois
Rivieres, www.musee-ursulines.qc.ca

Saskatchewan

*Cathedrale Notre-Dame de
L'Assomption,* Gravelbourg,
http://gravelbourgcocathedral.com

St. Peter's Abbey and Cathedral,
Muenster, www.stpetersabbey.ca

HANDS-ON THE ARTS: MUSEUMS AND THEATERS, U.S. AND CANADA

Alabama

Birmingham Museum of Art,
Birmingham, www.artsbma.org

Mobile Museum of Art, Mobile,
www.mobilemuseumofart.com

Alaska

Alaska Native Heritage Center,
Anchorage, www.alaskanative.net

*Anchorage Museum of History
and Art,* Anchorage,
www.anchoragemuseum.org

Arizona

Phippen Art Museum, Prescott,
www.phippenartmuseum.org

Phoenix Art Museum, Phoenix,
www.phxart.org

*Scottsdale Museum of Contemporary
Art,* Scottsdale, www.smoca.org

Arkansas

Arkansas Arts Center, Little Rock,
www.arkarts.com

Fort Smith Regional Art Museum,
Fort Smith, www.fsram.org

California

Los Angeles County Museum of Art,
Los Angeles, www.lacma.org

Santa Barbara Museum of Art,
Santa Barbara, www.sbmuseart.org

UC Berkeley Art Museum, Berkeley,
www.bampfa.berkeley.edu

San Francisco Art Institute,
San Francisco, www.sfai.edu

Colorado

Colorado Springs Fine Arts Center,
Colorado Springs,
www.csfineartscenter.org

Denver Art Museum, Denver,
www.denverartmuseum.org

The Art Center: Western Colorado Center for the Arts, Grand Junction, http://gjartcenter.org

Connecticut

Aldrich Museum of Contemporary Art, Ridgefield, www.aldrichart.org

Hill-Stead Museum, Farmington, www.hillstead.org

New Britain Museum of American Art, New Britain, www.nbmaa.org

Slater Memorial Museum, Norwich, www.slatermuseum.org/page.cfm?p=360

Wadsworth Atheneum Museum of Art, Hartford, www.thewadsworth.org

Delaware

Biggs Museum of American Art, Dover, www.biggsmuseum.org

Delaware Art Museum, Wilmington, www.delart.org

District of Columbia

Art Museum of the Americas, http://museum.oas.org

Freer and Arthur M. Sackler Galleries, Smithsonian, www.asia.si.edu

National Gallery of Art, www.nga.gov

National Museum of African Art, Smithsonian, http://africa.si.edu

Florida

Appleton Museum of Art, Ocala, www.appletonmuseum.org

Boca Raton Museum of Art, Boca Raton, www.bocamuseum.org

Charles Hosmer Morse Museum of American Art, Winter Park, www.morsemuseum.org

Cummer Museum of Art and Gardens, Jacksonville, www.cummer.org

Naples Museum of Art, Naples, www.thephil.org

Norton Museum of Art, West Palm Beach, www.norton.org

Georgia

Georgia Museum of Art, Athens, http://georgiamuseum.org

High Museum of Art, Atlanta, www.high.org

Marietta/Cobb Museum of Art, Marietta, www.mariettacobbartmuseum.org

Hawaii

Honolulu Museum of Art, Honolulu, Oahu, http://honolulumuseum.org

Lahaina Art Galleries, Lahaina, Maui, www.lahainagalleries.com

Idaho

Boise Art Museum, Boise, www.boiseartmuseum.org

Lewis and Clark Center for Arts and History, Lewiston, www.lcsc.edu/museum

Illinois

Art Institute of Chicago, Chicago, www.artic.edu

National Museum of Mexican Art, Chicago, www.nationalmuseumofmexicanart.org

Midwest Carvers' Museum, South Holland, http://www.southholland.org/index.php?page=Community/Org/carvers

Terra Museum of American Art, Chicago, www.terraamericanart.org

Indiana

Eiteljorg Museum of American Indians and Western Art, Indianapolis, www.eiteljorg.org

Indianapolis Museum of Art, Indianapolis, www.imamuseum.org

Columbus Museum of Art, Columbus, www.columbusmuseum.org

Snite Museum of Art, [Notre Dame campus], South Bend, http://sniteartmuseum.nd.edu

Swope Art Museum, Terre Haute, www.swope.org

Iowa

Des Moines Art Center, Des Moines,
www.desmoinesartcenter.org
Sioux City Art Center, Sioux City,
www.siouxcityartcenter.org

Kansas

Spencer Museum of Art,
Lawrence, www.spencerart.ku.edu
Wichita Center for the Arts,
Wichita, www.wcfta.com

Kentucky

Kentucky Museum of Art and Craft,
Louisville, www.kentuckyarts.org
Owensboro Museum of Fine Art,
Owensboro, www.omfa.us
Speed Art Museum, Louisville,
www.speedmuseum.org

Louisiana

Alexandria Museum of Art,
Alexandria, www.themuseum.org
New Orleans Museum of Art,
New Orleans, http://noma.org

Maine

*Farnsworth Art Museum and
the Wyeth Center,* Rockland,
www.farnsworthmuseum.org
Ogunquit Museum of American Art,
Ogunquit, www.ogunquitmuseum.org
Portland Museum of Art, Portland,
www.portlandmuseum.org
*Wendell Gilley Wood Carving
Museum,* Southwest Harbor,
www.wendellgilleymuseum.org

Maryland

African Art Museum of Maryland,
Fulton, www.africanartmuseum.org
Baltimore Museum of Art,
Baltimore, www.artbma.org
Schifferstadt Architectural Museum,
Frederick, www.frederickcounty-
landmarksfoundation.org
Ward Museum of Wildfowl Art,
Salisbury, www.wardmuseum.org

Massachusetts

Attleboro Art Museum, Attleboro,
http://attleboroartsmuseum.org
Museum of Fine Arts,
Boston, www.mfa.org
*National Center of Afro-American
Artists,* Boston, www.ncaaa.org
Norman Rockwell Museum at Stockbridge,
Stockbridge, www.nrm.org
Whistler House Museum of Art,
Lowell, www.whistlerhouse.org
Worcester Art Museum,
Worcester, www.worcesterart.org

Michigan

Art Center of Battle Creek, Battle Creek,
www.artcenterofbattlecreek.org
Detroit Institute of Arts,
Detroit, www.dia.org
Flint Institute of Arts,
Flint, www.flintarts.org

Minnesota

Minneapolis Institute of Arts,
Minneapolis, http://beta.artsmia.org

Mississippi

Ohr/O'Keefe Museum of Art,
Biloxi, www.georgeohr.org

Missouri

Nelson-Atkins Museum of Art,
Kansas City, www.nelson-atkins.org
St. Louis Art Museum,
St. Louis, www.slam.org

Montana

C.M. Russell Museum of Art,
Great Falls, http://cmrussell.org
Hockaday Museum of Art, Kalispell,
www.hockadaymuseum.org
Yellowstone Art Museum,
Billings, www.artmuseum.org

Nebraska

Joslyn Art Museum,
Omaha, www.joslyn.org
Museum of Nebraska Art,
Kearney, http://mona.unk.edu

Nevada

Las Vegas Art Museum, Las Vegas,
www.lasvegasartmuseum.org
Nevada Museum of Art,
Reno, www.nevadaart.org

New Hampshire

Hood Museum of Art, Hanover,
http://hoodmuseum.dartmouth.edu
New Hampshire Institute of Art,
Manchester, www.nhia.edu

New Jersey

Jane Voorhees Zimmerli Art Museum,
New Brunswick,
www.zimmerlimuseum.rutgers.edu
Noyes Museum of Art,
Oceanville, www.noyesmuseum.org

New Mexico

Georgia O'Keeffe Museum,
Santa Fe, www.okeeffemuseum.org
Roswell Museum and Art Center,
Roswell, http://roswellmuseum.org
Taos Art Museum at Fechin House,
Taos, www.taosartmuseum.org

New York

Albany Institute of History and Art,
Albany, www.albanyinstitute.org
Fenimore Art Museum, Cooperstown,
www.fenimoreartmuseum.org
Memorial Art Gallery,
Rochester, http://mag.rochester.edu
Metropolitan Museum of Art,
New York, www.metmuseum.org
The New Museum of Contemporary Art,
New York, www.newmuseum.org

North Carolina

Louise Wells Cameron Art Museum,
Wilmington,
www.cameronartmuseum.com
Mint Museum of Art,
Charlotte, www.mintmuseum.org
*Reynolda House Museum of American
Art,* Winston-Salem,
www.reynoldahouse.org

North Dakota

Bismarck Art and Galleries Association,
Bismarck, www.bismarck-art.org
Plains Art Museum,
Fargo, http://plainsart.org

Ohio

Akron Art Museum,
Akron, http://akronartmuseum.org
Cincinnati Art Museum, Cincinnati,
www.cincinnatiartmuseum.org
Dayton Art Institute,
Dayton, www.daytonartinstitute.org
Toledo Museum of Art,
Toledo, www.toledomuseum.org
Wexner Center for the Arts,
Columbus, http://wexarts.org
Zanesville Art Center,
Zanesville, www.zanesvilleart.org

Oklahoma

Fred Jones Jr. Museum of Art,
Norman, www.ou.edu/fjjma
Oklahoma City Museum of Art,
Oklahoma City, www.okcmoa.com
Philbrook Museum of Art,
Tulsa, http://philbrook.org

Oregon

*Favell Museum of Western Art and
Indian Artifacts,* Klamath Falls,
www.favellmuseum.org
Grants Pass Museum of Art,
Grants Pass, www.gpmuseum.com
Maude Kerns Art Center,
Eugene, www.mkartcenter.org
Oregon Shakespeare Festival,
Ashland, www.osfashland.org
Portland Art Museum, Portland,
www.portlandartmuseum.org

Pennsylvania

*Brandywine River Art Museum
[Wyeth family],* Chadds Ford,
www.brandywinemuseum.org
Carnegie Museum of Art,
Pittsburgh, www.cmoa.org

Philadelphia Museum of Art,
Philadelphia, www.philamuseum.org

Rhode Island
Museum of Art and Rhode Island
School of Design, Providence,
http://risdmuseum.org
Newport Art Museum, Newport,
www.newportartmuseum.org

South Carolina
Gibbes Museum of Art,
Charleston, www.gibbesmuseum.org
Sumter County Gallery of Art,
Sumter, www.sumtergallery.org

South Dakota
Redlin Art Center,
Watertown, www.redlinart.com
South Dakota Art Museum,
Brookings, www.sdstate.edu/
southdakotaartmuseum/

Tennessee
Fisk University Galleries,
Nashville, www.fisk.edu/CampusLife/
FiskUniversityGalleries.aspx
Hunter Museum of American Art,
Chattanooga, www.huntermuseum.org
Knoxville Museum of Art,
Knoxville, www.knoxart.org
Tullahoma Fine Arts Center,
Tullahoma, http://tullahomafinearts.
wordpress.com
Art Museum at the University of Memphis,
Memphis, www.memphis.edu/amum

Texas
Amon Carter Museum of American Art,
Fort Worth, www.cartermuseum.org
Austin Museum of Art,
Austin, http://amoa-arthouse.org
Brownsville Museum of Fine Art,
Brownsville, www.brownsvillemfa.org
San Antonio Museum of Art,
San Antonio, www.samuseum.org
The Museum of Fine Arts,
Houston, www.mfah.org

Utah
Utah Museum of Fine Arts,
University of Utah, Salt Lake City,
http://umfa.utah.edu

Vermont
Brattleboro Museum & Art, Brattleboro,
www.brattleboromuseum.org
Norman Rockwell Exhibit, Arlington,
www.normanrockwellexhibit.com
Robert Hull Fleming Museum,
Burlington, www.uvm.edu/~fleming

Virginia
Chrysler Museum of Art,
Norfolk, www.chrysler.org
Maier Museum of Art,
Lynchburg, http://maiermuseum.org
P. Buckley Moss Museum, Waynesboro,
www.pbuckleymoss.com
Virginia Museum of Fine Arts,
Richmond, www.vmfa.state.va.us

Washington
Maryhill Museum of Art, Goldendale,
www.maryhillmuseum.org
Museum of Northwest Art,
La Conner, www.museumofnwart.org
Northwest Museum of Arts & Culture,
Spokane, http://northwestmuseum.org
Seattle Art Museum,
Seattle, www.seattleartmuseum.org
Seattle Asian Art Museum,
Seattle, www.seattleartmuseum.org

West Virginia
Huntington Museum of Art,
Huntington, www.hmoa.org

Wisconsin
Leigh Yawkey Woodson Art Museum,
Wausau, www.lywam.org
Milwaukee Art Museum,
Milwaukee, http://mam.org
Museum of Woodcarving,
Shell Lake, www.shelllake.org/
museum-of-woodcarving

Wyoming

*Bradford Brinton Memorial Historic
    Ranch and Western Art Collection,*
    Big Horn, www.bbmandm.org
National Museum of Wildlife Art, Jackson,
    www.wildlifeart.org
Whitney Gallery of Western Art,
    Cody, www.bbhc.org/western-art/

Canada

Alberta

Art Gallery of Alberta,
    Edmonton, www.youraga.ca
Glenbow Museum,
    Calgary, www.glenbow.org
Esplanade Arts and Heritage Centre,
    Medicine Hat, www.esplanade.ca
Southern Alberta Art Gallery,
    Lethbridge, www.saag.ca

British Columbia

Kamloops Art Gallery,
    Kamloops, www.kag.bc.ca
Vancouver Art Gallery,
    Vancouver, www.vanartgallery.bc.ca
Vernon Public Art Gallery, Vernon,
    www.vernonpublicartgallery.com

Manitoba

Art Gallery of Southwestern Manitoba,
    Brandon, www.agsm.ca
Winnipeg Art Gallery,
    Winnipeg, http://wag.ca

New Brunswick

The Beaverbrook Art Gallery, Fredericton,
    http://beaverbrookartgallery.org/en
Galerie d'Art de l'Universite de Moncton,
    Moncton, www.umoncton.ca/umcm-ga

Nova Scotia

Art Gallery of Nova Scotia, Halifax,
    www.artgalleryofnovascotia.ca
Mt. St. Vincent University Art Gallery,
    Halifax, http://msvuart.ca

Ontario

Art Gallery of Algoma, Sault Ste. Marie,
    www.artgalleryofalgoma.com
Art Gallery of Ontario and the Grange,
    Toronto, www.ago.net
Kitchener-Waterloo Art Gallery,
    Kitchener, www.kwag.ca
MacLaren Art Centre,
    Barrie, http://maclarenart.com
McMaster Museum of Art,
    Hamilton, www.mcmaster.ca/museum
McMichael Canadian Art Collection,
    Kleinburg, www.mcmichael.com
National Gallery of Canada,
    Ottawa, www.gallery.ca
Robert McLaughlin Art Gallery,
    Oshawa, www.rmg.on.ca

Quebec

Amerindian and Inuit Museum,
    [art, sculpture, demonstrations],
    134 rue Pascal-Comeau, Godbout
Canadian Centre for Architecture,
    Montreal, www.cca.qc.ca
Lower St. Lawrence Museum,
    Riviere-du-Loup, www.mbsl.qc.ca
Musee D'Art Inuit Brousseau,
    Quebec, www.artinuit.ca
Segal Centre for Performing Arts,
    Montreal, www.segalcentre.org

Saskatchewan

Allen Sapp Gallery,
    North Battleford, www.allensapp.com
Art Gallery of Swift Current, Swift Current,
    www.artgalleryofswiftcurrent.org
MacKenzie Art Gallery,
    Regina, www.mackenzieartgallery.ca
Mendel Art Gallery & Civic Conservatory,
    Saskatoon, www.mendel.ca

EXPERIENTIAL HISTORICAL AND CULTURAL SITES, U.S. AND CANADA

Note: In addition to their hands-on educational enrichment value, the following sites may also provide volunteer and employment opportunities to students.

Alabama

Birmingham Civil Rights Institute, Birmingham, http://bcri.org

First White House of the Confederacy, Montgomery, www.firstwhitehouse.org

Alaska

Alaska Native Heritage Center, Anchorage, www.alaskanative.net

Alaska State Museum, Juneau, http://museums.alaska.gov

Anchorage Museum, Anchorage, www.anchoragemuseum.org

Sitka National Historical Park, Sitka, www.nps.gov/sitk

Arizona

Amerind Foundation Museum, Dragoon, www.amerind.org

Arizona State Museum, University of Arizona Campus, Tucson, www.statemuseum.arizona.edu

Casa Grande Ruins National Monument, Coolidge, www.nps.gov/cagr

Casa Malpais Pueblo, Springerville, www.casamalpais.org

Heard Museum, Phoenix, www.heard.org

Hubbell Trading Post National Historic Site, Ganado, www.nps.gov/hutr

Pioneer Living History Museum, Phoenix, www.pioneeraz.org

Arkansas

Fort Smith Museum of History, Fort Smith, www.fortsmithmuseum.com

Historic Arkansas Museum, Little Rock, www.historicarkansas.org

Museum of Regional History, Texarkana, www.texarkanamuseums.org

Historic Washington State Park, Washington, www.historicwashingtonstatepark.com

Parkin Archeological State Park, Parkin, www.arkansasstateparks.com/parkinarcheological

California

Please see listings under *Catholic Shrines/Historic Sites* for California Missions, most of which have on-site museums.

Bodie State Historic Park [gold mining 'ghost' town], Bodie, www.bodie.com

Chinatown, San Francisco, www.sanfranciscochinatown.com

Columbia State Historic Park [gold-rush town], Columbia, www.visitcolumbiacalifornia.com

Little Tokyo, Los Angeles, www.littletokyola.org

Los Angeles Holocaust Museum, Los Angeles, www.lamoth.org

Marshall Gold Discovery State Historic Park, Coloma, http://marshallgold.com

Shasta State Historic Park [gold-rush town], Shasta, http://saveoldshasta.com

Sonoma State Historic Park and Mission San Francisco Solano, Sonoma, www.sonomaparks.org

Sutter's Fort State Historic Park, Sacramento, www.suttersfort.org

Colorado

Black American West Museum and Heritage Center, Denver, www.blackamericanwestmuseum.org

History Colorado Center, Denver, www.historycoloradocenter.org

Manitou Cliff Dwellings, Manitou Springs, www.cliffdwellingsmuseum.com

Old Town Museum [village], Burlington, www.burlingtoncolo.com

Pikes Peak Ghost Town Museum,
Colorado Springs,
www.ghosttownmuseum.com

Trinidad History Museum, Trinidad,
www.historycolorado.org/museums/
trinidad-history-museum-o

Connecticut

Denison Homestead Museum,
Mystic, http://denisonhomestead.org

East Haddam Historical Society Museum,
East Haddam,
www.easthaddamhistory.org

Eli Whitney Museum,
Hamden, www.eliwhitney.org

Harriet Beecher Stowe Center, Hartford,
www.harrietbeecherstowecenter.org

Historic Ship/Submarine Force Museum
[nuclear powered sub], Naval Submarine
Base, Groton, www.ussnautilus.org

Maritime Aquarium at Norwalk,
Norwalk, www.maritimeaquarium.org

National Helicopter Museum, Stratford,
www.nationalhelicoptermuseum.org

Old State House, Hartford,
http://ctoldstatehouse.org

Simsbury Historical Society, Simsbury,
www.simsburyhistory.org

Delaware

Hagley Museum [interactive],
Wilmington, www.hagley.org

John Dickinson Plantation [18th century],
Dover, http://history.delaware.gov/
museums/jdp/jdp_main.shtml

Lewes Historical Society,
Lewes, www.historiclewes.org

Nanticoke Indian Museum, Millsboro, www.
nanticokeindians.org/museum.cfm

District of Columbia

NOTE: Those who wish to tour the White
House, Capitol, Supreme Court, and House
and Senate Galleries may contact their
senators/representatives, well in advance
of a visit, to obtain tickets/passes for these
tours.

African-American Civil War Memorial,
www.afroamcivilwar.org

Anacostia Community Museum,
http://anacostia.si.edu

Explorers Hall, [National Geographic
Museum], http://events.
nationalgeographic.com/events/
national-geographic-museum

The Smithsonian Institution,
www.si.edu/Museums
Including but not limited to:
National Air and Space Museum
National Museum of American History
National Museum of Natural History

United States Holocaust Memorial
Museum, www.ushmm.org

U.S. Navy Memorial and Naval Heritage
Center, www.navymemorial.org

Voice of America, www.insidevoa.com/
info/voa_studio_tour_2/2399.html

Florida

American Police Hall of Fame and
Museum, Titusville,
www.aphf.org/museum.html

Castillo de San Marcos National Monument,
St. Augustine, www.nps.gov/casa

Florida Holocaust Museum, St. Petersburg, www.flholocaustmuseum.org

Gamble Plantation and Judah Benjamin
Confedereate Memorial,
Ellenton, www.cantiniere.org/
Cantinieres_UDC/Gamble_Mansion.html

Government House Museum, St. Augustine,
www.staugustinegovernment.com/
visitors/gov-house.cfm

Heritage Village,
Largo, www.pinellascounty.org/heritage

St. Augustine Old Jail and Museum
Complex, St. Augustine,
www.trolleytours.com/st-augustine

Miami-Dade Cultural/History Center,
Miami, www.historymiami.org

Mission San Luis [and village],
Tallahassee, www.missionsanluis.org

Morikami Museum and Japanese
Gardens, Delray Beach,
www.morikami.org

National Armed Services and Law Enforcement Memorial Museum, Dunedin, www.naslemm.com

National Naval Aviation Museum, Pensacola, www.navalaviationmuseum.org

Oldest House, St. Augustine, www.nps.org/casa

St. Petersburg Museum of History, St. Petersburg, www.spmoh.com

The Holocaust Memorial Resource and Education Center, Maitland, www.holocaustedu.org

Georgia

Albany Civil Rights Movement Museum, Albany, www.albanycivilrightsinstitute.org

Archibald Smith Plantation Home, Roswell, www.archibaldsmithplantation.org

Atlanta History Center, Atlanta, www.atlantahistorycenter.com

Callaway Plantation, Washington, www.historyofwilkes.org/ sites-callaway.html

Chickamauga Battlefield and Museum, Georgia/Tennessee border, www.nps.gov/chch

Chieftains Museum [Cherokee], Rome, http://chieftainsmuseum.org

Georgia Agrirama [living history], Tifton, www.abac.edu/museum

Hofwyl-Broadfield Plantation, Brunswick, www.gastateparks.org/ HofwylBroadfield

Martin Luther King Jr. National Historic Site, Atlanta, www.nps.gov/malu

Ocmulgee National Monument [archaeological site], Macon, www.nps.gov/ocmu

Port Columbus National Civil War Naval Museum, Columbus, http://portcolumbus.org

The Antebellum Plantation, Stone Mountain, www.stonemountainpark. com/activities.aspx

Hawaii

Bailey House Museum, Maui, www.mauimuseum.org

Hawaii's Plantation Village, Oahu, www.hawaiiplantationvillage.org

Pearl Harbor, Oahu, www.pearlharborhistoricsites.org

Wo Hing Museum, Lahaina, Maui, www.lahainarestoration.org/wohing.html

Idaho

Fort Hall Replica, Upper Ross Park, Pocatello, www.forthall.net

National Oregon/California Trail Center, Montpelier, www.oregontrailcenter.org

The Museum of Idaho, Idaho Falls, www.museumofidaho.org

Illinois

Center for American Archeology, Kampsville, www.caa-archeology.org

Walnut Grove Pioneer Village, Glenview, www.scottcountyiowa.com/ conservation/walnut.php

Lincoln Home National Historic Site, Springfield, www.nps.gov/liho

Lincoln Log Cabin State Historic Site, Lerna, www.lincolnlogcabin.org

Lincoln's New Salem Historic Site, Petersburg, www.lincolnsnewsalem.com

Museum of Broadcast Communications, Chicago, www.museum.tv

Naper Settlement, Naperville, www.napersettlement.org

Octave Chanute Aerospace Museum, Rantoul, www.aeromuseum.org

Stephenson County Historical Museum [Underground Railroad], Freeport, www.stephcohs.org

Ulysses S. Grant Home State Historic Site, Galena, www.granthome.com

Indiana

Conner Prairie, Fishers, www.connerprairie.org

Evansville Museum of Arts, History and Science, Evansville, www.emuseum.org

Indiana State Museum, Indianapolis,
    www.indianamuseum.org
Lincoln Boyhood National Memorial
    and Living Historical Farm, Dale,
    www.nps.gov/libo
Northern Indiana Center for History,
    South Bend, centerforhistory.org
President Benjamin Harrison
    Home, Indianapolis,
    www.presidentbenjaminharrison.org
The Indiana Historical Society,
    Indianapolis, www.indianahistory.org
Wilbur Wright Birthplace and Museum,
    Hagerstown, www.wwbirthplace.com
Working Men's Institute
    [19th century commune/
    Utopian village], New Harmony,
    http://workingmensinstitute.org

Iowa
Herbert Hoover National Historic Site,
    West Branch,
    www.nps.gov/heho/index.htm
Humboldt County Historical Association,
    Dakota City,
    www.humboldtiowahistory.org
Iowa State Capitol, Des Moines,
    www.legis.iowa.gov/Resources/
    tourCapitol.aspx
Iowa State Historical Building,
    Des Moines, www.iowahistory.org
Living History Farms, Urbandale,
    www.lhf.org
Pella Historical Village, Pella, www.
    pellatuliptime.com/historical-village

Kansas
Cloud County Historical Society
    Museum, Concordia,
    www.cloudcountymuseum.org
Fort Scott National Historic Site,
    Fort Scott, www.nps.gov/fosc/index.htm
Frontier Army Museum, Leavenworth,
    http://usacac.army.mil/cac2/CSI/
    FrontierArmyMuseum.asp
Kansas Museum of History, Topeka, www.
    kshs.org/museum

Prairie Museum of Art and History, Colby,
    www.prairiemuseum.org

Kentucky
Abraham Lincoln Birthplace National
    Historic Site, Hodgenville,
    www.nps.gov/abli/index.htm
Adsmore Living History Museum,
    Princeton, www.adsmore.org
Bittersweet Cabin Village/Museum,
    Renfro Valley,
    www.bittersweetcabinvillage.com
Civil War Museum of the Western
    Theater, Bardstown,
    www.civil-war-museum.org
Mary Todd Lincoln House, Lexington,
    http://mtlhouse.org
Mountain Homeplace [history village],
    Staffordsville,
    www.visitpaintsvilleky.com/homeplace
General George Patton Museum
    of Leadership, Fort Knox,
    www.generalpatton.org
Shaker Museum, South Union [adjacent to
    Catholic homeschool-friendly *Fathers*
    of Mercy Generalate—orthodox order
    of priests], www.shakermuseum.com
Kentucky State Capitol, Frankfort,
    http://capitol.ky.gov
Thomas Edison House, Louisville,
    www.edisonhouse.org

Louisiana
Acadian Cultural Center, Lafayette
Longfellow-Evangeline Historic Site,
    Martinville, www.stateparks.com/
    longfellow-evangeline_state_historic_
    site_in_louisiana.html
National World War II Museum,
    New Orleans,
    www.nationalww2museum.org
Rosedown Plantation Historic Site,
    Francisville, www.crt.state.la.us/parks/
    irosedown.aspx
San Francisco Plantation, Garyville,
    www.sanfranciscoplantation.org

Maine

Abbe Native American Museum, Bar Harbor, www.abbemuseum.org

Acadian Village, Van Buren, www.nps.gov/maac/planyourvisit/acadvillage.htm

Maine Historical Society Museum, Portland, www.mainehistory.org/museum_overview.shtml

Cole Land Transportation Museum, Bangor, www.colemuseum.org

Joshua L. Chamberlain Museum, Brunswick, http://pejepscothistorical.org/chamberlain

Maine State Museum, Augusta, http://mainestatemuseum.org

Old Lincoln County Jail and Museum, Wiscasset, www.lincolncountyhistory.org/OJAboutBuilding.html

Museums of Old York [nine historic buildings], York, www.oldyork.org

Shaker Museum, New Gloucester, www.shaker.lib.me.us/museum.html

Washburn-Norlands Living History Center, Livermore, www.norlands.org

Maryland

Antietam National Battlefield, Sharpsburg, www.nps.gov/ancm

Fort McHenry National Monument, Baltimore, www.nps.gov/fomc

Hampton National Historic Site [plantation], Towson, www.historichampton.org

Maryland Historical Society, Baltimore, www.mdhs.org

Maryland State House, Annapolis, http://msa.maryland.gov/msa/mdstatehouse/html/home.html

Patuxent River Naval Air Museum, Lexington Park, paxmuseum.com

USS Constellation, Baltimore, www.historicships.org/constellation.html

Massachusetts

Bunker Hill Monument and Museum, Charlestown, www.nps.gov/bost/historyculture/bhm.htm

Concord Museum, Concord, www.concordmuseum.org

Faneuil Hall, Boston, www.thefreedomtrail.org/freedom-trail/faneuil-hall.shtml

Fruitlands Museums [Bronson Alcott commune, 1843], Harvard, www.fruitlands.org

Historic Deerfield [village], Deerfield, www.historic-deerfield.org

Jackson Homestead [Underground Railroad], Newton, newtonma.gov/gov/historic/jackson

Lexington Battle Green, Lexington, www.lexingtonhistory.org

Mayflower Society Museum, Plymouth, www.themayflowersociety.com/museum

Old North Church, Boston, http://oldnorth.com

Paul Revere House, Boston, www.paulreverehouse.org

Peabody Essex Museum, Salem, www.pem.org

Plimoth Plantation, Plymouth, www.plimoth.org

Robert Peabody Museum of Archeology, Andover, www.andover.edu/Museums/MuseumOfArchaeology

Semitic Museum [Mesopotamian history], Cambridge [Harvard University], www.semiticmuseum.fas.harvard.edu

USS Constitution and Museum [Charlestown Navy Yard], Charlestown, www.ussconstitutionmuseum.org

Michigan

Alfred P. Sloan Museum, Flint, www.sloanlongway.org/Sloan-Museum

Henry Ford Museum and Greenfield Village, Dearborn, www.thehenryford.org

Holocaust Memorial Center, Farmington
  Hills, www.holocaustcenter.org
Air Zoo, Portage, www.airzoo.org
*Marquette Mission Park and Museum of
  Ojibwa Culture,* St. Ignace,
  http://museumofojibwaculture.net

Minnesota

Runestone Museum, Alexandria,
  www.runestonemuseum.org
The Depot Museum, Duluth,
  www.lsrm.org

Mississippi

*Beauvoir: The Jefferson Davis Home and
  Presidential Library,* Biloxi,
  www.beauvoir.org
Corinth Civil War Interpretive Center,
  Corinth, www.nps.gov/shil/
  historyculture/corinth.htm
University Museums, [University of
  Mississippi], Oxford,
  http://museum.olemiss.edu
Vicksburg National Military Park,
  Vicksburg, www.nps.gov/vick

Missouri

'Arabia' Steamboat Museum,
  Kansas City, www.1856.com
*Henry County Museum and Cultural
  Arts Center* [history village], Clinton,
  http://henrycountymomuseum.org
Holocaust Museum and Learning Center,
  St. Louis, www.hmlc.org
Kansas City Museum, Kansas City,
  http://kansascitymuseum.org
*Mark Twain Boyhood Home
  and Museum,* Hannibal,
  www.marktwainmuseum.org

Montana

*Lewis and Clark National Historic Trail
  Interpretive Center,* Great Falls,
  www.fs.usda.gov/lcnf
*Little Bighorn Battlefield National
  Monument,* Crow Agency,
  www.nps.gov/libi
Montana Historical Society Museum,
  Helena, http://mhs.mt.gov/museum/

Museum of the Rockies, [Montana
  State University], Bozeman,
  www.museumoftherockies.org

Nebraska

Boys Town, Omaha, www.boystown.org
Fort Kearny State Historical Park, Kearney,
  http://outdoornebraska.ne.gov/Parks/
  state_historical_parks.asp
Nebraska History Museum, Lincoln,
  www.nebraskahistory.org/sites/mnh
Plainsman Museum, Aurora,
  www.plainsmanmuseum.org
Strategic Air and Space Museum,
  Ashland, www.sasmuseum.com
Stuhr Museum of the Prairie Pioneer
  [living history], Grand Island,
  www.stuhrmuseum.org

Nevada

Lost City Museum of Archeology,
  Overton,
  http://museums.nevadaculture.org
Nevada State Museum, Carson City,
  http://museums.nevadaculture.org
Virginia City [historic silver boom town],
  www.visitvirginiacitynv.com

New Hampshire

American Independence Museum, Exeter,
  www.independencemuseum.org
Canterbury Shaker Village,
  Canterbury Center, www.shakers.org
Clark House Museum Complex
  [village], Wolfeboro,
  www.wolfeborohistoricalsociety.org
Fort at No. 4 Living History Museum,
  Charlestown, www.fortat4.org
Manchester Historic Association,
  Manchester,
  www.manchesterhistoric.org
Mt. Kearsarge Indian Museum,
  Warner, www.indianmuseum.org

New Jersey

*Ellis Island National Monument/Statue
  of Liberty,* South Ferry from Jersey
  City, www.ellisisland.org/genealogy/
  ellis_island.asp

Morristown National Historic Park,
Morristown, www.nps.gov/morr
Historic Cold Spring Village, Cape May,
www.hcsv.org
Waterloo Village [living history],Stanhope,
www.winakungatwaterloo.org

New Mexico

Archdiocese of Santa Fe Museum,
Santa Fe, www.archdiocesesantafe.org/
Offices/Archives/Archives.html
Aztec Ruins National Monument,
Aztec, www.nps.gov/azru
New Mexico Farm and Ranch
Heritage Museum, Las Cruces,
www.nmfarmandranchmuseum.org
Old Town, Albuquerque,
www.albuquerqueoldtown.com
Palace of the Governors, Santa Fe,
www.palaceofthegovernors.org
Roswell Museum and Art Center,
Roswell, http://roswellmuseum.org
Taos Pueblo, Taos, www.taospueblo.com

New York

Adirondack Museum, Blue Mountain Lake,
www.adkmuseum.org
Brooklyn Museum, Brooklyn,
www.brooklynmuseum.org
Cobblestone Society Museum and Village,
Albion, www.cobblestonemuseum.org
Corning-Painted Post Historical Society
Museum Complex [village], Corning,
www.pattersoninnmuseum.org
Federal Hall National Memorial,
Lower Manhattan, www.nps.gov/feha
Harriett Tubman House,
Auburn, http://harriethouse.org
Old Fort Niagara,
Youngstown, http://oldfortniagara.org
Sainte Marie Among the Iroquois
[recreated Jesuit mission/living
history Iroquois village], Liverpool,
www.onondagacountyparks.com/
sainte-marie-among-the-iroquois/

Statue of Liberty National Monument
and Ellis Island, Liberty Island,
www.nps.gov/stli
The Farmers' Museum, Cooperstown,
www.farmersmuseum.org

North Carolina

Airborne and Special Operations Museum,
Fayetteville, www.asomf.org
Charlotte Museum of History and
Hezekiah Alexander Homesite,
Charlotte, www.charlottemuseum.org
CSS Neuse [Confederate ironclad] Historic
Site/Gov. Caswell Memorial, Kinston,
www.nchistoricsites.org/neuse
Greensboro Historical Museum,
Greensboro, www.greensborohistory.org
Historic Stagville [plantation],
Durham, www.stagville.org
Museum of the Cherokee Indian,
Cherokee, www.cherokeemuseum.org
North Carolina Museum of History,
Raleigh, www.ncdcr.gov/ncmoh
Wright Bros. National Memorial, Kill Devil
Hills, www.firstflightfoundation.org

North Dakota

Fort Abraham Lincoln State Park,
Mandan, www.parkrec.nd.gov/
parks/falsp/falsp.html
Geographical Center Museum and
Prairie Village Museum, Rugby,
www.prairievillagemuseum.com
Lewis and Clark Trail Museum,
Alexander, www.nps.gov/lecl

Ohio

Akron Police Museum, Akron,
www.downtownakron.com/
go/akron-police-museum
Campus Martuis Museum, Washington
Marietta,
http://campusmartiusmuseum.org
Cincinnati History Museum,
Cincinnati, www.cincymuseum.org/
historymuseum

Edison Birthplace Museum,
Milan, www.tomedison.org
Historic Zoar Village,
Zoar, http://historiczoarvillage.com
Hubbard House Underground Railroad
Museum, Ashtabula,
www.hubbardhouseugrrmuseum.org
National Road/Zane Grey Museum,
Norwich, www.ohiohistory.org/
museums-and-historic-sites/
museum--historic-sites-by-name/
national-road
National Underground Railroad
Freedom Center, Cincinnati,
http://freedomcenter.org
Ross County Historical Society Museum,
Chillicothe, www.rosscountyhistorical.
org/museum.html
Sunwatch Indian Village and
Archaeological Park,
Dayton, www.sunwatch.org
The National Afro-American Museum
and Cultural Center, Wilberforce,
http://www.ohiohistory.org/
museums-and-historic-sites/
museum--historic-sites-by-name/
national-afro-american-museum--
cultural-center
Western Reserve Historical Society,
Cleveland, www.wrhs.org
Wright Brothers Memorial,
Wright-Patterson Air Force Base,
Springfield Pike, Dayton,
www.nps.gov/wrbr

Oklahoma
Choctaw Nation Museum, Tuskahoma,
www.choctawnationculture.com/
museum/choctaw-nation-capitol-
museum.aspx
Elk City Old Town Museum Complex,
Elk City, http://visitelkcity.com/
museums.aspx

Har-Ber Village [interactive historical
village], Grove,
www.har-bervillage.com
Ft. Sill National Historic Landmark
Museum, Lawton,
http://sill-www.army.mil/Museum
National Cowboy and Western Heritage
Museum, Oklahoma City,
www.nationalcowboymuseum.org
Oklahoma History Center, Oklahoma City,
www.okhistory.org/historycenter
Woolaroc Ranch, Museum, and Wildlife
Preserve, Bartlesville,
www.woolaroc.org

Oregon
Eastern Oregon Museum, Haines,
http://culturaloregon.com/western-
heritage-eastern-oregon-museum/
Fort Clatsop [Lewis and Clark], Astoria,
www.nps.gov/lewi
Fort Klamath Museum, Fort Klamath,
www.co.klamath.or.us/museum/
Profile%2oFKM.htm
Heritage Museum,
Astoria, www.cumtux.org
Kam Wah Chung Museum [19th century
Chinese immigrants], John Day,
www.oregonstateparks.org
Klamath County Museum, Klamath Falls,
www.co.klamath.or.us/museum/
Profile%2oKCM.htm
Lane County Historical Society
and Museum, Eugene,
www.lanecountyhistoricalsociety.org
Lincoln County Historical Society, Newport,
www.oregoncoast.history.museum
Museum of Science and History,
Jacksonville, www.themosh.org
National Historic Oregon Trail
Interpretive Center, Baker City,
www.blm.gov/or/oregontrail
Oregon Historical Society and Oregon
History Museum, Portland,
www.ohs.org

Tamastslikt Cultural Institute,
Pendleton, www.tamastslikt.org

Pennsylvania

Gettysburg National Military Park,
Gettysburg, www.nps.gov/gett

Independence National Historical Park
Visitor Center, Philadelphia, http://
phlvisitorcenter.com/national-park

National Civil War Museum, Harrisburg,
www.nationalcivilwarmuseum.org

State Museum of Pennsylvania, Harrisburg, www.statemuseumpa.org

Valley Forge National Historic Park,
Valley Forge/King of Prussia,
www.nps.gov/vafo

Washington Crossing Historic Park,
Washington Crossing, www.ushistory.
org/washingtoncrossing

Rhode Island

Museum of Newport History,
Newport, www.newporthistorical.org

Slater Mill Historic Village,
Pawtucket, www.slatermill.org

South Carolina

Fort Sumter National Monument,
Charleston Harbor, www.nps.gov/fosu

Hampton Plantation State Historic Site,
McClellanville,
www.southcarolinaparks.com/hampton

Patriots Point Naval and Maritime Museum,
Mount Pleasant, www.patriotspoint.org

South Carolina Confederate Relic Room and
Museum, Columbia, www.crr.sc.gov

South Carolina Law Enforcement
Officers' Hall of Fame,
Columbia, www.scdps.gov/hof

South Carolina State Museum,
Columbia, www.scmuseum.org

The Old Exchange and Provost Dungeon,
Charleston, http://oldexchange.org

South Dakota

Custer State Park, Custer, http://gfp.
sd.gov/state-parks/directory/custer

Mitchell Prehistoric Indian Village and
Archeodome Research Center, Mitchell,
www.mitchellindianvillage.org

Tennessee

Belle Meade Plantation, Nashville,
http://bellemeadeplantation.com

Cannonsburgh Historic Village, Murfreesboro, www.murfreesborotn.gov/index.
aspx?NID=164

Chickamauga and Chattanooga
National Military Park, Civil War
Battleground, www.nps.gov/chch

Chucalissa Archaeological Site, Memphis,
www.memphis.edu/chucalissa

Davy Crockett Tavern Museum, Morristown, www.crocketttavernmuseum.org

Historic Collinsville [living history], Southside, www.historiccollinsville.com

Mississippi River Museum,
Memphis, www.mudisland.com

Museum of Appalachia, Clinton,
www.museumofappalachia.org

National Civil Rights Museum, Memphis,
www.civilrightsmuseum.org

Red Clay State Historic Park, Cleveland,
www.tn.gov/environment/parks/RedClay

Sequoyah Birthplace Museum, Vonore,
www.sequoyahmuseum.org

Shiloh National Military Park, Civil War
Battleground, www.nps.gov/shil

Texas

Bullock Texas State History Museum,
Austin, www.thestoryoftexas.com

Dallas Heritage Village at Old City Park,
Dallas, www.dallasheritagevillage.org

El Paso Museum of Archaeology, El Paso,
www.elpasotexas.gov/arch_museum

Holocaust Museum Houston,
Houston, http://hmh.org

Panhandle-Plains Historical Museum,
Canyon, www.panhandleplains.org

San Jacinto Battlefield Monument and
Museum of History, La Porte,
www.sanjacinto-museum.org

The Alamo, San Antonio,
www.thealamo.org

Utah
Anasazi State Park Museum, Boulder,
http://stateparks.utah.gov/park/
anasazi-state-park-museum

Vermont
Bennington Museum, Bennington,
www.benningtonmuseum.org
Shelburne Museum and Village, Shelburne,
http://shelburnemuseum.org

Virginia
Agecroft Hall [recreated 15th cent. English
farm], Richmond, www.agecrofthall.com
*Appomattox Court House National
Historical Park,* 3 miles north of
Appomattox, www.nps.gov/apco
Booker T. Washington National Monument,
Hardy, www.nps.gov/bowa
Brandon Plantation, Burrowsville,
www.cr.nps.gov/nr/travel/jamesriver/
bra.htm
*Fredericksburg and Spotsylvania
Military Park* [Civil War battlefields],
Fredericksburg, www.nps.gov/frsp
Jamestown Settlement,
Williamsburg, www.historyisfun.org/
Jamestown-Settlement.htm
Kenmore Plantation and Gardens,
Fredericksburg, www.kenmore.org
Mariners' Museum, Newport News,
www.marinersmuseum.org
Monticello [home of Thomas Jefferson],
Charlottesville, www.monticello.org
Mount Vernon, Mount Vernon,
www.mountvernon.org
*Museum and White House of the Confed-
eracy,* Richmond, www.moc.org
*Pamplin Historical Park/Museum of the
Civil War Soldier,* Petersburg,
www.pamplinpark.org
*Southwest Virginia Museum Historical
State Park,* Big Stone Gap,
www.swvamuseum.org

*The Legacy Museum of African-
American Heritage,* Lynchburg,
http://legacymuseum.org
The Manassas Museum, Manassas,
www.manassascity.org/index.
aspx?NID=211
Virginia Holocaust Museum, Richmond,
www.va-holocaust.com
Virginia State Capitol [designed by Jefferson],
Richmond, www.virginiacapitol.gov
Yorktown Victory Center, Yorktown,
www.historyisfun.org/
Yorktown-Victory-Center.htm
Wolf Creek Indian Village and Museum,
Bastian, www.indianvillage.org

Washington
Cashmere Museum and Pioneer Village,
Cashmere, www.cashmeremuseum.org
Fort Vancouver National Historic Site
[fur trading], Vancouver,
www.nps.gov/fova
Fort Walla Walla Museum Complex,
Walla Walla,
www.fortwallawallamuseum.org
*Grant County Historical Museum and
Village,* 742 N. Basin St., Ephrata
Mt. St. Helen's Forest Learning Center,
Kelso, http://mountsthelens.com/
Forest-Learning-Center.html
*Klondike Gold Rush - Seattle Unit
National Historical Park,*
Seattle, www.nps.gov/klse
Makah Cultural and Research Museum,
Neah Bay,
www.makah.com/mcrchome.html
Museum of Flight, Seattle,
www.museumofflight.org
Naval Memorial Museum Ship,
[USS Turner Joy], Bremerton,
www.ussturrerjoy.org
Seattle Metropolitan Police Museum, Seattle,
www.seametropolicemuseum.org
State Capital Museum, Olympia,
www.washingtonhistory.org/visit/scm

Tribal Cultural Center and Museum,
    1515 Lafayette St., Steilacoom
Washington State History Museum,
    Tacoma, www.washingtonhistory.org/
    visit/wshm
Wenatchee Valley Museum and Cultural
    Center, Wenatchee, www.wenatcheewa.
    gov/Index.aspx?page=32
Wing Luke Asian Museum,
    Seattle, www.wingluke.org

West Virginia

Fort New Salem [living history village], Salem,
    www.fortnewsalemfoundation.org
Grave Creek Mound Historic Site
    [Indian mounds], Moundsville,
    www.wvculture.org/museum/
    GraveCreekmod.html
Harpers Ferry National Historical Park
    [exhibits/museums], 20 miles south-
    west of Frederick, MD,
    www.nps.gov/hafe
West Virginia Independence Hall Museum,
    Wheeling, www.wvculture.org/
    museum/wvihmod.html
West Virginia Penitentiary [1867],
    Moundsville, www.wvpentours.com
West Virginia State Capitol
    [and Cultural Center], Charleston,
    www.wvculture.org/museum/
    State-Museum-Index.html

Wisconsin

EAA Airventure Museum, Oshkosh,
    www.airventuremuseum.org
Milwaukee Public Museum,
    Milwaukee, www.mpm.edu
Old World Wisconsin [historical village],
    Eagle, http://oldworldwisconsin.
    wisconsinhistory.org
Ozaukee County Pioneer Village,
    Saukville, www.co.ozaukee.wi.us/
    ochs/PioneerVillage.htm
Wisconsin Maritime Museum, Manitowoc,
    www.wisconsinmaritime.org

Wyoming

The Brinton Museum,
    Big Horn, www.bbmandm.org
The Plains Indian Museum, Cody,
    www.bbhc.org/explore/plains-indians
Wyoming Pioneer Memorial Museum,
    Douglas, http://wyoparks.state.wy.us/
    Site/SiteInfo.aspx?siteID=32
Wyoming State Museum, Cheyenne,
    http://wyomuseum.state.wy.us
Wyoming Territorial Prison State Historic
    Site [living history village], Laramie,
    www.wyomingterritorialprison.com

Canada

Alberta

Bar U Ranch National Historic Site,
    Longview, www.pc.gc.ca/lhn-nhs/ab/
    baru/index.aspx
Buffalo Nations Luxton Museum, Banff,
    http://buffalonationsmuseum.com
Chinese Cultural Centre Museum,
    Calgary, www.culturalcentre.ca
Dunvegan Provincial Park [Early Roman
    Catholic mission and fort], Dunvegan,
    www.history.alberta.ca/dunvegan/
    default.aspx
Fort Calgary Historic Park,
    Calgary, www.fortcalgary.com
Glenbow Museum,
    Calgary, www.glenbow.org
Grande Prairie Museum,
    Grande Prairie, www.cityofgp.com/
    index.aspx?page=174&recordid=32
Head-Smashed-In Buffalo Jump
    Interpretive Centre, Fort Macleod,
    history.alberta.ca/headsmashedin
Heritage Park Historical Village,
    Calgary, www.heritagepark.ca
Medicine Hat Museum and Art Gallery,
    1302 Bomford Crescent, Medicine Hat
Museum of the Northwest Mounted
    Police, Fort Macleod,

www.albertasouthwest.com/
the_fort_museum_of_the_north_west_
mounted_police

Nikka Yuko Japanese Garden,
Lethbridge, www.nikkayuko.com

Rocky Mountain House Historic Site
[fur trading post], Rocky Mountain
House, www.pc.gc.ca/lhn-nhs/ab/
rockymountain/index.aspx

Royal Alberta Museum, Edmonton,
www.royalalbertamuseum.ca

Ukrainian Cultural Heritage Village,
Edmonton, www.history.alberta.ca/
ukrainianvillage

Vital Grandin Centre/Bishop's Palace
[home of Alberta's first bishop], St.
Albert, http://www.history.alberta.ca/
fatherlacombe/default.aspx

British Columbia

Barkerville Historic Town,
Hwy. 26, 80 km east of Quesnel,
www.barkerville.ca

Fort St. James National Historic Site,
[off of Hwy. 27], Fort St. James,
www.pc.gc.ca/lhn-nhs/bc/stjames/
index.aspx

Fort Steele Heritage Town,
Fort Steele, www.fortsteele.ca

Historic Hat Creek Ranch,
Cache Creek, http://hatcreekranch.ca

Kamloops Museum and Archives,
Kamloops, www.kamloops.ca/
museum/index.shtml

'Ksan Historical Village and Museum,
Hazelton, www.ksan.org

*Langley Centennial Museum and
National Exhibition Centre,* Fort
Langley, www.langleymuseum.org

Museum of the Cariboo Chilcotin, Williams
Lake, www.cowboy-museum.com

Nanaimo District Muiseum, Nanaimo,
www.nanaimomuseum.ca

North Vancouver Museum and Archives,
North Vancouver,
www.northvanmuseum.ca

*Osoyoos and District Museum and
Archives,* Osoyoos,
www.osoyoosmuseum.ca

Parliament Buildings, Victoria,
www.victoriabc.ca/victoria/
parliamentbuildings.htm

Penticton Museum, Penticton,
www.pentictonmuseum.com

Port Moody Station Museum, Port Moody,
http://portmoodymuseum.org

Princeton and District Museum and Archives,
Princeton, http://princetonmuseum.org/
Princeton_Museum/Index.html

Quesnel and District Museum and Archives,
Quesnel, www.quesnelmuseum.ca

*Quw'utsun' Cultural and Conference
Centre,* Duncan, www.quwutsun.ca

Royal British Columbia Museum,
Victoria, http://royalbcmuseum.bc.ca

Walter Wright Pioneer Village, Dawson
Creek, www.dawsoncreek.ca/residents/
parks/walter-wright-pioneer-village

Manitoba

Air Force Heritage Park and Museum,
Winnipeg, www.mhs.mb.ca/docs/
sites/airforceheritagemuseum.shtml

*Broken Beau Historical Society Pioneer
Museum,* Beausejour, www.mhs.mb.ca/
docs/sites/brokenbeaumuseum.shtml

*Commonwealth Air Training Plan
Museum,* Brandon Airport, Brandon,
www.airmuseum.ca

Cooks Creek Heritage Museum,
Cooks Creek, www.cchm.ca

Dalnavert Museum and Visitors' Centre,
Winnipeg, www.mhs.mb.ca/info/
museums/dalnavert

Eskimo Museum, Churchill,
www.visitnorthernmanitoba.ca/
index.php?pageid=ATT003

*Fort la Reine Museum and Pioneer
Village,* Portage la Prairie,
www.fortlareinemuseum.ca

*Lake Winnipeg Visitor Centre and New
Iceland Heritage Museum,*

Gimli, http://www.nihm.ca/exhibits/
visitorCentre.html

Lower Ft. Garry National Historic Site,
Selkirk, www.pc.gc.ca/eng/lhn-nhs/
mb/fortgarry/index.aspx

Manitoba Legislative Building,
Winnipeg, www.gov.mb.ca/mit/
legtour/legbld.html

Manitoba Museum [includes science
gallery and planetarium], Winnipeg,
www.manitobamuseum.ca

Royal Canadian Mint,
Winnipeg, www.mint.ca

*Royal Regiment of Canadian Artillery
Museum,* Shilo,
www.rcamuseum.com

Saint Boniface Museum,
Winnipeg, http://msbm.mb.ca

Western Canada Aviation Museum,
Winnipeg, http://wcam.mb.ca

New Brunswick

Acadian Historical Village, Caraquet,
www.vhanb.ca/index_en.cfm

Albert County Museum, Hopewell Cape,
www.albertcountymuseum.ca

*Canadian Forces Base Gagetown Military
Museum,* Canadian Forces Base,
Oromocto, www.museumgagetown.
ca/EngRNBR.htm

Ft. Beausejour National Historic Site,
Aulac, www.pc.gc.ca/eng/lhn-nhs/nb/
beausejour/index.aspx

Kings Landing Historical Settlement,
Prince William,
http://kingslanding.nb.ca

Legislative Assembly Building, Fredericton,
www.gnb.ca/legis

Madawaska Historical Museum,
http://patrimoinemadvic.com/en/
musee.php?cat=
Madawaska+Historical+Museum

Miramichi History Museum,
182 Wellington St., Miramichi

Moncton Museum, Moncton,
www.moncton.ca/Residents/
Recreation_Parks_and_Culture/
Museums_and_Heritage/Moncton_
Museum.htm

New Brunswick Museum,
Saint John, www.nbm-mnb.ca

Royal Canadian Legion War Museum,
575 Peter Ave., Bathurst

York-Sunbury Museum, Fredericton,
www.yorksunburymuseum.com

Newfoundland

Barbour Living Heritage Village,
Newton, www.barbour-site.com

Mary March Provincial Museum,
Grand Falls-Windsor,
www.therooms.ca/mmpm

*Provincial Museum of Newfoundland
and Labrador,* St. John's,
www.therooms.ca/museum

Trinity Historical Society Museum, Trinity,
www.trinityhistoricalsociety.com

Twillingate Museum,
Twillingate, www.tmacs.ca

Nova Scotia

*Alexander Graham Bell National Historic
Site,* Baddeck, www.pc.gc.ca/lhn-nhs/
ns/grahambell/index.aspx

Amos Seaman School Museum
[one room school house], 5518
Barronsfield Rd., River Hebert

Battle of Restigouche National Historic Site,
Pointe a-la-Croix, www.pc.gc.ca/eng/
lhn-nhs/qc/ristigouche/index.aspx

Black Cultural Centre for Nova Scotia,
Dartmouth, www.bccns.com

*Cape Breton Centre for Heritage and
Science,* Sydney, www.oldsydney.com/
museums/centre.html

*Fort Anne National Historic Site and
Museum,* Annapolis Royal,
www.pc.gc.ca/eng/lhn-nhs/ns/
fortanne/index.aspx

Fortress of Louisbourg National Historic
Site, Louisburg,
www.fortressoflouisbourg.ca
Grand-Pre National Historic Site,
Grand-Pre, www.grand-pre.com
Greenwood Military Aviation Museum,
Greenwood, http://gmam.ca
Halifax Citadel National Historic Site,
Halifax, www.pc.gc.ca/eng/lhn-nhs/
ns/halifax/index.aspx
Marconi National Historic Site, Glace
Bay, www.pc.gc.ca/eng/lhn-nhs/ns/
marconi/index.aspx
Maritime Museum of the Atlantic,
Halifax, http://museum.gov.ns.ca/
mmanew/en/home/default.aspx
Nova Scotia Museum of Industry,
Stellarton, http://museum.gov.ns.ca/
moi/en/home/default.aspx
Port-Royal National Historic Site: The
Habitation, Port-Royal,
www.pc.gc.ca/eng/lhn-nhs/ns/
portroyal/index.aspx
Sherbrooke Village, Sherbrooke,
http://museum.gov.ns.ca/sv/index.php
Yarmouth County Museum and
Archives, Yarmouth,
yarmouthcountymuseum.ednet.ns.ca

Ontario

Ameliasburgh Historical Museum and
Pioneer Village, Ameliasburgh,
http://prince-edward-county.com/
ameliasburgh-museum
Assiginack Museum, Manitoulin Island,
www.manitoulin-island.com/
museums/assiginack_complex.htm
Black Creek Pioneer Village,
Toronto, www.blackcreek.ca
Bowmanville Museum, Bowmanville,
www.claringtonmuseums.com/
bowmanville-museum
Canada Aviation and Space Museum,
Ottawa, http://aviation.technomuses.ca

Champlain Trail Museum and Pioneer
Village, Pembroke,
www.champlaintrailmuseum.com
Correctional Service of Canada Museum
[old penitentiary], Kingston,
www.penitentiarymuseum.ca
Diefenbunker, Canada's Cold War
Museum, Carp, www.diefenbunker.ca
Doon Heritage Crossroads, Kitchener,
www.waterlooregionmuseum.com/
doon-heritage-village.aspx
Elgin County Pioneer Museum,
St. Thomas, www.elgincounty.ca/
museum
Fanshawe Pioneer Village, London,
www.fanshawepioneervillage.ca
Fort Henry, Kingston, www.forthenry.com/
index.cfm/en/home
Georgina Pioneer Village and Archives,
Keswick, www.georginapioneervillage.ca
Heritage House Museum, Smiths Falls,
www.smithsfalls.ca/
heritage-house-museum.cfm
Old Historic Fort Erie, Fort Erie,
www.niagaraparksheritage.com/
old-fort-erie
Huron Historic Gaol and Governor's
House, Goderich,
www.huroncounty.ca/museum
Huron-Ouendat Village, Midland,
http://huroniamuseum.com
Joseph Brant Museum, Burlington,
www.museumsofburlington.com/
joseph-brant
Loyalist Cultural Centre/Allison House &
Grounds, Adolphustown Loyalist Park,
Adolphustown, www.historicplaces.ca/
en/rep-reg/place-lieu.aspx?id=8842
Markham Museum and Historic Village,
Markham, www.markham.ca/wps/
portal/Markham/RecreationCulture/
MarkhamMuseum

HISTORICAL AND CULTURAL SITES

Military Communications and Electronics Museum, Kingston, www.c-and-e-museum.org

Mississauga Chinese Centre, Mississauga, http://mississaugachinesecentre.com

Museum on the Boyne, Alliston, http://newtecumseth.ca/visitors/museum-on-the-boyne-2

Muskoka Heritage Place, Huntsville, www.muskokaheritageplace.org

Ontario Legislative Buildings, Toronto, www.ontla.on.ca/web/home.do

Ontario Provincial Police Museum, Orillia, www.opp.ca/museum/en/index.php

Parliament Buildings, Parliament Hill, Ottawa, www.parl.gc.ca

Peninsula and St. Edmunds Township Museum, Tobermory, www.tobermory.org/page/St._Edmunds_Township_Museum

Pickering Museum Village, Greenwood, www.pickering.ca/en/museum.asp

Royal Canadian Mounted Police Stables, Ottawa, www.rcmp-grc.gc.ca/mr-ce/centre-eng.htm

Royal Ontario Museum, Toronto, www.rom.on.ca

Ska-Nah-Doht Iroquoian Village and Museum, London, www.ltvca.ca/Ska-Nah-Doht.html

Thessalon Township Heritage Park and Museum, Thessalon, www.thesslibcap.com/business/museum

Thunder Bay Museum, Thunder Bay, www.thunderbaymuseum.com

Timber Village Museum, Blind River, www.blindriver.com/site/welcome/index.php?pid=75

Toronto Police Museum and Discovery Centre, Toronto, www.torontopolice.on.ca/museum

Uncle Tom's Cabin Historic Site, Dresden, www.heritagetrust.on.ca/Uncle-Tom-s-Cabin-Historic-Site/Home.aspx

Upper Canada Village, Morrisburg, www.uppercanadavillage.com/index.cfm/en/home

Wellington County Museum and Archives, Fergus, www.wellington.ca/en/discover/museumandarchives.asp

Woodland Cultural Centre [First Nations People], Brantford, www.woodland-centre.on.ca

Prince Edward Island

Anne of Green Gables Museum at Silver Bush Home, Park Corner, www.annemuseum.com

Founders' Hall, Charlottetown, www.foundershall.ca

LeVillage de L'Acadie, Hwy. 11, Mont-Carmel

North Cape Complex [wind test site and interpretive centre], North Cape, www.northcape.ca

Orwell Corner Historic Village, Orwell, http://orwellcorner.ca

Province House National Historic Site, Charlottetown, www.pc.gc.ca/lhn-nhs/pe/provincehouse/index.aspx

Woodleigh Replicas and Gardens, Hwy. 234, Kensington

Quebec

Acadian Historical Museum of Quebec, Hwy. 132, Bonaventure

Amerindian Museum of Mashteuiatsh, Mashteuiatsh, www.museeilnu.ca

Champlain Trail Museum and Pioneer Village, Pembroke, www.champlaintrailmuseum.com

Coteau-du-Lac National Historic Site, Coteau-du-Lac, www.pc.gc.ca/lhn-nhs/qc/coteaudulac/index.aspx

Fort Chambly National Historic Site, Chambly, www.pc.gc.ca/lhn-nhs/qc/fortchambly/index.aspx

Fort Temiscamingue National Historic Site, Vilee-Marie, www.pc.gc.ca/eng/lhn-nhs/qc/temiscamingue/index.aspx

Fur Trade Interpretation Centre,
 1645 rue Ouiatchouan, Mashteuiatsch
Gaspesie Museum, Gaspe,
 www.museedelagaspesie.ca
Levis Forts National Historic Site,
 Levis, www.pc.gc.ca/lhn-nhs/qc/
 levis/index.aspx
Louis S. Saint-Laurent National Historic
 Site, Compton, www.pc.gc.ca/eng/
 lhn-nhs/qc/stlaurent/index.aspx
Macaulay Heritage Park,
 33 Union St., Picton
McCord Museum of Canadian History,
 Montreal, www.mccord-museum.qc.ca
Missisquoi Museum, Stanbridge-East,
 www.museemissisquoi.ca
Museum of Civilization, Quebec,
 www.mcq.org
Museum of Early Canadians,
 St-Jean-Port-Joli,
 www.chaudiereappalaches.com/en/
 travel-quebec/la-cote-du-sud/
 saint-jean-port-joli/musee-des-
 anciens-canadiens/museum-and-
 interpretation-center
Muskoka Lakes Museum, Port Carling,
 www.mlmuseum.com
Old Port of Quebec Interpretation
 Centre, 100 rue St-Andre, Quebec
Pentanguishene Centennial Museum,
 Pentanguishene,
 www.pencenmuseum.com
Peterborough Museum and Archives,
 Peterborough,
 peterboroughmuseumandarchives.ca
Petrolia Discovery [living history],
 Petrolia, http://petroliadiscovery.com
Pierre Boucher Museum, Trois Rivieres,
 www.museepierreboucher.com
Pioneer Village, Drummondville,
 www.villagequebecois.com
Quebec Museum, rue Bougainville
 and St-Louis Gate, Quebec

Scugog Shores Historical Museum
 Village, Port Perry,
 www.scugogshoresmuseum.com
The Citadel of Quebec,
 Quebec, www.lacitadelle.qc.ca
The Fur Trade at Lachine National
 Historic Site, Lachine, www.pc.gc.ca/
 eng/lhn-nhs/qc/lachine/index.aspx
The Jesuit House [museum]/Maison des
 Jésuites de Sillery, Sillery,
 www.maisonsdupatrimoine.com/fr
The Stewart Museum, Montreal,
 www.stewart-museum.org
Val-Jalbert Historic Village,
 Chambord, www.valjalbert.com

Saskatchewan

Ancient Echoes Interpretive Centre,
 Herschel, www.ancientechoes.ca
Batoche National Historic Site,
 Wakaw, www.pc.gc.ca/lhn-nhs/sk/
 batoche/index.aspx
Diefenbaker Canada Centre, Saskatoon,
 www.usask.ca/diefenbaker
Fort Walsh National Historic Site,
 Maple Creek, www.pc.gc.ca/lhn-nhs/
 sk/walsh/index.aspx
Homestead Museum, Hwy. 51, Biggar
Indian Head Museum, Indian Head,
 www.facebook.com/
 IndianHeadMuseum
Legislative Building,
 Regina, www.legassembly.sk.ca
Prairie West Historical Centre, Eston,
 www.saskmuseums.org/museums/
 museum_search.php?city=Eston
Rotary Museum of Police and Corrections,
 Prince Albert, www.historypa.com/
 museums/police_corrections.html
Royal Saskatchewan Museum,
 Regina, www.royalsaskmuseum.ca
Sukanen Ship Pioneer Village and Museum,
 Moose Jaw, www.sukanenmuseum.ca
Ukrainian Museum of Canada,
 Saskatoon, www.umc.sk.ca

Western Development Museum's 1910 Boomtown, Saskatoon, www.wdm.ca/stoon.html

Western Development Museum's Heritage Farm and Village, North Battleford, www.wdm.ca/nb.html

Weyburn Area Heritage Village, Weyburn, www.saskmuseums.org/museums/museum_search.php?id=223

Wood Mountain Post Provincial Historic Park, www.woodmountain.ca/Oldpost.HTML

Yukon Territory

Dawson City Museum, Dawson City, www.dawsonmuseum.ca

Kluane Museum of Natural History, Burwash Landing, www.yukonmuseums.ca/museum/kluane/kluane.html

Macbride Museum, Whitehorse, www.macbridemuseum.com

SS Klonkide II National Historic Site, Whitehorse, www.pc.gc.ca/eng/lhn-nhs/yt/ssklondike/natcul.aspx

Yukon Transportation Museum, Whitehorse, http://goytm.ca

EXPERIENTIAL SCIENCE SITES, U.S. AND CANADA

Note: In addition to their hands-on educational enrichment value, the following sites may also provide volunteer and employment opportunities to students. ***Please note that industrial sites often have special requirements for visitors! It is best to contact sites in advance of visit.***

Alabama

Alabama Museum of Natural History, Tuscaloosa, http://amnh.ua.edu

DeSoto Caverns Park, Childersburg, http://desotocavernspark.com

Gulf Coast Exploreum Science Center, Mobile, www.exploreum.com

U.S. Space and Rocket Center, Huntsville, http://rocketcenter.com

Alaska

Alaska Raptor Center, Sitka, www.alaskaraptor.org

Alaska Sealife Center, Seward, www.alaskasealife.org

Macaulay Salmon Hatchery, Juneau, http://dipac.net/New%20VC%20Website/visit.html

Arizona

Arizona Science Center, Phoenix, www.azscience.org

Asarco Mineral Discovery Center, Sahuarita, www.asarco.com/about-us/our-locations/asarco-mineral-discovery-center

Boyce Thompson Arboretum State Park, Superior, http://azstateparks.com/Parks/BOTH

Colossal Cave Mountain Park, Vail, www.colossalcave.com

Hoover Dam, Lake Mead, www.usbr.gov/lc/hooverdam/service

Vatican Observatory, Tucson, www.vaticanobservatory.org

Arkansas

Blanchard Springs Caverns,
Fifty-Six, www.blanchardsprings.org
Mid-America Science Museum, Hot
Springs, www.midamericamuseum.org
Museum of Discovery, Little Rock,
http://museumofdiscovery.org

California

Aquarium of the Pacific, Long Beach,
www.aquariumofpacific.org
Birch Aquarium at Scripps Institution of
Oceanography, La Jolla,
http://aquarium.ucsd.edu
California Science Center, Los Angeles,
www.californiasciencecenter.org
Chabot Space and Science Center,
Oakland, www.chabotspace.org
Discovery Museum Science & Space Center,
Sacramento, www.thediscovery.org
Exploratorium, San Francisco,
www.exploratorium.edu
Monterey Bay Aquarium, Monterey,
www.montereybayaquarium.org
Natural History Museum of Los Angeles
County, Los Angeles, www.nhm.org
Palomar Observatory, Palomar Mountain,
www.astro.caltech.edu/palomar
Reuben H. Fleet Science Center,
San Diego, www.rhfleet.org
The Arboretum, Arcadia,
www.arboretum.org

Colorado

Cave of the Winds, Manitou Springs,
http://caveofthewinds.com
Denver Museum of Nature and Science,
Denver, www.dmns.org
University of Colorado Museum of
Natural History, Boulder,
http://cumuseum.colorado.edu

Connecticut

Bruce Museum of Arts and Science,
Greenwich, http://brucemuseum.org
Discovery Museum, Bridgeport,
www.discoverymuseum.org
Millstone Discovery Center,
278 Main, Niantic
Mystic Aquarium, Mystic,
www.mysticaquarium.org

Delaware

Delaware Museum of Natural History,
Wilmington, www.delmnh.org
Iron Hill Museum of Natural History,
Newark, http://ironhill-museum.org

District of Columbia

Department of the Interior Museum,
www.doi.gov/interiormuseum/index.cfm
National Museum of Health and Medicine
[Walter Reed Army Medical Complex]
6900 Georgia Ave.
National Museum of Natural History,
Smithsonian, www.mnh.si.edu

Florida

Butterfly World, Coconut Creek,
www.butterflyworld.com
Everglades Wonder Gardens and Natural
History Museum, Bonita Springs,
www.evergladeswondergardens.net
Graves Museum of Archaeology and
Natural History, Dania Beach,
www.gravesmuseum.org
Kennedy Space Center Visitor Complex,
Cocoa, www.kennedyspacecenter.com
Miami Museum of Science and Planetarium,
Miami, www.miamisci.org
Museum of Science and Industry,
Tampa, www.mosi.org
Museum of Discovery and Science,
Fort Lauderdale, www.mods.org
Museum of Science and History,
Jacksonville, www.themosh.org
South Florida Science Center and
Aquarium, West Palm Beach,
www.sfsciencecenter.org
The Florida Aquarium, Tampa,
www.flaquarium.org

SCIENCE SITES

Georgia

Day Butterfly Center, Pine Mountain,
www.callawaygardens.com/
things-to-do/attractions/
day-butterfly-center

Fernbank Museum of Natural History,
Atlanta, www.fernbankmuseum.org

Fernbank Science Center,
Atlanta, www.fernbank.edu

National Science Center's Fort Discovery,
Augusta, www.nscdiscovery.org

Okefenokee Swamp Park,
Waycross, www.okeswamp.com

Tellus Science Museum, Cartersville,
http://tellusmuseum.org

*The Marine Education Center and
Aquarium,* Savannah,
www.marex.uga.edu/aquarium/
publicAquarium.html

Hawaii

Maui Ocean Center, Wailuku,
www.mauioceancenter.com

Sea Life Park, Waimanalo Beach,
www.sealifeparkhawaii.com

The Bernice Pauahi Bishop Museum,
Honolulu, www.bishopmuseum.org

Idaho

Discovery Center of Idaho, Boise,
www.scidaho.org

*Hagerman Fossil Beds National
Monument,* Hagerman,
www.nps.gov/hafo/index.htm

Herrett Center for Arts and Science,
Twin Falls, http://herrett.csi.edu

Idaho Museum of Natural History,
Pocatello, http://imnh.isu.edu

Illinois

*Adler Planetarium and Museum of
Astronomy,* Chicago,
www.adlerplanetarium.org

Fermi National Accelerator Laboratory,
Batavia, www.fnal.gov

Museum of Science and Industry,
Chicago, www.msichicago.org

SciTech Hands-On Museum, Aurora,
http://scitechmuseum.org

Shedd Aquarium, Chicago,
www.sheddaquarium.org

Indiana

*Foellinger-Freimann Botanical
Conservatory,* Fort Wayne,
www.botanicalconservatory.org

Holcomb Observatory and Planetarium,
Indianapolis,
www.butler.edu/holcomb-observatory

Science Central, Fort Wayne,
http://sciencecentral.org

Squire Boone Caverns & Village, Mauck-
port, www.squireboonecaverns.com

Wonderlab, Bloomington,
www.wonderlab.org

Wyandotte Caves, Wyandotte,
www.nature.nps.gov/
nnl/site.cfm?Site=WYCA-IN

Iowa

Science Center of Iowa,
Des Moines, www.sciowa.org

Kansas

Exploration Place,
Wichita, www.exploration.org

Kansas Cosmosphere and Space Center,
Hutchinson, www.cosmo.org

Natural History Museum, Lawrence,
http://naturalhistory.ku.edu/

Sternberg Museum of Natural History,
Hays, http://sternberg.fhsu.edu

Kentucky

*American Cave Museum and Hidden
River Cave,* Horse Cave,
http://hiddenrivercave.com

*Gheens Science Hall and Rauch
Planetaruim,* Louisville,
http://louisville.edu/planetarium

Kentucky Science Center, Louisville,
www.kysciencecenter.org

Mammoth Cave National Park, Mammoth
Cave, www.nps.gov/maca/index.htm

Newport Aquarium, Newport,
www.newportaquarium.com
*Owensboro Museum of Science and
History,* Owensboro,
www.owensboromuseum.org

Louisiana
Audubon Aquarium of the Americas,
New Orleans,
www.auduboninstitute.org/
visit/aquarium
Audubon Nature Institute, New Orleans,
www.auduboninstitute.org
Sci-Port: Louisiana's Science Center,
Shreveport, www.sciport.org

Maine
Mount Desert Oceanarium,
Bar Harbor and Southwest Harbor,
www.theoceanarium.com
Southworth Planetarium,
Portland, www.usm.maine.edu/planet

Maryland
Calvert Marine Museum, Solomons,
www.calvertmarinemuseum.com
*Maryland Science Center and Davis
Planetarium,* Baltimore,
www.mdsci.org
National Aquarium, Baltimore,
www.aqua.org
National Museum of Health and Medicine,
Silver Spring, www.medicalmuseum.mil

Massachusetts
Cape Cod Museum of Natural History,
Brewster, www.ccmnh.org
Harvard Museum of Natural History,
Cambridge, www.hmnh.harvard.edu
Museum of Science and Planetarium,
Boston, www.mos.org
New England Aquarium,
Boston, www.neaq.org
The Butterfly Place [atrium], Westford,
https://butterflyplace-ma.com
*Woods Hole Oceanographic
Institution's Exhibit Center,*
Woods Hole, www.whoi.edu

Michigan
Cranbrook Institute of Science, Bloomfield
Hills, http://science.cranbrook.edu
Michigan Science Center,
Detroit, www.mi-sci.org
Longway Planetarium,
Flint, http://sloanlongway.org/
Longway-Planetarium

Minnesota
Great Lakes Aquarium,
Duluth, http://glaquarium.org
Minnesota Landscape Arboretum,
Chaska, www.arboretum.umn.edu
Mystery Cave, Wykoff,
www.dnr.state.mn.us/state_parks/
forestville_mystery_cave
Science Museum of Minnesota,
St. Paul, www.smm.org

Mississippi
J.L. Scott Marine Education Center, Ocean
Springs, www.usm.edu/gcrl/mec
*INFINITY Science Center (NASA
Visitor Center),* Bay St. Louis,
www.visitinfinity.com
Mississippi Museum of Natural Science,
Jackson,
www.mdwfp.com/museum.aspx
*Russell C. Davis Planetarium/Ronald
McNair Space Theater,*
Jackson, www.jacksonms.gov/
visitors/planetarium

Missouri
Fantastic Caverns, Springfield,
www.fantasticcaverns.com
Meramec Caverns, Stanton,
www.americascave.com
St. Louis Science Center,
St. Louis, www.slsc.org

Montana
Lewis and Clark Caverns State Park,
Whitehall, http://stateparks.mt.gov/
lewis-and-clark-caverns

Mineral Museum, Butte,
www.mbmg.mtech.edu/museum/
museum.asp

Nebraska

Ashfall Fossil Beds State Historical Park,
Royal, http://ashfall.unl.edu

Nevada

Fleischmann Planetarium,
[University of Nevada], Reno,
http://planetarium.unr.nevada.edu

Las Vegas Natural History Museum,
Las Vegas, www.lvnhm.org

New Hampshire

The Christa McAuliffe Planetarium,
Concord, www.starhop.com

See Science Center, Manchester,
www.see-sciencecenter.org

The Science and Nature Center at
Seabrook Station, Seabrook,
www.nexteraenergyresources.com/
what/nuclear_seabrook_center.shtml

New Jersey

Franklin Mineral Museum, Franklin,
www.franklinmineralmuseum.com

Rutgers Geology Museum, New Brunswick,
http://geologymuseum.rutgers.edu

Adventure Aquarium, Camden,
www.adventureaquarium.com

New Mexico

Albuquerque Aquarium and the Rio
Grande Botanic Garden,
Albuquerque, www.bioparksociety.org

Bradbury Science Museum,
Los Alamos, www.lanl.gov/museum

Carlsbad Cavern,
Carlsbad, www.nps.gov/cave

Mineral Museum, [New Mexico
Institute of Mining and Technology
campus], Socorro,
https://geoinfo.nmt.edu/museum

New Mexico Museum of Space
History, Alamogordo,
www.nmspacemuseum.org

New York

American Museum of Natural History,
Midtown Manhattan, www.amnh.org

Howe Caverns, Howes Cave,
www.howecaverns.com

Milton J. Rubenstein Museum of
Science and Technology, Syracuse,
www.most.org

New York Botanical Garden,
Bronx, www.nybg.org

Rochester Museum and Science Center,
Rochester, www.rmsc.org

North Carolina

Aurora Fossil Museum, Aurora,
www.aurorafossilmuseum.com

Discovery Place, Charlotte,
www.discoveryplace.org

North Carolina Maritime Museum, Beaufort,
www.ncmaritimemuseums.com/
beaufort.html

North Carolina Museum of
Life and Science, Durham,
http://lifeandscience.org

North Carolina Museum of Natural Sciences,
Raleigh, http://naturalsciences.org

The Schiele Museum of Natural History,
Gastonia, www.schielemuseum.org

Ohio

Cincinnati Museum Center at Union
Terminal [history and science],
Cincinnati, www.cincymuseum.org

COSI [Center of Science and Industry],
Columbus, http://cosi.org

Imagination Station, Toledo,
www.imaginationstationtoledo.org

Franklin Park Conservatory and
Botanical Garden, Columbus,
www.fpconservatory.org

Great Lakes Science Center,
Cleveland, www.glsc.org

Ohio Agricultural Research and
Development Center, Wooster,
www.oardc.ohio-state.edu

Ohio Caverns, West Liberty,
www.ohiocaverns.com

Oklahoma

Science Museum Oklahoma, Oklahoma
City, www.sciencemuseumok.org

Southern Plains Range Research Station,
Woodward, http://oaes.okstate.edu/
frsu/southern-plains-research-station

Oregon

Columbia River Maritime Museum,
Astoria, www.crmm.org

Hatfield Marine Science Center,
Newport, http://hmsc.oregonstate.edu

High Desert Museum, Bend,
www.highdesertmuseum.org

John Inskeep Environmental Learning
Center, Oregon City,
www.clackamas.edu/
Environmental_Learning_Center.aspx

Lava River Cave,
Bend, www.fs.usda.gov/
recarea/centraloregon/
recreation/otheractivities/
recarea/?recid=38396&actid=102

University of Oregon Museum of Natural
and Cultural History [natural sciences,
geology, archeology], Eugene,
http://natural-history.uoregon.edu

Oregon Caves, Cave Junction,
www.nps.gov/orca

Oregon Coast Aquarium,
Newport, http://aquarium.org

Oregon Museum of Science and Industry,
Portland, www.omsi.edu

World Forestry Center, Portland,
www.worldforestry.org

Pennsylvania

Carnegie Science Center, Pittsburgh,
www.carnegiesciencecenter.org

Franklin Institute Science Museum,
Philadelphia, www2.fi.edu

North Museum of Natural History
and Science, Lancaster,
www.northmuseum.org

Penn's Cave and Wildlife Park, Centre
Hall, www.pennscave.com

University of Pennsylvania Museum
of Archaeology/Anthropology,
Philadelphia, www.penn.museum

South Carolina

Edisto Island Serpentarium, Edisto Island,
www.edistoserpentarium.com

Ripley's Aquarium, Myrtle Beach,
www.ripleyaquariums.com/myrtlebeach

South Carolina Aquarium,
Charleston, http://scaquarium.org

World of Energy [nuclear, coal, water],
Seneca, www.duke-energy.com/
visitor-centers/world-of-energy.asp

South Dakota

Jewel Cave National Monument,
Custer, www.nps.gov/jeca

Museum of Geology, Rapid City,
www.sdsmt.edu/Museum-of-Geology

Washington Pavilion of Arts and Science,
Sioux Falls, www.washingtonpavilion.org

Tennessee

Adventure Science Center, Nashville,
www.adventuresci.com

American Museum of Science and Energy
[WWII 'Manhattan Project'], Oak Ridge,
http://amse.org

East Tennessee Discovery Center
and Planetarium, Knoxville,
www.etdiscovery.org

Mississippi River Museum,
Memphis, www.mudisland.com/
c-3-mississippi-river-museum.aspx

Ripley's Aquarium of the Smokies,
Gatlinburg,
www.ripleyaquariums.com/gatlinburg

Tennessee Aquarium,
Chattanooga, www.tennaqua.org

Tuckaleechee Caverns, Townsend,
www.tuckaleecheecaverns.com

Texas

Caverns of Sonora, Sonora,
http://cavernsofsonora.com

Fort Worth Museum of Science and
History, Fort Worth,
www.fwmuseum.org
Houston Museum of Natural Science,
Houston, www.hmns.org
Insights: El Paso Science Center,
El Paso, www.insightselpaso.org
Space Center Houston, Houston,
http://spacecenter.org
Texas State Aquarium, Corpus Christi,
www.texasstateaquarium.org
Perot Museum of Nature and Science,
Dallas, www.perotmuseum.org
Witte Museum [natural science
and history], San Antonio,
www.wittemuseum.org

Utah
Clark Planetarium, Salt Lake City,
http://clarkplanetarium.org

Vermont
Fairbanks Museum and Planetarium,
St. Johnsbury,
www.fairbanksmuseum.org
Montshire Museum of Science, Norwich,
www.montshire.org

Virginia
Luray Caverns, Luray,
http://luraycaverns.com
NASA Visitor Center, Wallops Flight
Facility, Chincoteague,
http://sites.wff.nasa.gov/wvc/
Norfolk Botanical Garden, Norfolk,
http://norfolkbotanicalgarden.org
North Anna Nuclear Information Center,
Mineral, www.dom.com/about/stations/
nuclear/north-anna/north-anna-nuclear-
information-center.jsp
Science Museum of Western Virginia
and Hopkins Planetarium,
Roanoke, www.smwv.org
Skyline Caverns, Front Royal,
www.skylinecaverns.com
Surry Nuclear Information Center, Surry,
www.dom.com/about/stations/nuclear/
surry/surry-nuclear-information-center.jsp

Virginia Aquarium and Marine
Science Museum, Virginia Beach,
www.virginiaaquarium.com

Washington
Bonneville Dam Visitor Center,
North Bonneville,
www.nwp.usace.army.mil/Locations/
ColumbiaRiver/Bonneville.aspx
Castle Rock Mt. St Helens Exhibit Hall,
Castle Rock, www.mountsthelens.com/
visitorcenters.html
Columbia River Exhibition of History,
Science and Technology, Richland,
www.crehst.org
Naval Undersea Museum, Keyport,
www.navalunderseamuseum.org
Seattle Aquarium, Seattle,
www.seattleaquarium.org
Stonerose Interpretive Center and
Eocene Fossil Site, Republic,
http://stonerosefossil.org

West Virginia
Lost World Caverns, Lewisburg,
www.lostworldcaverns.com
National Radio Astronomy Observatory,
Green Bank, https://science.nrao.edu
Science Center of West Virginia,
500 Bland St., Bluefield
Smoke Hole Caverns, south of Petersburg,
www.smokehole.com/caverns.htm
Youth Museum of Southern West
Virginia, Beckley,
www.beckley.org/youth_museum

Wisconsin
Cave of the Mounds, Blue Mounds,
www.caveofthemounds.com
Discovery World, Milwaukee,
www.discoveryworld.org
Museum of Minerals and Crystals,
Dodgeville
Olbrich Botanical Gardens, Madison,
www.olbrich.org

Wyoming
Tate Geological Museum, Casper,
www.caspercollege.edu/tate

The Draper Natural History Museum,
Cody, www.bbhc.org

Canada

Alberta

Aero Space Museum of Calgary,
Calgary, www.asmac.ab.ca

Alberta Birds of Prey Centre,
Coaldale, www.burrowingowl.com

Telus World of Science—Calgary,
www.sparkscience.ca

*Bomber Command Museum
of Canada,* Nanton,
www.bombercommandmuseum.ca

*Banff Park Museum National Historic
Site,* Banff, www.pc.gc.ca/eng/
lhn-nhs/ab/banff/index.aspx

Telus World of Science—Edmonton,
www.telusworldofscienceedmonton.com

British Columbia

British Columbia Aviation Museum,
Sidney, www.bcam.net

Butchart Gardens, Brentwood Bay,
www.butchartgardens.com

Butterfly World and Gardens,
Coombs, www.nature-world.com

Canadian Museum of Flight, Langley,
www.canadianflight.org

Centre of the Universe, Victoria,
www.nrc-cnrc.gc.ca/eng/outreach/cu

*Courtenay and District Museum and
Palaeontology Centre,* Courtenay,
www.courtenaymuseum.ca

*Dominion Radio Astrophysical Observa-
tory,* Penticton, www.nrc-cnrc.gc.ca/
eng/solutions/facilities/drao.html

George Reifel Migratory Bird Sanctuary,
Delta, www.reifelbirdsanctuary.com

*Kootenay Gallery of Art, History and
Science,* Castlegar,
www.kootenaygallery.com

Pacific Museum of the Earth, Vancouver,
www.eos.ubc.ca/resources/museum

Okanagan Science Centre,
Vernon, www.okscience.ca

Princeton and District Museum & Archives
[fossils/minerals/mining], Princeton,
http://princetonmuseum.org/
Princeton_Museum

Telus World of Science—Vancouver,
www.scienceworld.ca

Scout Island Nature Centre,
Williams Lake,
www.scoutislandnaturecentre.ca

Victoria Butterfly Gardens, Brentwood
Bay, www.butterflygardens.com

Manitoba

Assiniboine Park Conservatory,
Winnipeg, www.assiniboinepark.ca/
attractions/conservatory.php

Marine Museum of Manitoba, Selkirk,
www.marinemuseum.ca

Sandilands Forest Centre, Hadashville,
www.thinktrees.org/Sandilands_
Forest_Discovery_Centre.aspx

New Brunswick

Aquarium and Marine Centre,
Shippagan, http://aquariumnb.ca

Huntsman Marine Science Centre, St.
Andrews, www.huntsmanmarine.com

Irving Eco-Centre [La Dune de Bouctouche],
Bouctouche, www.jdirving.com/
environment.aspx?id=318

Mactaquac Hydroelectric Dam, Trans-
Canada Hwy. 451 Hwy. 105, Mactaquac

Miramichi History Museum, 182 Wellington
St., Miramichi

Point Lepreau Nuclear Generating Station,
Hwy. 790 [exit 86 off Hwy. 1], Lepreau

Newfoundland

Discovery Centre, Woody Point,
Gros Morne National Park,
http://woodypoint.ca

Johnson Geo Centre, St. John's,
www.geocentre.ca

Newfoundland Insectarium, Reidville,
www.nfinsectarium.com

North Atlantic Aviation Museum, Gander,
www.northatlanticaviationmuseum.com
The Fluvarium [freshwater ecology],
St. John's, http://fluvarium.ca

Nova Scotia
Annapolis Royal Historic Gardens,
Annapolis Royal,
www.historicgardens.com
Annapolis Tidal Power Generating
Station, Annapolis Royal,
www.nspower.ca/en/home/
aboutnspower/makingelectricity/
renewable/annapolis.aspx
Discovery Centre, Halifax,
www.discoverycentre.ns.ca
Joggins Fossil Centre, Joggins,
http://jogginsfossilcliffs.net/centre
Museum of Natural History, Halifax,
http://museum.gov.ns.ca/mnhnew

Ontario
Bancroft Mineral Museum, Bancroft,
www.princesssodalitemine.ca
Bruce Nuclear Power Visitors' Centre,
Tiverton, www.brucepower.com/
community/visitorscentre
Canada Science and Technology
Museum, Ottawa,
www.sciencetech.technomuses.ca
Canadian Museum of Nature,
Ottawa, www.nature.ca
Darlington Nuclear Generating Station,
Bowmanville, www.opg.com/power/
nuclear/darlington/index.asp
David Dunlap Observatory,
Richmond Hill, www.theddo.ca
Earth Sciences Museum, Waterloo,
https://uwaterloo.ca/
earth-sciences-museum
Niagara Parks Botanical Gardens [School
of Horticulture], Niagara Falls,
www.niagaraparks.com/niagara-falls-
attractions/botanical-gardens.html
Niagara Parks Butterfly Conservatory,
Niagara Falls, www.niagaraparks.com/

niagara-falls-attractions/butterfly-
conservatory.html
Ontario Science Centre, Toronto,
www.ontariosciencecentre.ca
Royal Botanical Gardens,
Burlington, www.rbg.ca
Wye Marsh Wildlife Centre, Midland,
www.wyemarsh.com

Prince Edward Island
Basin Head Fisheries Museum, www.
peimuseum.com/index.php3?
number=1042966&lang=E

Quebec
Belle Terre Botanic Garden and Arboretum,
Otter Lake, http://arbnet.org/
morton-register/canada/belle-terre-
botanic-garden-and-arboretum.html
Botanical Garden of Montreal,
Montreal, http://espacepourlavie.ca/
en/botanical-garden
City of Energy, Shawinigan,
www.citedelenergie.com
Cosmodome, [science center, space
flight], Laval, www.cosmodome.org
Miguasha Park, [fossils], Miguasha,
www.quebecmaritime.ca/en/
company/miguasha-national-park/
activities
Montreal Biodome [ecosystems],
Olympic Park, Montreal, http://
espacepourlavie.ca/en/biodome
Montreal Planetarium, Montreal,
http://espacepourlavie.ca/en/planetarium
Montreal Science Centre, Montreal,
www.montrealsciencecentre.com
Museum of the Bee, Ste-Anne-de-Beaupre,
www.musee-abeille.com
Museum of Nature and Sciences, Sherbrooke,
www.naturesciences.qc.ca/en/museum
St-Felicien Zoological Park [and recreated
19th century village], St-Felicien,
www.zoosauvage.org
The City of Gold, Val-D'Or,
www.citedelor.com

SCIENCE SITES

The Marine Mammal Interpretation Centre,
    Tadoussac, www.quebecmaritime.ca/en/
    company/marine-mammal-interpretation-
    centre-cimm/activities

Saskatchewan

Living Forestry Museum, Nipawin,
    www.nipawin.com/attractions-museum.html

Nipawin Hydroelectric Station and Dam,
    Nipawin, http://nipawin.com/
    attractions-dam.html

Saskatchewan Science Centre, Regina,
    www.sasksciencecentre.com

Yukon Territory

Northern Lights Centre, Watson Lake,
    www.northernlightscentre.ca

FORMS *and* CHARTS

Class Lesson Plan Form

Course Title: U.S. History

Text Titles: A Basic History of the U.S.

Experiential Learning Activity: Underground RR excavation

Field Work Contact/phone: n/a

Week	Pages/Chapter	Supplemental Materials and Essay Topics	Experiential Learning
1	Ch. 1	subscribe to American History magazine	
2	Ch. 2		
3	Ch. 3	Read Saint Among Savages	Canadian Martyrs site, NY: visit
4	Ch. 4		shrine for Ch.4
5	Ch. 5	Essay: St. Isaac Jogues and 17th century	
6	Ch. 6	North America	
7	Ch. 7	Self-test Ch. 1-6	
8	Ch. 8		Create map of 1803 North
9	Ch. 9	Find biography of Lewis and Clark	America; include state and
10	Ch. 10	read archaeological magazines Aunt Erin sent	Canadian boundaries; trace
11	Ch. 11		route of Lewis and Clark
12	Ch. 12	Self-test Ch. 7-12	
13	Ch. 13		
14	Ch. 14		
15		Read slavery: CCC 2414, & 'On the	
16	Ch. 15	Abolition of Slavery,' Leo XIII	Volunteer: Underground Railroad
17		Begin Ken Burn's Civil War video series;	excavation site
18		practice taking notes!!!!	
19	Ch. 16	Essay: The Civil War and the Theory of	
20	Ch. 17	Nullification: Is Secession Constitutional?	
21	Ch. 18		
22		Self-test, Ch. 13-18	re: Ch. 19--immigration: Visit
23	Ch. 19		Ellis Island Memorial in
24	Ch. 20	Read, Research, Write: The Contributions of	New York
25	Ch. 21	Catholic Immigrants to U.S. Society	
26	Ch. 22		
27	Ch. 23		
28	Ch. 24	Read: The Grunt Padre and When Hell Was	Volunteer: Veterans' Clinic;
29	Ch. 25	in Session [Viet Nam]	interview Viet Nam veteran
30			
31		Watch The Great Courses video: United	
32		States and the Middle East: 1914-9/11	
33	Ch. 26		
34		Research Paper: U.S. Foreign Relations and	Visit mosque
35		Islam	
36		Final Test	

Sample: Community College/Vocational Track

Class Lesson Plan Form

Course Title: Environmental Science

Text Titles: Our Environment

Experiential Learning Activity: Soil and Water volunteer

Field Work Contact/phone: Soil and Water office 234-5678

Week	Pages/Chapter	Supplemental Materials and Essay Topics	Experiential Learning
1	Ch. 1		
2	Ch. 2	Read Eco-Scam	
3	Ch. 3		
4	Ch. 4		
5	Ch. 5	internet research, reclaimed coal lands	
6	Ch. 6	and local sites	Soil and Water Volunteer
7	Ch. 7		Orientation
8	Ch. 8	internet research: Clear-cut harvest-	
9	Ch. 9	ing, replanting, and the well-managed	
10	Ch. 10	forest	Visit re-claimed coal lands
11	Ch. 11		
12	Ch. 12	Read, Research, Write: Successful	
13	Ch. 13	reclamation projects	Photographic essay of reclaimed coal
14	Ch. 14		lands and methods used
15		Self-test Ch.1-13	
16	Ch. 15		
17			
18		Internet research: environmental	Visit and interview farmer about
19	Ch. 16	regulations and their effect on	environmental regulations
20	Ch. 17	farmers; short essay	
21	Ch. 18		
22			
23	Ch. 19	Pollution control on the Mississippi River	
24	Ch. 20	drainage	
25	Ch. 21		Volunteer: water quality testing
26	Ch. 22		
27	Ch. 23		
28	Ch. 24		
29	Ch. 25	Essay: Animals OR Man or Animals	Call Wildlife Control to see about
30		AND Man?	'shadowing' an officer for the day
31			
32			
33	Ch. 26	Self-test	
34			
35			
36			

Class Lesson Plan Form

Course Title: Botany

Text Titles: Plant Agriscience

Experiential Learning Activity: Northside Nursery

Field Work Contact/phone: 123-456-7890

Week	Pages/Chapter	Supplemental Materials and Essay Topics	Experiential Learning
1	Ch. 1		
2	Ch. 2		
3	Ch. 3		
4	Ch. 4	Video: Germination Variables, remem-	
5	Ch. 5	ber to take notes!	each Tuesday afternoon after Holy
6	Ch. 6		Mass: community volunteer hours—
7	Ch. 7	plant heirloom tomato seeds in green-	parish and parochial school grounds-
8	Ch. 8	house; watch for germination time	keeping: photograph work and note
9	Ch. 9		in Journal each day
10	Ch. 10	Self-test: chapters 1-9	
11	Ch. 11		
12	Ch. 12		
13	Ch. 13		
14	Ch. 14	experiment with grow-lights vs. natu-	MWF, 10 a.m.–12: Northside Nursery
15		ral light	job, photograph work and note in
16	Ch. 15		Journal daily
17		Essay on plant disease and prevention	
18			
19	Ch. 16		
20	Ch. 17	Video: grafting techniques	
21	Ch. 18	practice grafts	demonstration of fruit tree grafting
22			techniques to homeschool group; may
23	Ch. 19	Self-test: chapters 10-18	use for Speech credit instead of
24	Ch. 20		Botany? Photograph and record in
25	Ch. 21	Internet research, County Exten-	Journal
26	Ch. 22	sion visit: organic tomato hornworm	
27	Ch. 23	eradication measures	
28	Ch. 24		harvest first tomatoes from green-
29	Ch. 25		house; sell to Fran's Organic Fruit
30			Stand
31		Research and Write: Invasive Plants	
32		of Alberta and Their Control	
33	Ch. 26		
34			
35			
36			

Class Lesson Plan Form

Course Title:

Text Titles:

Experiential Learning Activity:

Field Work Contact/phone:

Week	Pages/Chapter	Supplemental Materials and Essay Topics	Experiential Learning
1			
2			
3			
4			
5			
6			
7			
8			
9			
10			
11			
12			
13			
14			
15			
16			
17			
18			
19			
20			
21			
22			
23			
24			
25			
26			
27			
28			
29			
30			
31			
32			
33			
34			
35			
36			

Monthly Hours' Chart

Month: _____

Class	1	2	3	4	5	6	7	8	9	10	11	12	13	14	15	16	17	18	19	20	21	22	23	24	25	26	27	28	29	30	31	Totals
Biology		45																														
composition		20																														
Literature		55																														
computer composition																																
U.S. History		75																														
Geography																																
Algebra I																																
P.E.																																
Music																																

Enter minutes spent on subject

Minutes that might be 'banked', that might be used with other courses, or for use with composing a Minutes could be used for Comp., not Biology, e.g., essay English class only; for Biology [one class only; Computer per course to for all]. Allow three lines per course to record extra minutes.

Monthly Hours' Chart

Month:

Class	1	2	3	4	5	6	7	8	9	10	11	12	13	14	15	16	17	18	19	20	21	22	23	24	25	26	27	28	29	30	31	Totals

High School: From Freshman to Graduate

Sample

Note Required Subjects for High School Graduation [see Table of Contents]

Freshman Year Courses:

Ag. Science/Botany

U.S. History

P. E.

Speech

English Lit and Comp

Basic Math for Occupational and Vocational Students

Sophomore Year Courses:

Junior Year Courses:

Remember to refer to *Required Subjects for High School Graduation* [see Table of Contents] when creating your four-year plan!

Senior Year Courses:

High School: From Freshman to Graduate

Note Required Subjects for High School Graduation [see Table of Contents]

Freshman Year Courses:

Sophomore Year Courses:

Junior Year Courses:

Senior Year Courses:

High School: From Freshman to Graduate

Academic Transcript
Sample

NAME: Thomas J. Broughton
SEX: M
BIRTHDATE: 9/08/1991
BIRTHPLACE: Peterborough, ON, Canada
GRADE: 12

SCHOOL: Sapientia Academy
ADDRESS: 18252 Little Flower Rd.
Sursum Corda, CA 98765

CURRENT SUMMARY

CREDIT HOURS COMPLETED: 24
ACCUMULATED GPA: 4.0

YR SEM	COURSE	MARK	CREDIT
1	HEALTH	4.0	.50
1	ALGEBRA I	4.0	.50
1	BIOLOGY	4.0	.50
1	P.E.	4.0	.50
1	ENGLISH I	4.0	.50
1	SPANISH I	4.0	.50
2	ALGEBRA I	4.0	.50
2	BIOLOGY	4.0	.50
2	P.E.	4.0	.50
2	ENGLISH I	4.0	.50
2	SPANISH I	4.0	.50
2	SPEECH	4.0	.50
04-05			
GPA 4.0	CREDIT HRS	6.0	
1	GEOGRAPHY	4.0	.50
1	ALGEBRA II	4.0	.50
1	CHEMISTRY	4.0	.50
1	P.E.	4.0	.50
1	ENGLISH II	4.0	.50
1	SPANISH II	4.0	.50
2	ALGEBRA II	4.0	.50
2	CHEMISTRY	4.0	.50
2	MUSIC	4.0	.50
2	ENGLISH II	4.0	.50
2	SPANISH II	4.0	.50
2	WOODSHOP	4.0	.50
05-06			
GPA 4.0	CREDIT HRS	6.0	

YR SEM	COURSE	MARK	CREDIT
1	GOVERNMENT	4.0	.50
1	GEOMETRY	4.0	.50
1	SOCIAL PROBLEMS	4.0	.50
1	PHYSICS	4.0	.50
1	ENGLISH III	4.0	.50
1	SPANISH III	4.0	.50
2	GEOMETRY	4.0	.50
2	PHYSICS	4.0	.50
2	SOCIAL PROBLEMS	4.0	.50
2	ENGLISH III	4.0	.50
2	SPANISH III	4.0	.50
2	APOLOGETICS	4.0	.50
06-07			
GPA 4.0	CREDIT HRS	6.0	
1	US HISTORY	4.0	.50
1	TRIGONOMETRY	4.0	.50
1	AERONAUTIC SCI	4.0	.50
1	THEOLOGY	4.0	.50
1	ENGLISH IV	4.0	.50
1	SPANISH IV	4.0	.50
2	TRIGONOMETRY	4.0	.50
2	AERONAUTIC SCI	4.0	.50
2	THEOLOGY	4.0	.50
2	ENGLISH IV	4.0	.50
2	SPANISH IV	4.0	.50
2	US HISTORY	4.0	.50
07-08			
GPA 4.0	CREDIT HRS	6.0	

- Credits: 1 full year=1.0 credits;
1 semester, or 1/2 year= .50 credits

- Grading: A=4.0
B=3.0
C=2.0
D=1.0

- total grades for semester, then
average grades to figure GPA

180 hours of instruction=1 credit hour
Credit hours required for graduation=22

Date Graduated:

Academic Transcript

NAME:		SCHOOL:
SEX:		ADDRESS:
BIRTHDATE:		
BIRTHPLACE:		
GRADE:		

CURRENT SUMMARY			
HOURS COMPLETED:			
ACCUMULATED GPA:			

YR	SEM	COURSE	MARK	CREDIT

YR	SEM	COURSE	MARK	CREDIT

180 hours of instruction=1 credit hour
Credit hours required for graduation=22

Date Graduated:

Sample: Personalization may be added to diploma, either by hand or by computer, as in this example. [See next page.]

Sapientia Academy

This certifies that

Thomas Joseph Broughton

has satisfactorily completed a Course of Study prescribed for graduation from this School and is thereby awarded this Diploma.

Given this _____ day of _____, 20___.

_____
Superintendent – Principal

This certifies that

has satisfactorily completed a Course of Study prescribed for graduation from this School and is thereby awarded this Diploma.

Given this _____ *day of* _____ *, 20* _____ *.*

_____

Superintendent — Principal